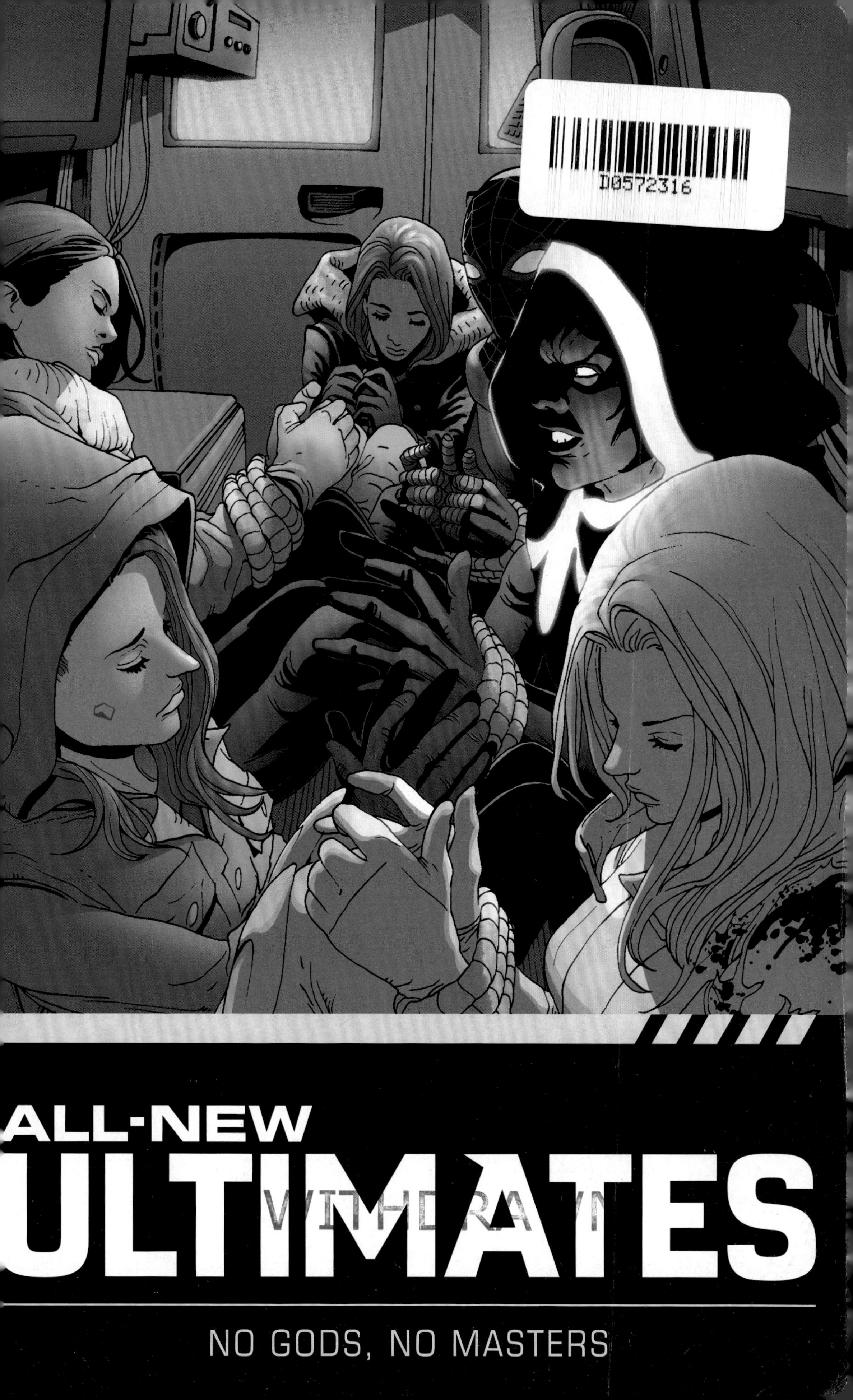

ALL-NEW ULTIMATES

NO GODS, NO MASTERS

COLLECTION EDITOR: SARAH BRUNSTAD
ASSOCIATE MANAGING EDITOR: ALEX STARBUCK
EDITORS, SPECIAL PROJECTS: JENNIFER GRÜNWALD & MARK D. BEAZLEY
SENIOR EDITOR, SPECIAL PROJECTS: JEFF YOUNGQUIST
SVP PRINT, SALES & MARKETING: DAVID GABRIEL
BOOK DESIGNER: RODOLFO MURAGUCHI

EDITOR IN CHIEF: AXEL ALONSO
CHIEF CREATIVE OFFICER: JOE QUESADA
PUBLISHER: DAN BUCKLEY
EXECUTIVE PRODUCER: ALAN FINE

ALL-NEW ULTIMATES VOL. 2: NO GODS, NO MASTERS. Contains material originally published in magazine form as ALL-NEW ULTIMATES #7-12. First printing 2015. ISBN# 978-0-7851-5428-0. Published by MARVEL WORLDWIDE, INC., a subsidiary of MARVEL ENTERTAINMENT, LLC. OFFICE OF PUBLICATION: 135 West 50th Street, New York, NY 10020. Copyright © 2014 and 2015 Marvel Characters, Inc. All rights reserved. All characters featured in this issue and the distinctive names and likenesses thereof, and all related indicia are trademarks of Marvel Characters, Inc. No similarity between any of the names, characters, persons, and/or institutions in this magazine with those of any living or dead person or institution is intended, and any such similarity which may exist is purely coincidental. **Printed in Canada.** ALAN FINE, EVP - Office of the President, Marvel Worldwide, Inc. and EVP & CMO Marvel Characters B.V.; DAN BUCKLEY, Publisher & President - Print, Animation & Digital Divisions; JOE QUESADA, Chief Creative Officer; TOM BREVOORT, SVP of Publishing; DAVID BOGART, SVP of Operations & Procurement, Publishing; C.B. CEBULSKI, SVP of Creator & Content Development; DAVID GABRIEL, SVP Print, Sales & Marketing; JIM O'KEEFE, VP of Operations & Logistics; DAN CARR, Executive Director of Publishing Technology; SUSAN CRESPI, Editorial Operations Manager; ALEX MORALES, Publishing Operations Manager; STAN LEE, Chairman Emeritus. For information regarding advertising in Marvel Comics or on Marvel.com, please contact Niza Disla, Director of Marvel Partnerships, at ndisla@marvel.com. For Marvel subscription inquiries, please call 800-217-9158. **Manufactured between 1/16/2015 and 2/23/2015 by SOLISCO PRINTERS, SCOTT, QC, CANADA.**

10 9 8 7 6 5 4 3 2 1

ALL-NEW ULTIMATES

NO GODS, NO MASTERS

WRITER:
MICHEL FIFFE

ARTISTS:
GIANNIS MILONOGIANNIS (#7-9) &
AMILCAR PINNA (#10-12) WITH **TERRY PALLOT** (INKER, #12)

INKERS, #11:
AMILCAR PINNA, TERRY PALLOT, LORENZO RUGGIERO
& LE BEAU UNDERWOOD

COLOR ARTISTS:
JORDIE BELLAIRE (#7-8),
ESTHER SANZ (#9) &
NOLAN WOODARD (#10-12)

LETTERER:
VC'S CLAYTON COWLES

COVER ARTIST:
DAVID NAKAYAMA

EDITOR:
EMILY SHAW

SENIOR EDITOR:
MARK PANICCIA

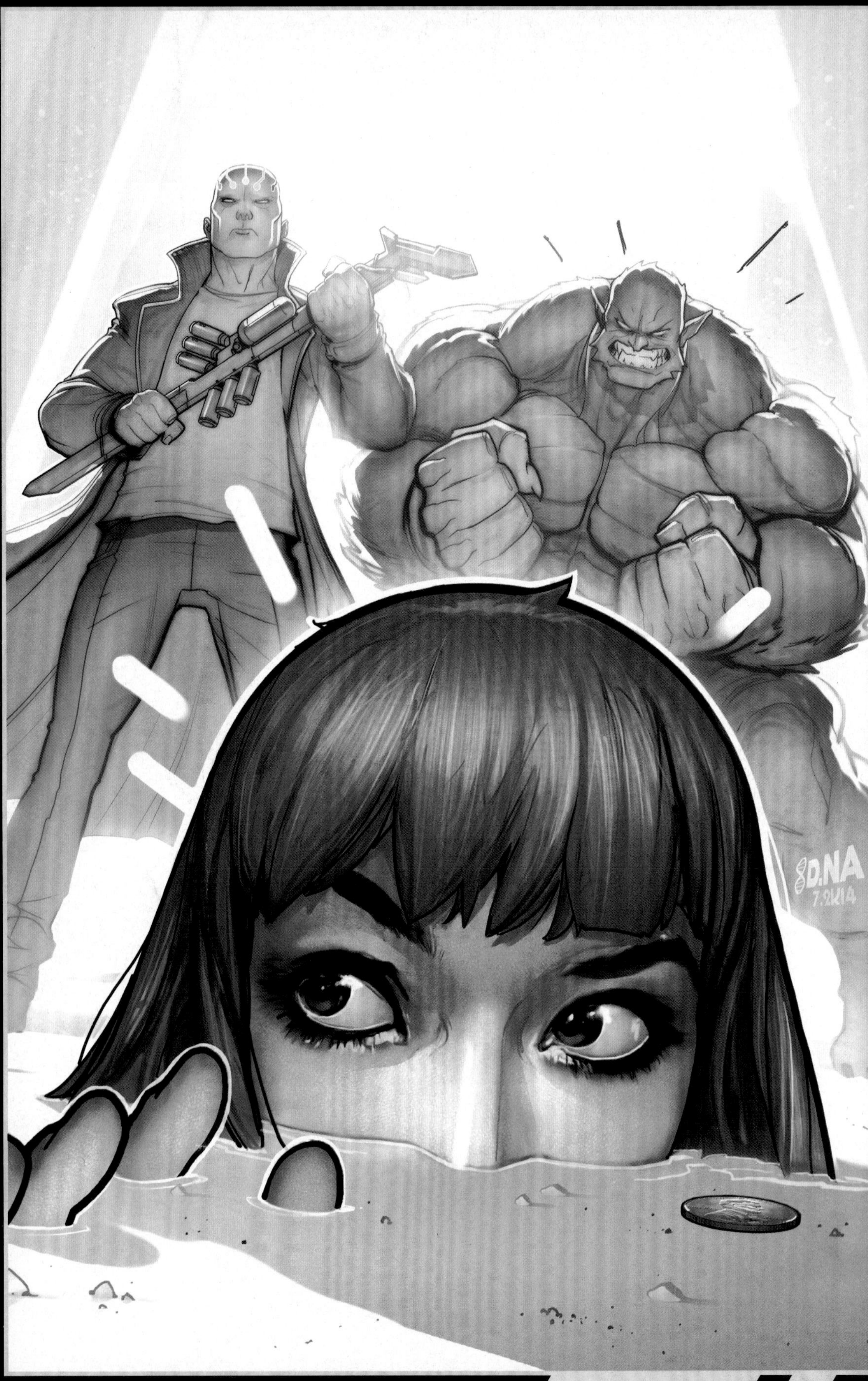
D.NA
7.2K14

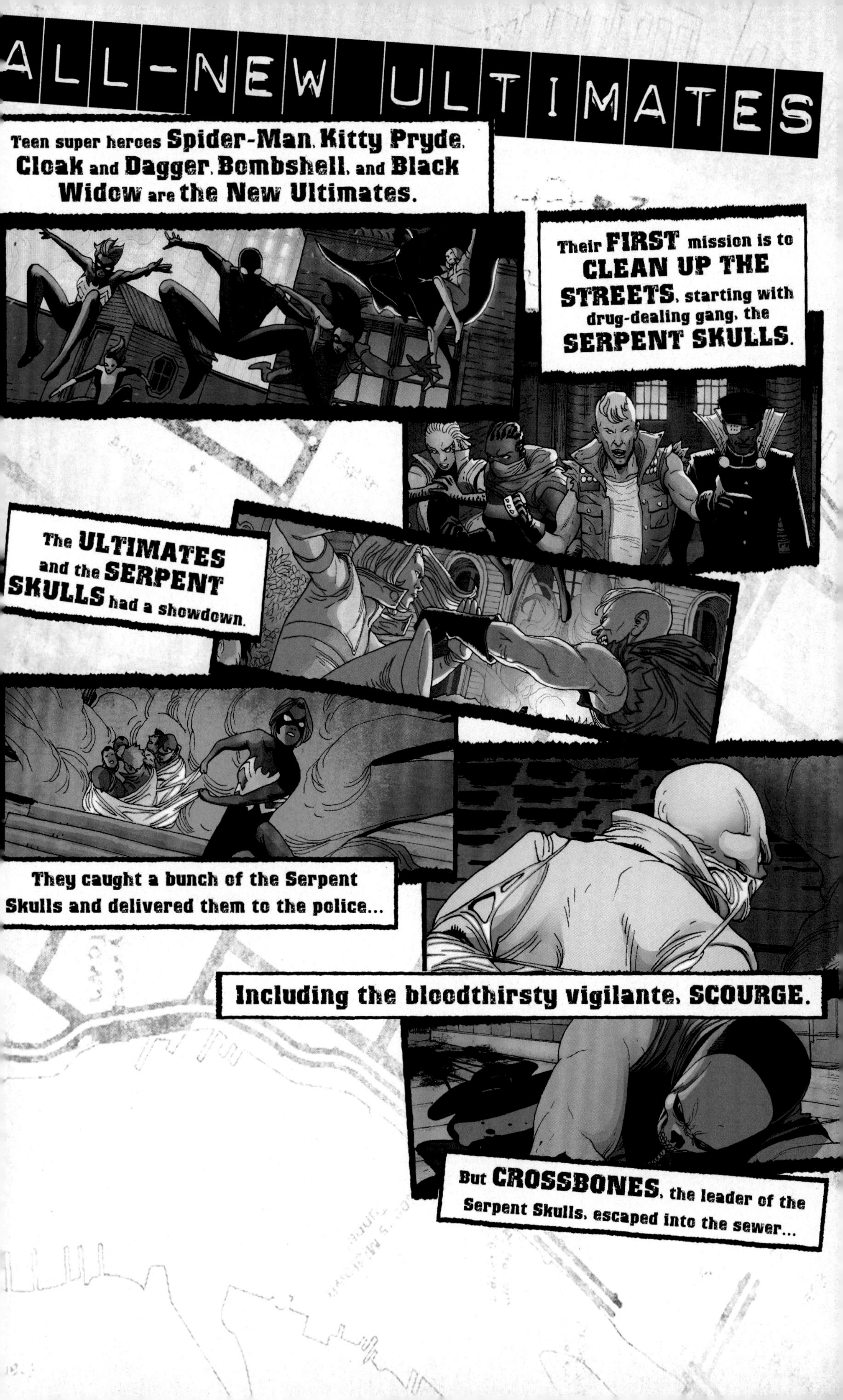
ALL-NEW ULTIMATES
Teen super heroes Spider-Man, Kitty Pryde, Cloak and Dagger, Bombshell, and Black Widow are the New Ultimates.
Their FIRST mission is to CLEAN UP THE STREETS, starting with drug-dealing gang, the SERPENT SKULLS.
The ULTIMATES and the SERPENT SKULLS had a showdown.
They caught a bunch of the Serpent Skulls and delivered them to the police...
Including the bloodthirsty vigilante, SCOURGE.
But CROSSBONES, the leader of the Serpent Skulls, escaped into the sewer...

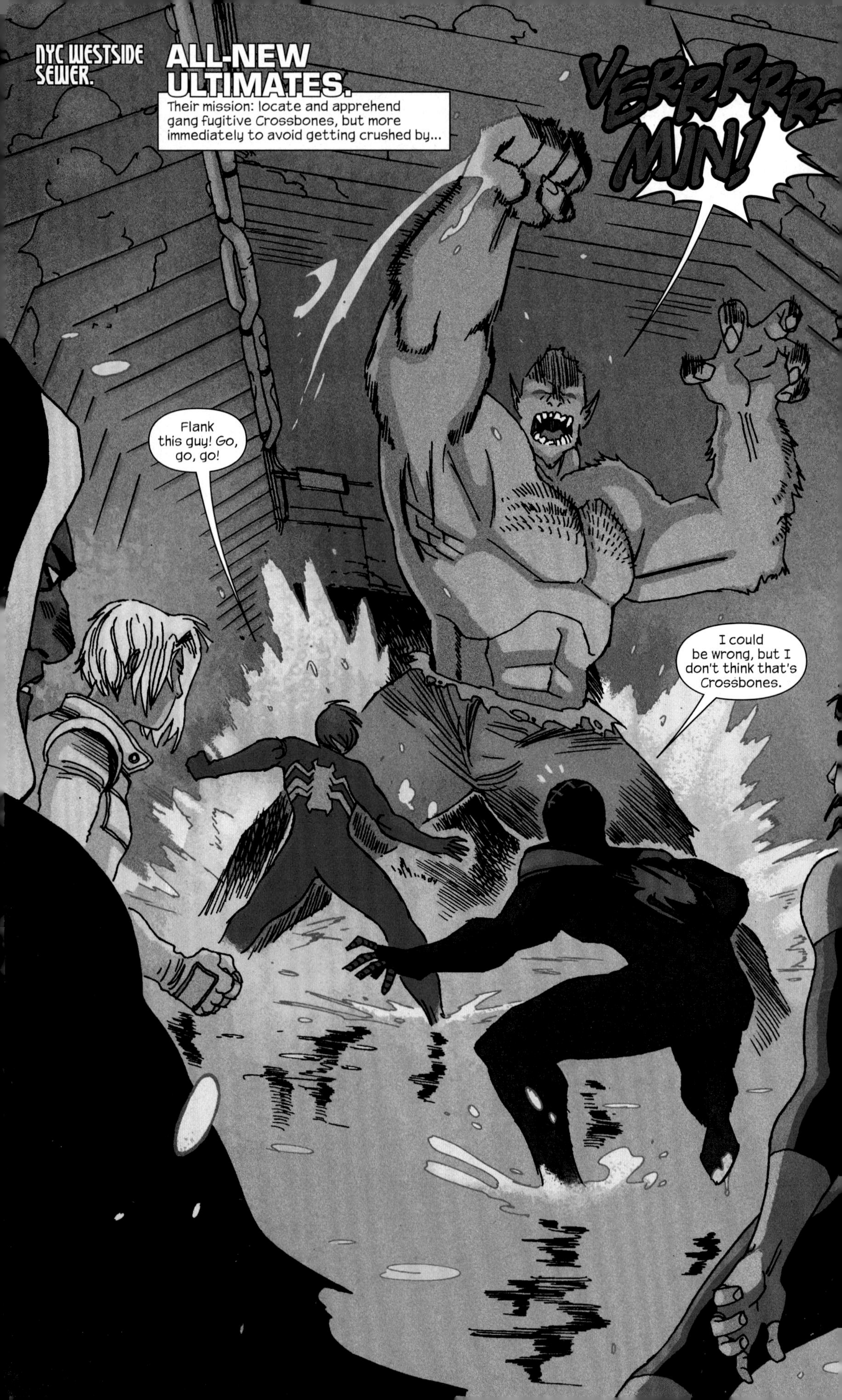
NYC WESTSIDE SEWER.
ALL-NEW ULTIMATES.
Their mission: locate and apprehend gang fugitive Crossbones, but more immediately to avoid getting crushed by...
VERRRRR-MIN!
Flank this guy! Go, go, go!
I could be wrong, but I don't think that's Crossbones.

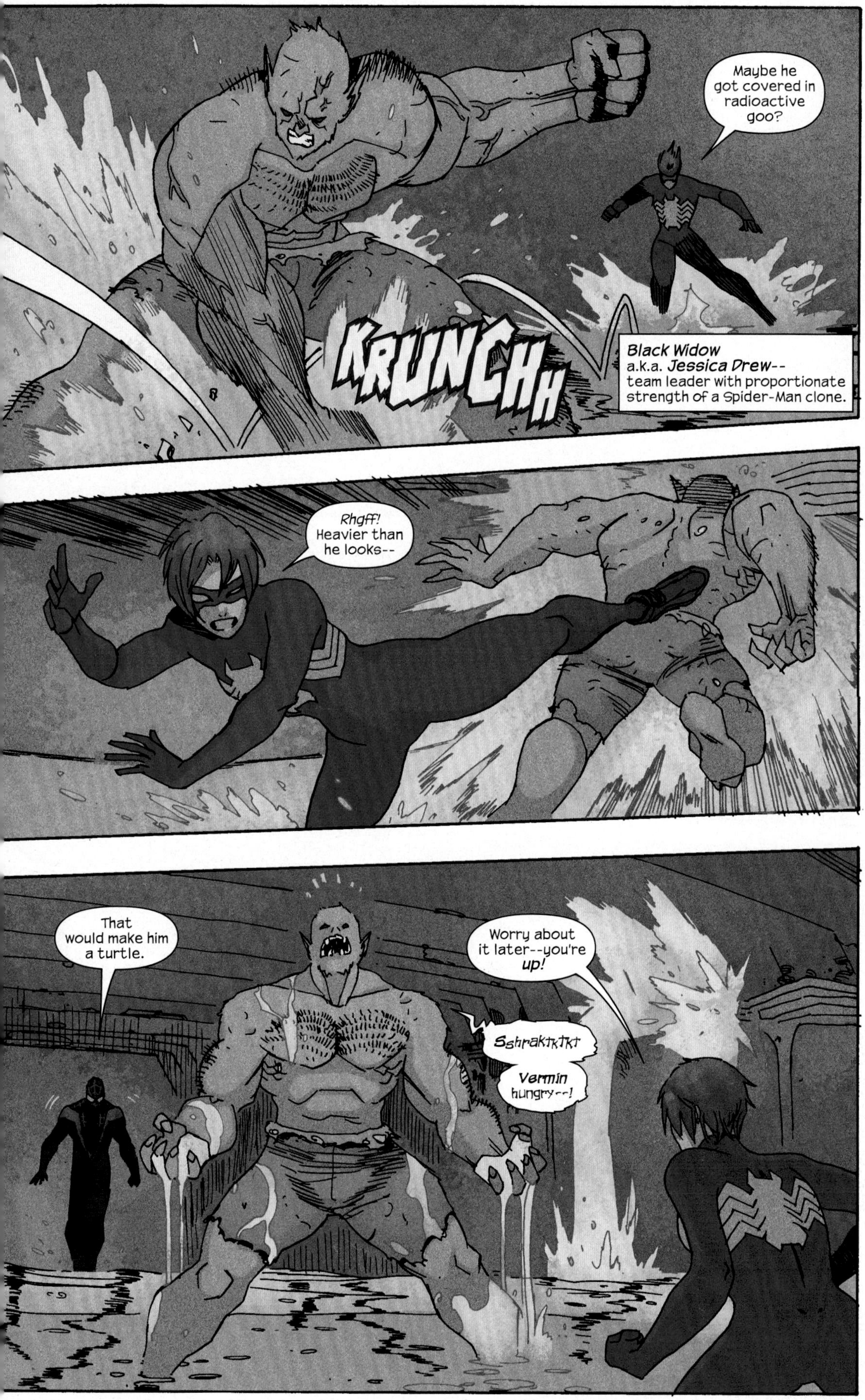

Maybe he got covered in radioactive goo?
KRUNCHH
Black Widow
a.k.a. Jessica Drew--
team leader with proportionate strength of a Spider-Man clone.
Rhgff! Heavier than he looks--
That would make him a turtle.
Worry about it later--you're up!
Sshraktktkt
Vermin hungry--!

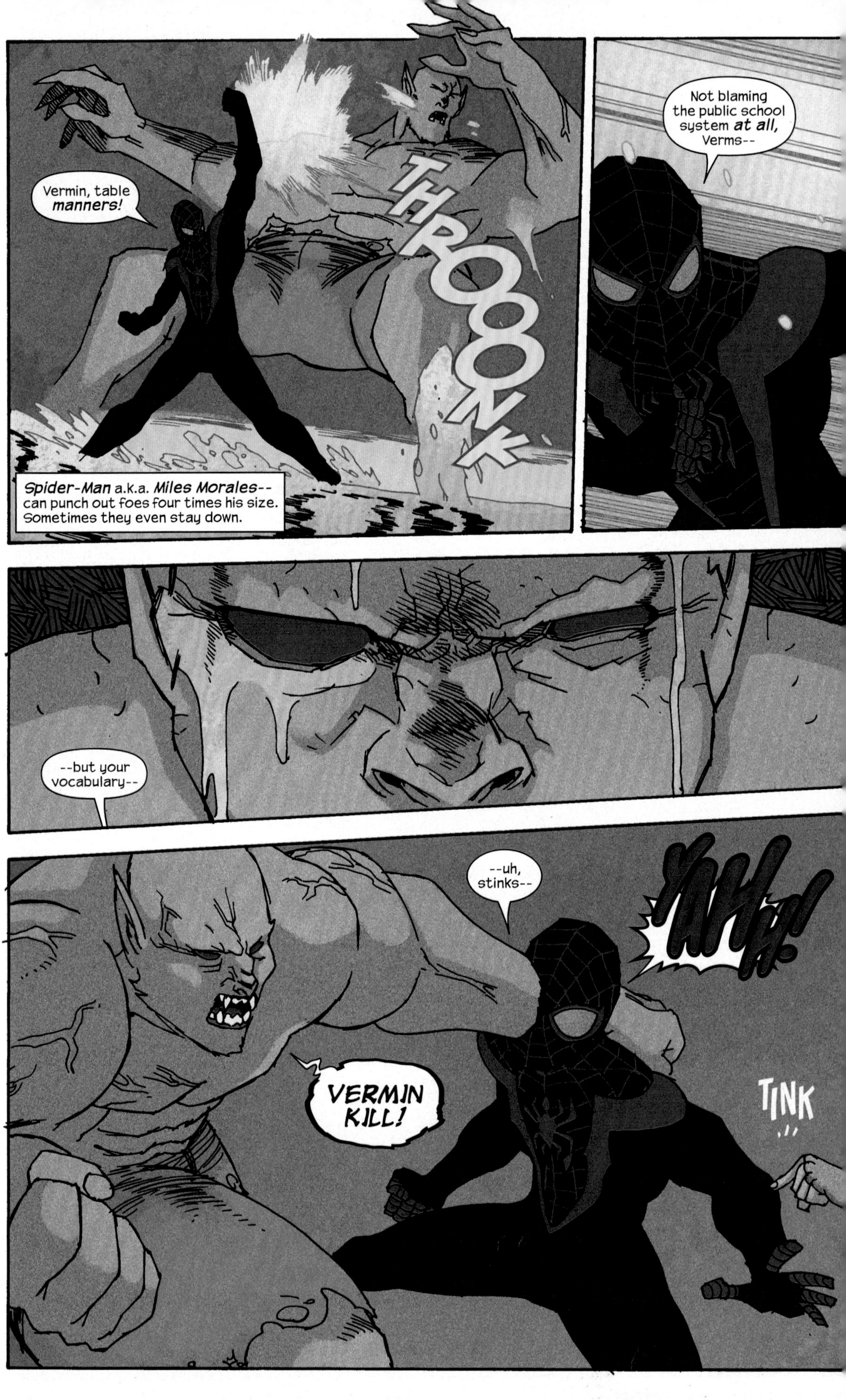
Vermin, table manners!
THROOONK
Spider-Man a.k.a. Miles Morales--
can punch out foes four times his size.
Sometimes they even stay down.
Not blaming the public school system at all, Verms--
--but your vocabulary--
--uh, stinks--
YAHH!
VERMIN KILL!
TINK

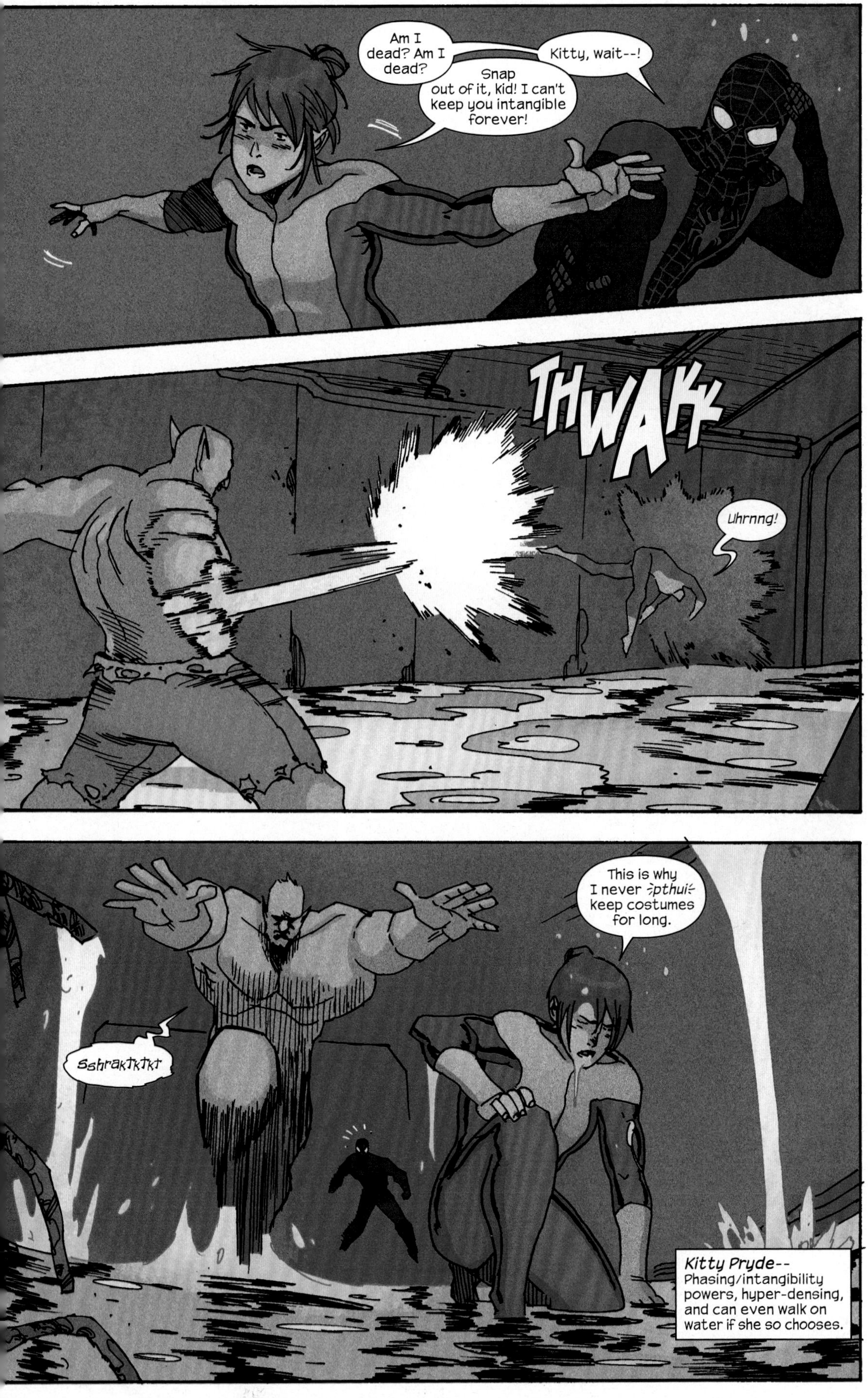
Am I dead? Am I dead?
Kitty, wait--!
Snap out of it, kid! I can't keep you intangible forever!
THWAKK
Uhrnng!
This is why I never ~pthui~ keep costumes for long.
Sshraktktkt
Kitty Pryde--
Phasing/intangibility powers, hyper-densing, and can even walk on water if she so chooses.

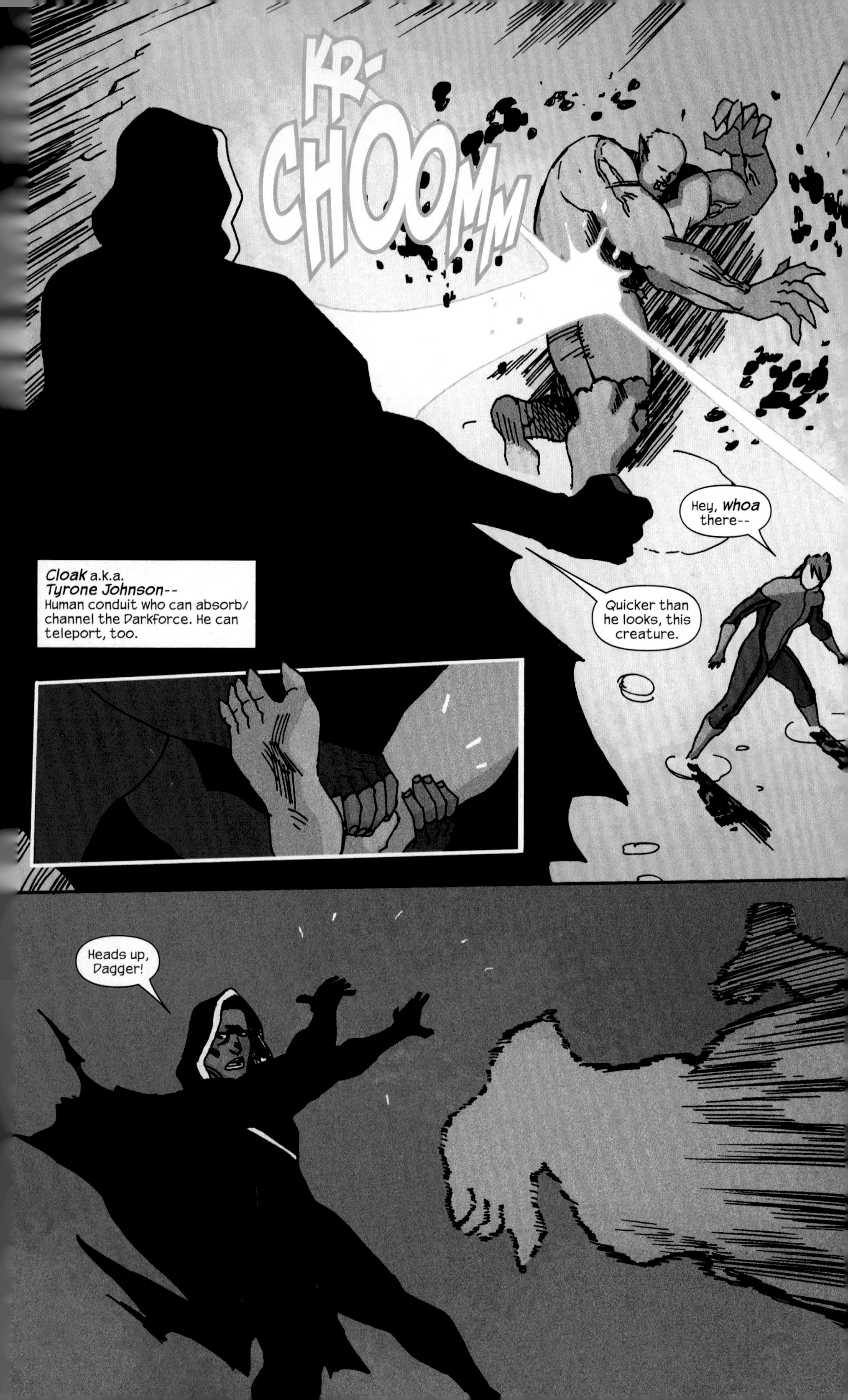
KR-CHOOMM
Hey, whoa there--
Cloak a.k.a. Tyrone Johnson-- Human conduit who can absorb/ channel the Darkforce. He can teleport, too.
Quicker than he looks, this creature.
Heads up, Dagger!

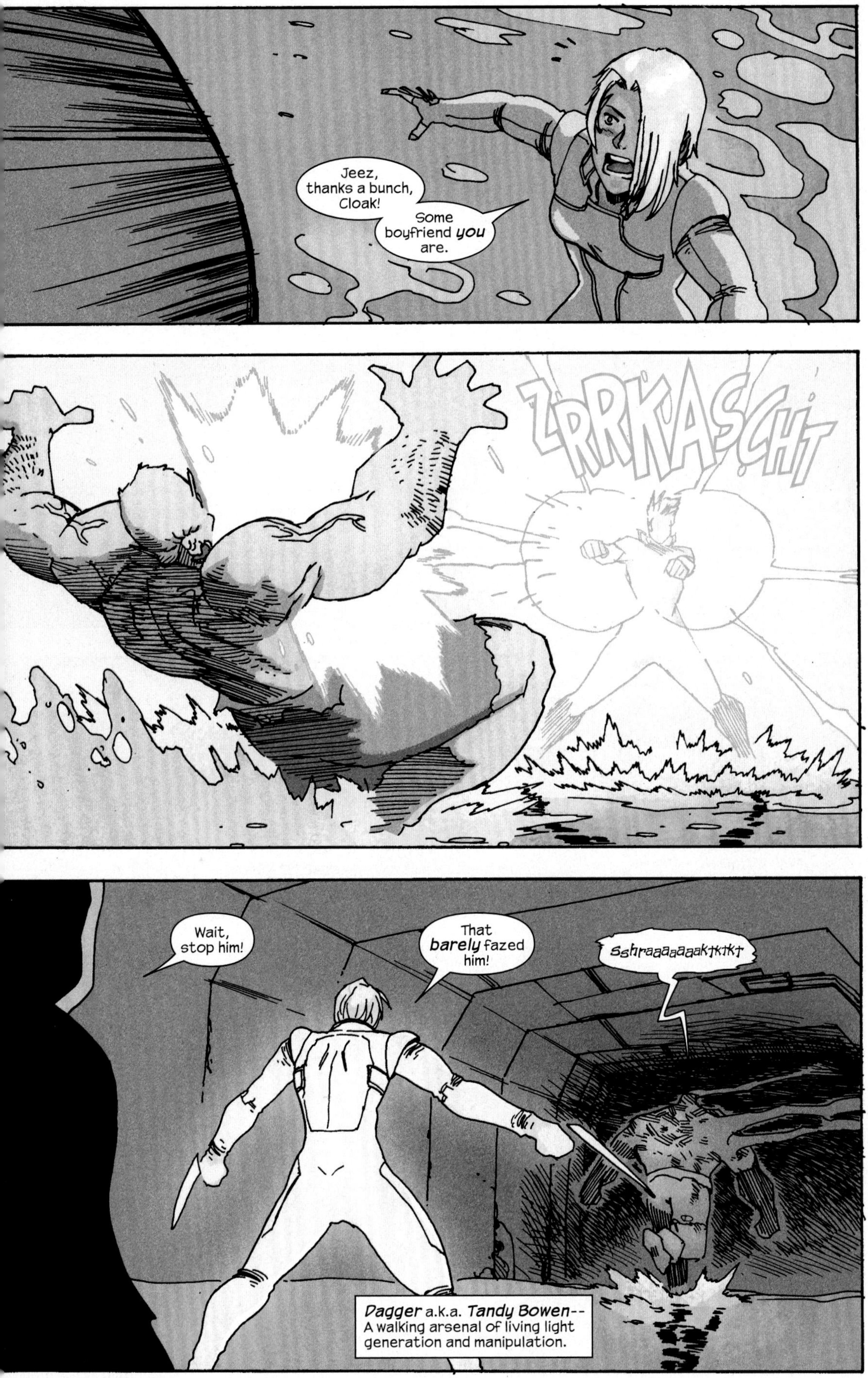

Jeez, thanks a bunch, Cloak!
Some boyfriend *you* are.
ZRRKASCHT
Wait, stop him!
That *barely* fazed him!
Sshraaaaaaaaktktkt
Dagger a.k.a. *Tandy Bowen*-- A walking arsenal of living light generation and manipulation.

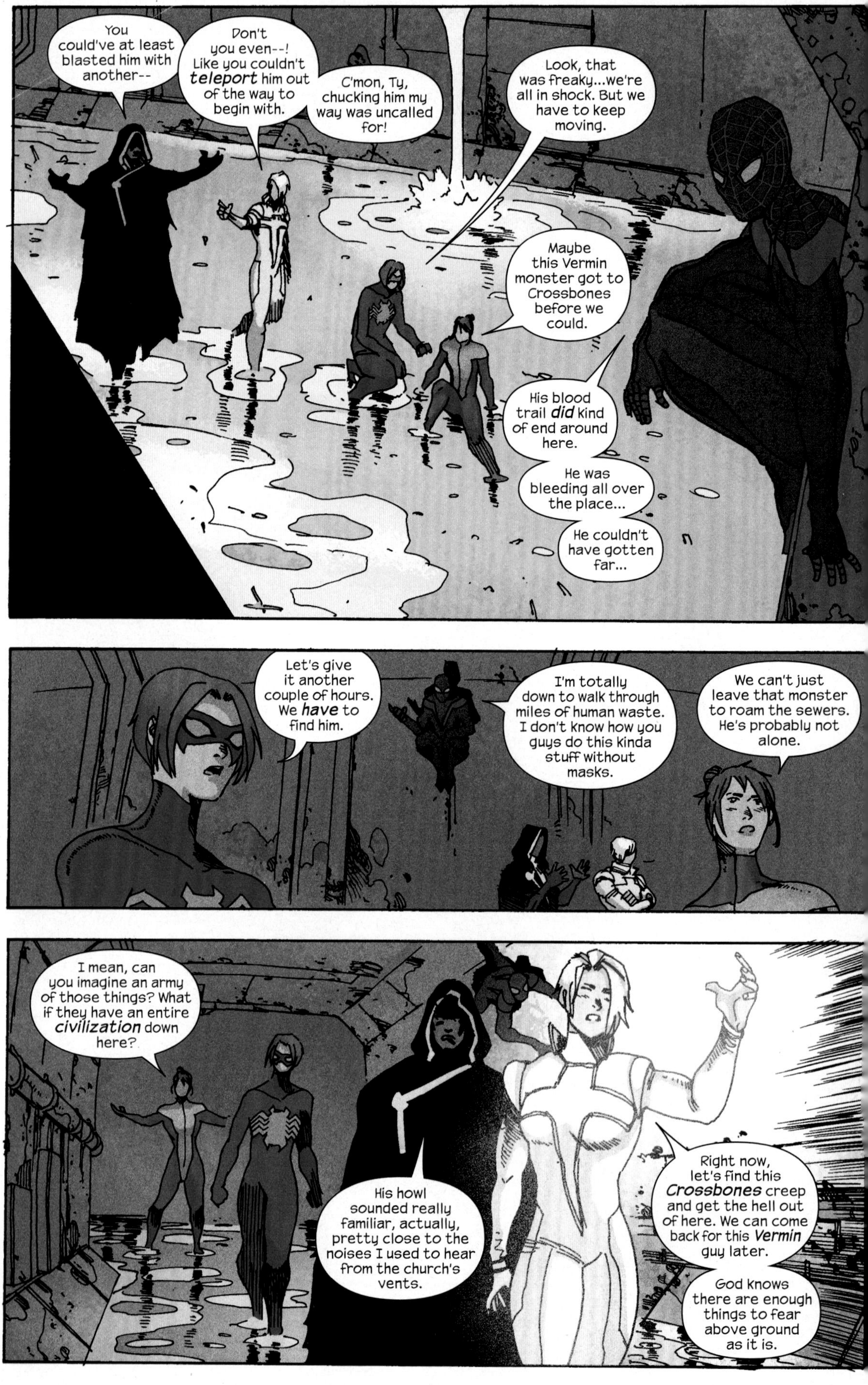

You could've at least blasted him with another--
Don't you even--! Like you couldn't *teleport* him out of the way to begin with.
C'mon, Ty, chucking him my way was uncalled for!
Look, that was freaky...we're all in shock. But we have to keep moving.
Maybe this Vermin monster got to Crossbones before we could.
His blood trail *did* kind of end around here.
He was bleeding all over the place...
He couldn't have gotten far...
Let's give it another couple of hours. We *have* to find him.
I'm totally down to walk through miles of human waste. I don't know how you guys do this kinda stuff without masks.
We can't just leave that monster to roam the sewers. He's probably not alone.
I mean, can you imagine an army of those things? What if they have an entire *civilization* down here?
His howl sounded really familiar, actually, pretty close to the noises I used to hear from the church's vents.
Right now, let's find this *Crossbones* creep and get the hell out of here. We can come back for this *Vermin* guy later.
God knows there are enough things to fear above ground as it is.

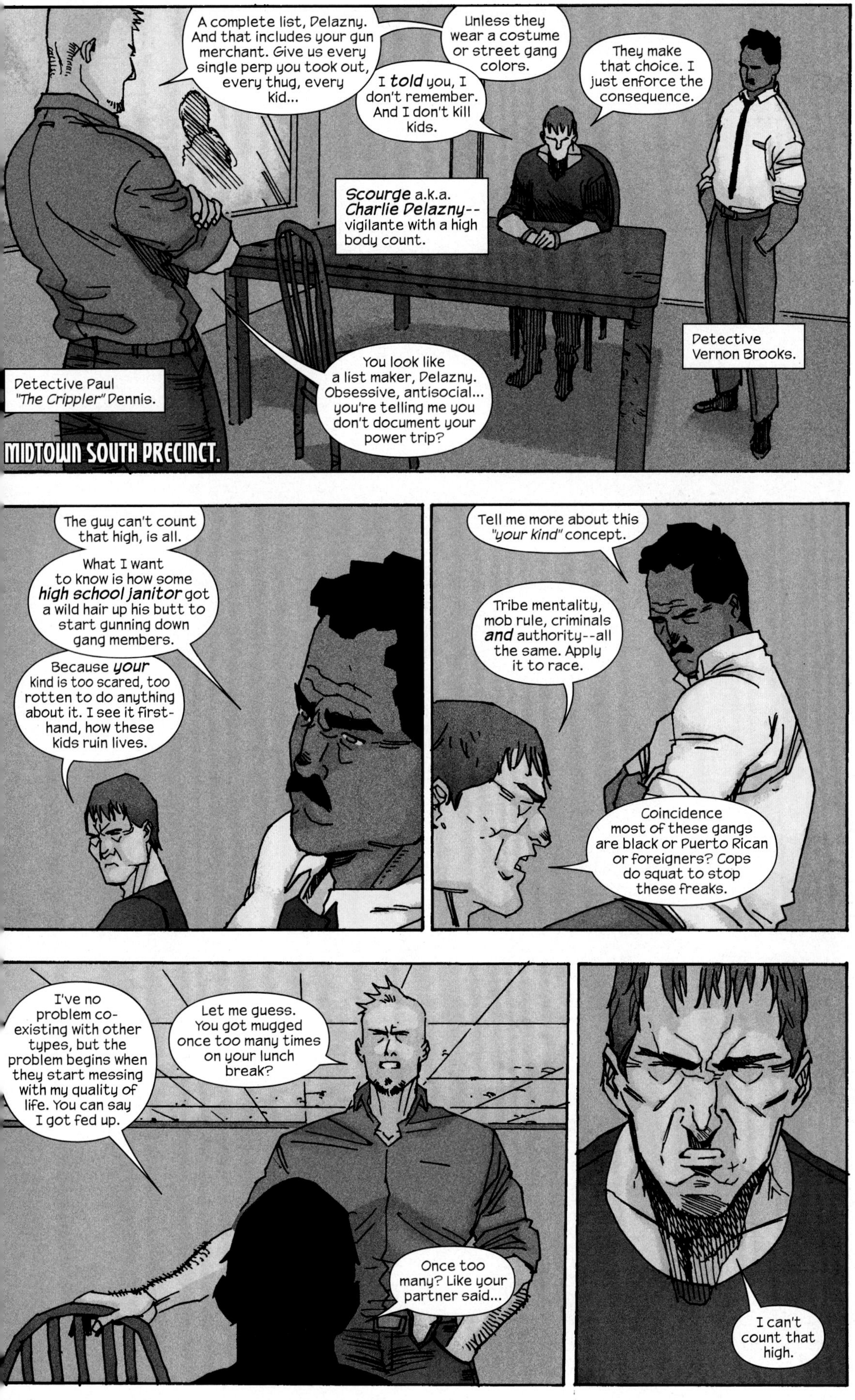
MIDTOWN SOUTH PRECINCT.
Detective Paul "The Crippler" Dennis.
Scourge a.k.a. Charlie Delazny--vigilante with a high body count.
Detective Vernon Brooks.
A complete list, Delazny. And that includes your gun merchant. Give us every single perp you took out, every thug, every kid...
I told you, I don't remember. And I don't kill kids.
Unless they wear a costume or street gang colors.
They make that choice. I just enforce the consequence.
You look like a list maker, Delazny. Obsessive, antisocial... you're telling me you don't document your power trip?
The guy can't count that high, is all.
What I want to know is how some high school janitor got a wild hair up his butt to start gunning down gang members.
Because your kind is too scared, too rotten to do anything about it. I see it first-hand, how these kids ruin lives.
Tell me more about this "your kind" concept.
Tribe mentality, mob rule, criminals and authority--all the same. Apply it to race.
Coincidence most of these gangs are black or Puerto Rican or foreigners? Cops do squat to stop these freaks.
I've no problem co-existing with other types, but the problem begins when they start messing with my quality of life. You can say I got fed up.
Let me guess. You got mugged once too many times on your lunch break?
Once too many? Like your partner said...
I can't count that high.

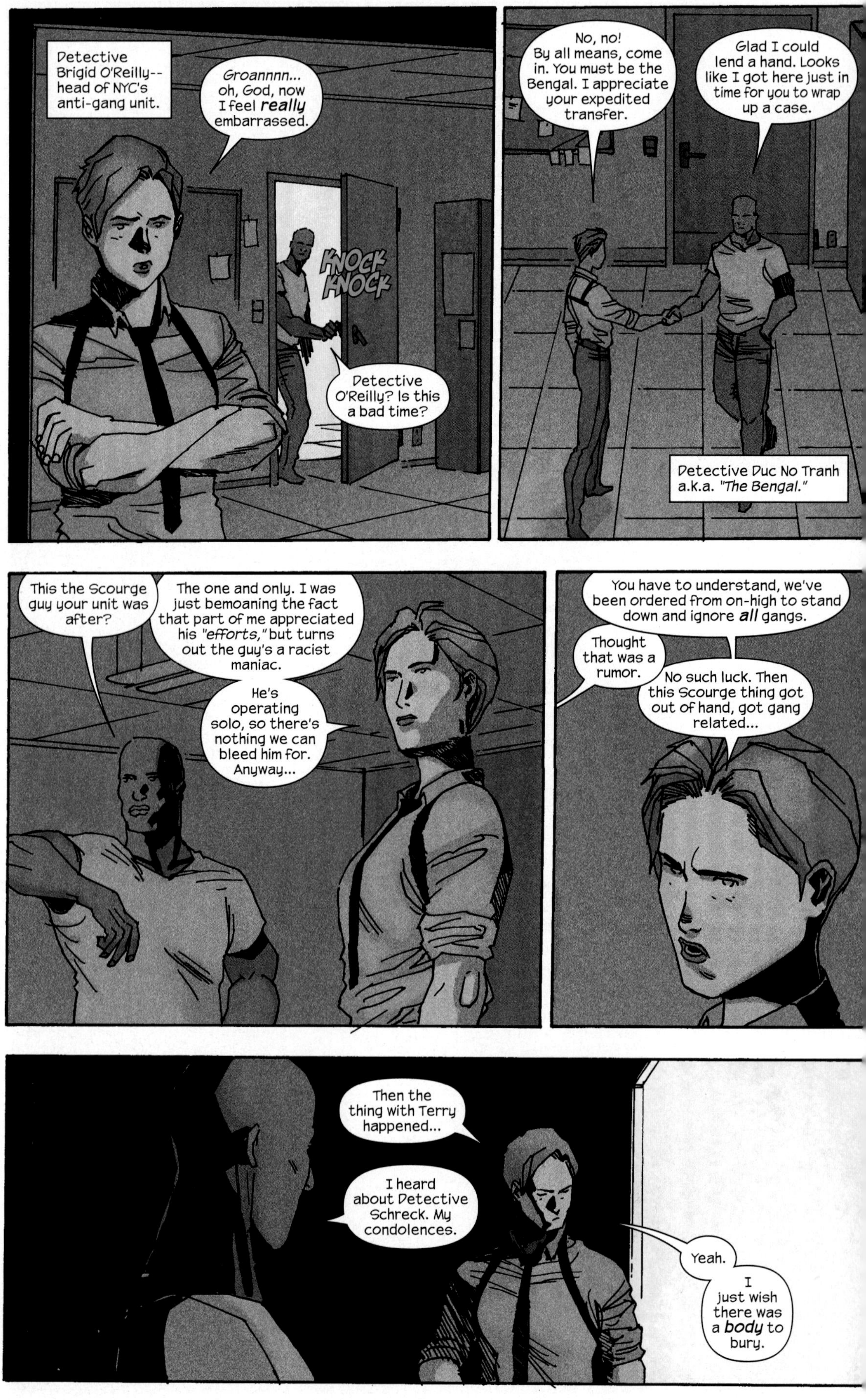

Detective Brigid O'Reilly-- head of NYC's anti-gang unit.
Groannnn... oh, God, now I feel *really* embarrassed.
KNOCK KNOCK
Detective O'Reilly? Is this a bad time?
No, no! By all means, come in. You must be the Bengal. I appreciate your expedited transfer.
Glad I could lend a hand. Looks like I got here just in time for you to wrap up a case.
Detective Duc No Tranh a.k.a. *"The Bengal."*
This the Scourge guy your unit was after?
The one and only. I was just bemoaning the fact that part of me appreciated his *"efforts,"* but turns out the guy's a racist maniac.
He's operating solo, so there's nothing we can bleed him for. Anyway...
You have to understand, we've been ordered from on-high to stand down and ignore *all* gangs.
Thought that was a rumor.
No such luck. Then this Scourge thing got out of hand, got gang related...
Then the thing with Terry happened...
I heard about Detective Schreck. My condolences.
Yeah.
I just wish there was a *body* to bury.

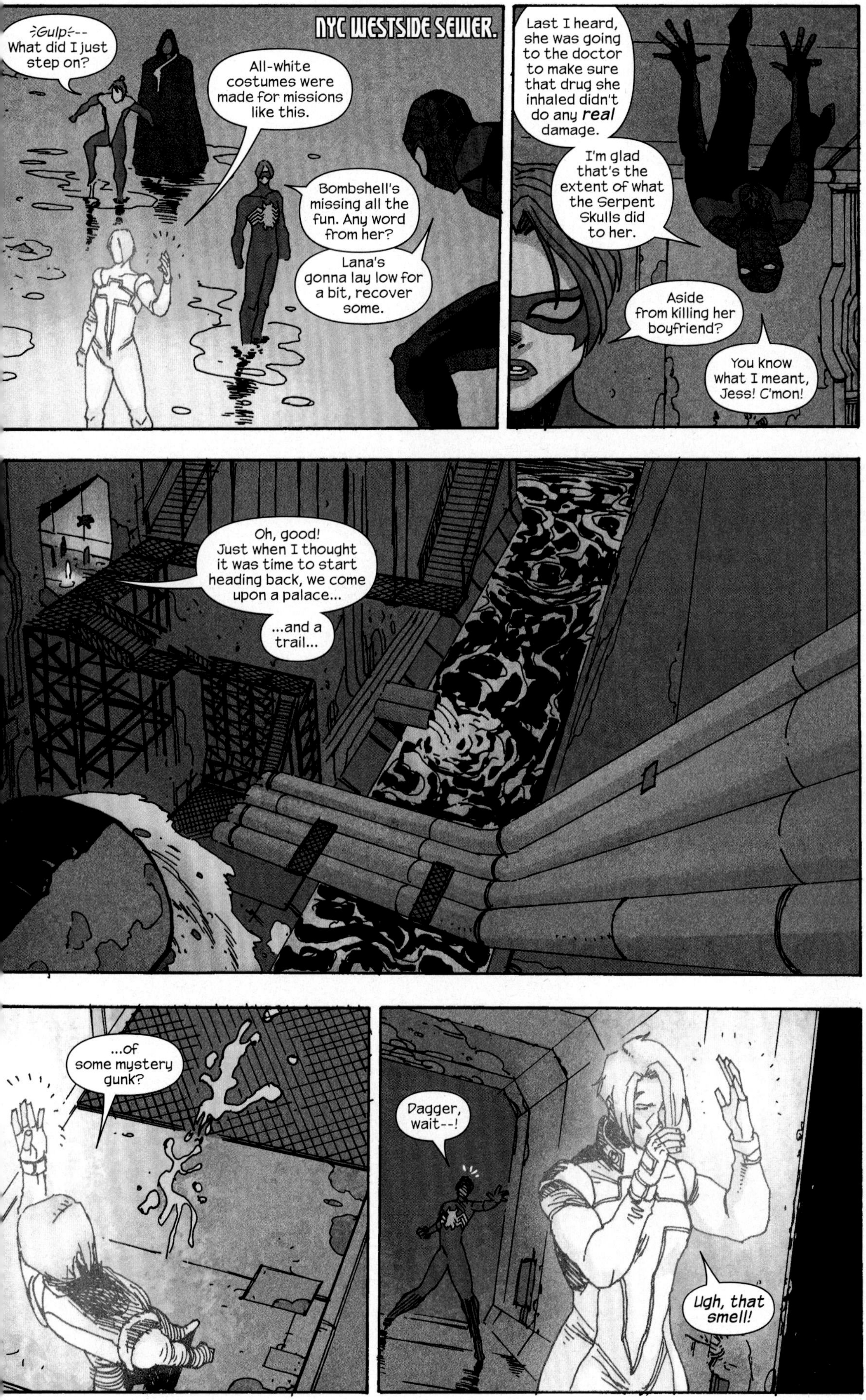
NYC WESTSIDE SEWER.
-Gulp--- What did I just step on?
All-white costumes were made for missions like this.
Bombshell's missing all the fun. Any word from her?
Lana's gonna lay low for a bit, recover some.
Last I heard, she was going to the doctor to make sure that drug she inhaled didn't do any *real* damage.
I'm glad that's the extent of what the Serpent Skulls did to her.
Aside from killing her boyfriend?
You know what I meant, Jess! C'mon!
Oh, good! Just when I thought it was time to start heading back, we come upon a palace...
...and a trail...
...of some mystery gunk?
Dagger, wait--!
Ugh, that smell!

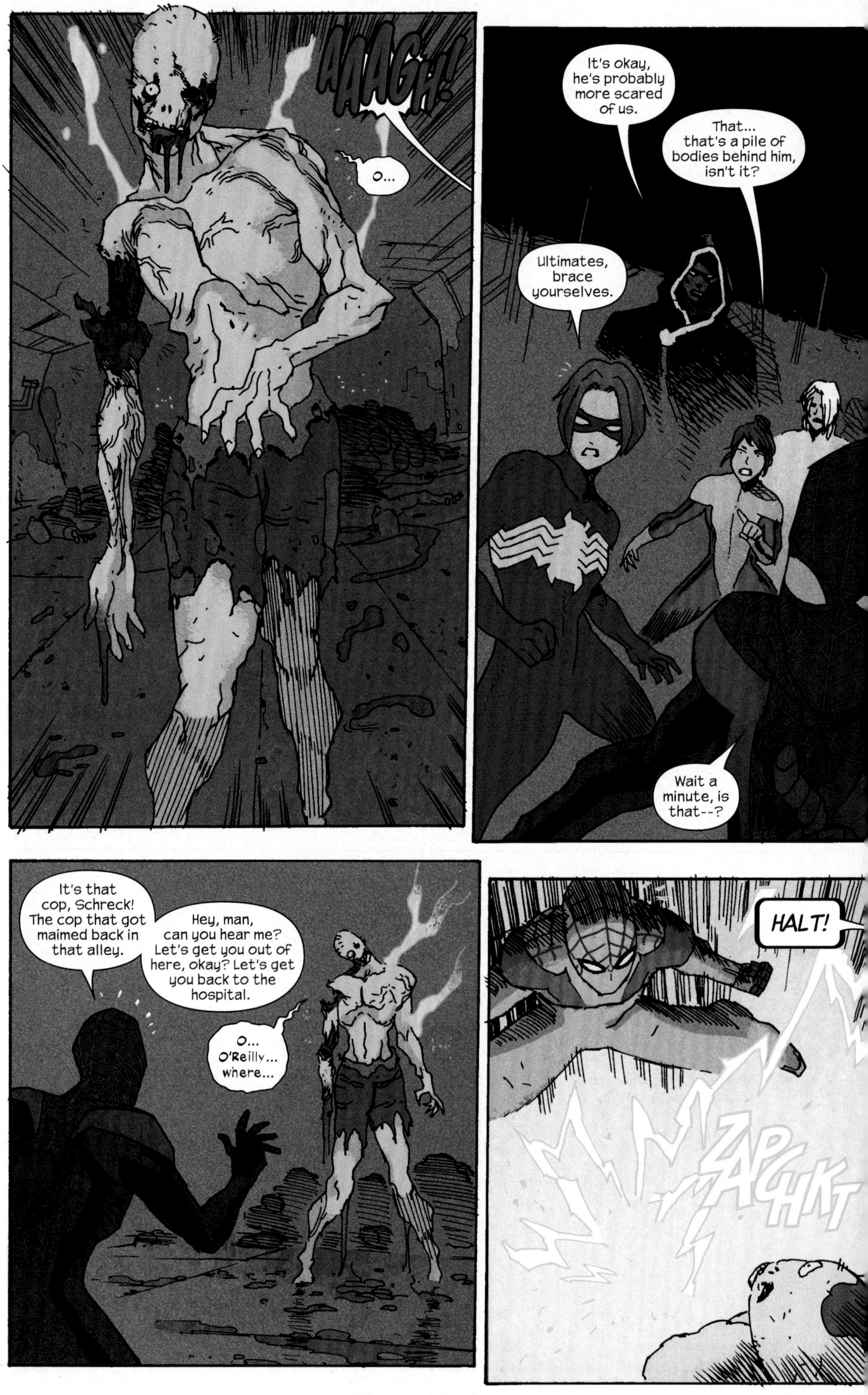
AAAGH!
O...
It's okay, he's probably more scared of us.
That... that's a pile of bodies behind him, isn't it?
Ultimates, brace yourselves.
Wait a minute, is that--?
It's that cop, Schreck! The cop that got maimed back in that alley.
Hey, man, can you hear me? Let's get you out of here, okay? Let's get you back to the hospital.
O... O'Reilly... where...
HALT!
ZAPCHKT

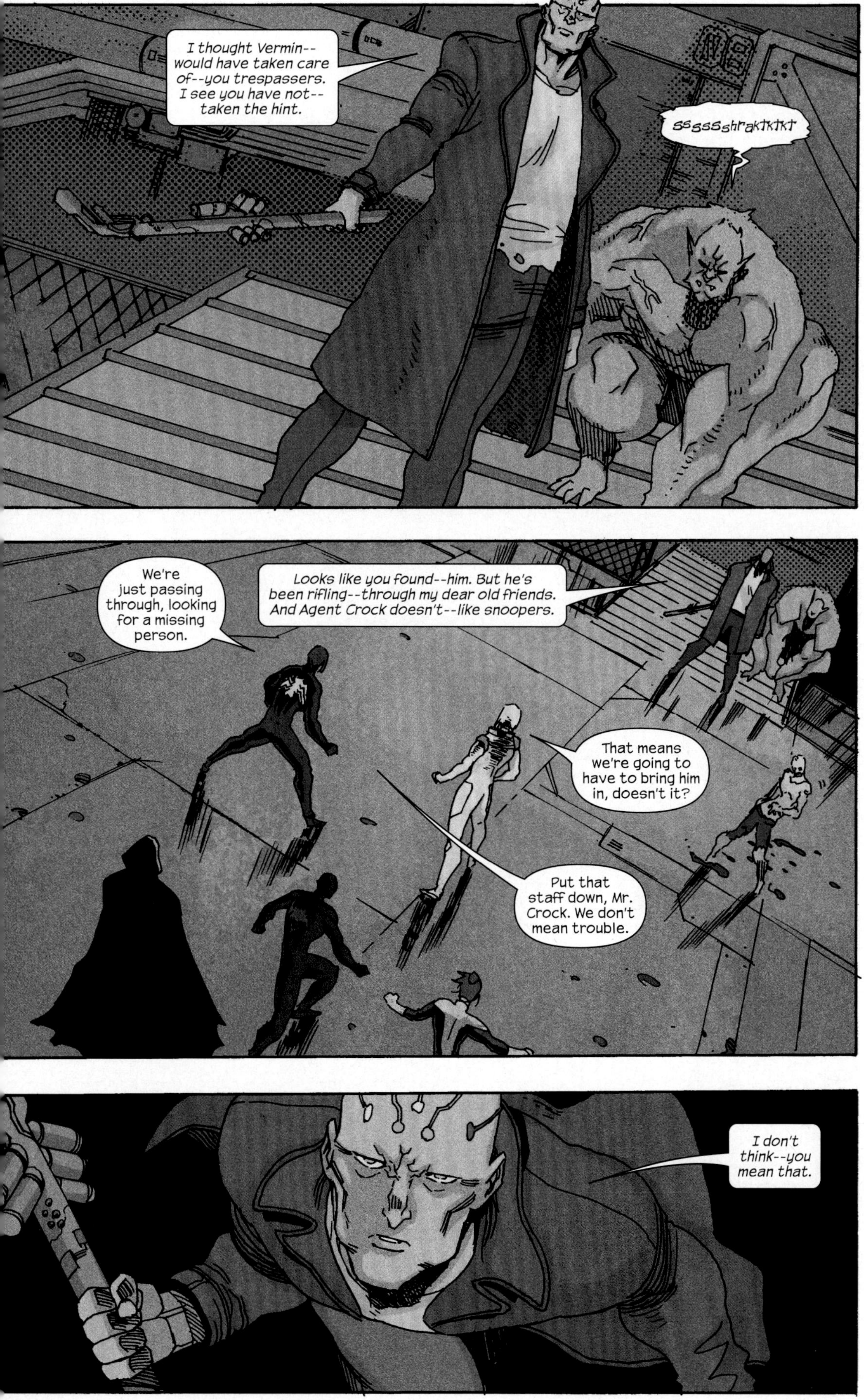
I thought Vermin--would have taken care of--you trespassers. I see you have not--taken the hint.
Ssssssshrakktkkt
We're just passing through, looking for a missing person.
Looks like you found--him. But he's been rifling--through my dear old friends. And Agent Crock doesn't--like snoopers.
That means we're going to have to bring him in, doesn't it?
Put that staff down, Mr. Crock. We don't mean trouble.
I don't think--you mean that.

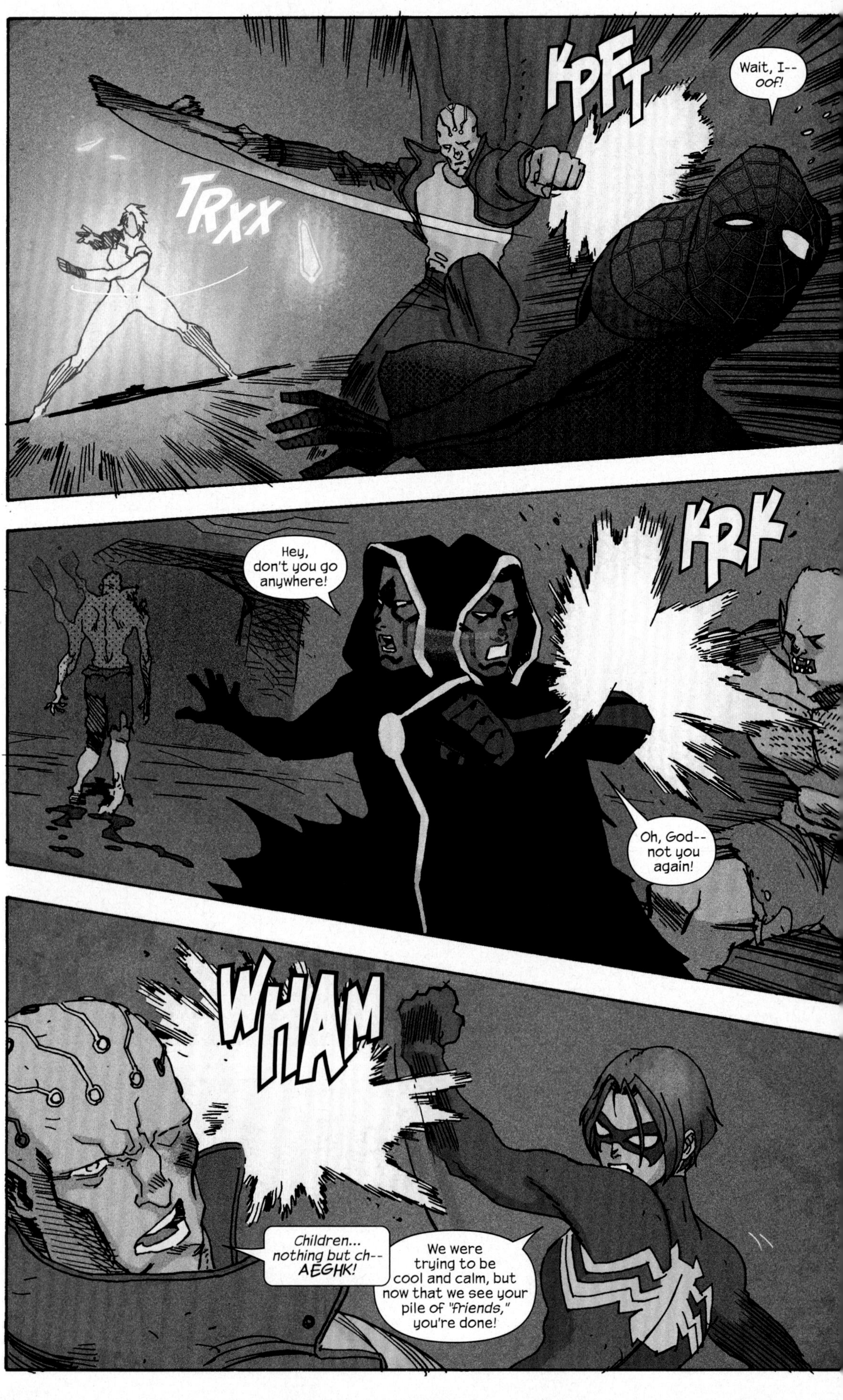

TRXX
KPFT
Wait, I-- oof!
Hey, don't you go anywhere!
KRK
Oh, God-- not you again!
WHAM
Children... nothing but ch-- AEGHK!
We were trying to be cool and calm, but now that we see your pile of "friends," you're done!

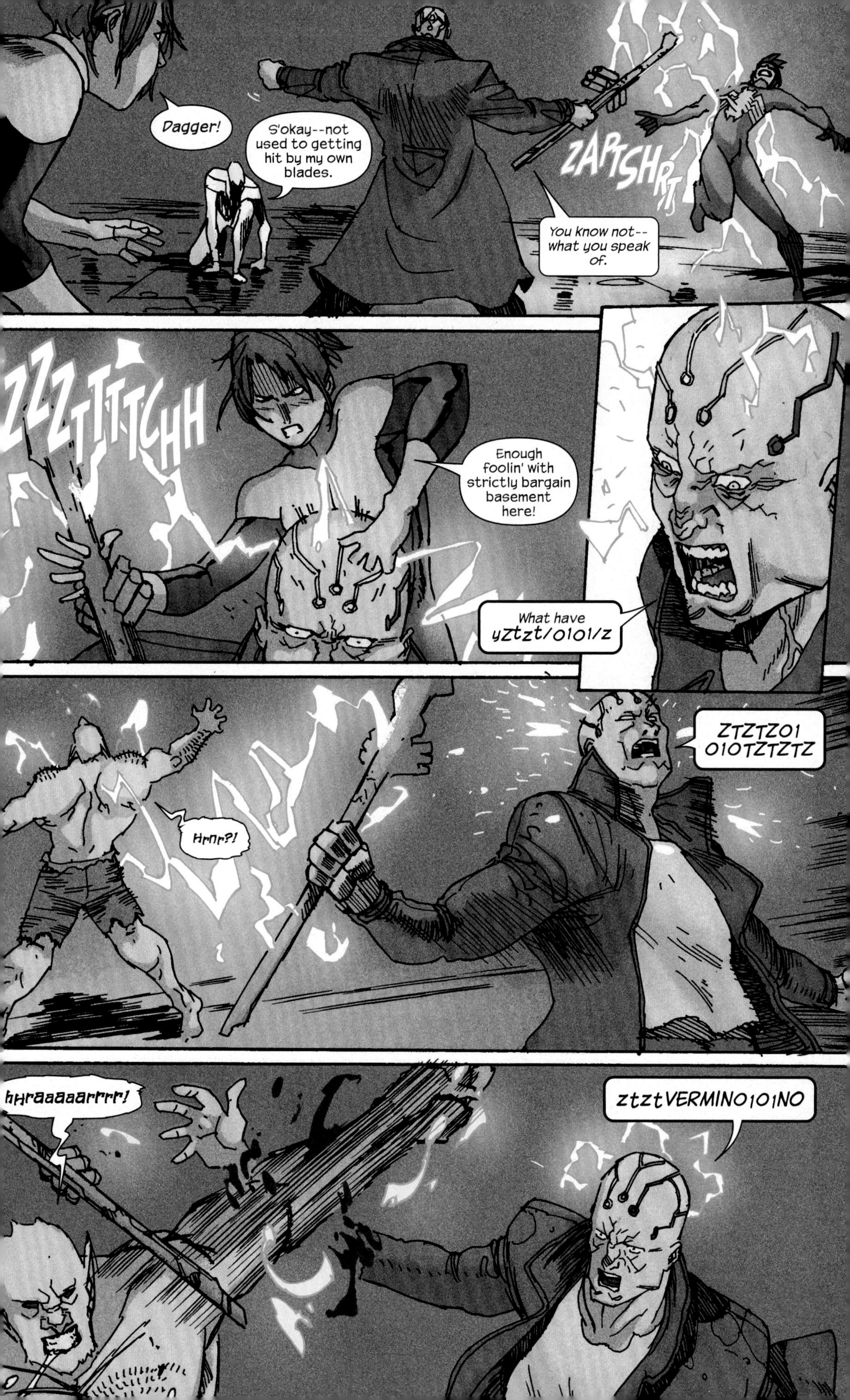
Dagger!
S'okay--not used to getting hit by my own blades.
ZARTSHRT
You know not--what you speak of.
ZZZTTTTCHH
Enough foolin' with strictly bargain basement here!
What have yztzt/0101/z
ZTZTZ01 010TZTZTZ
Hrnr?!
hHraaaaarrrr!
ztztVERMIN0101NO

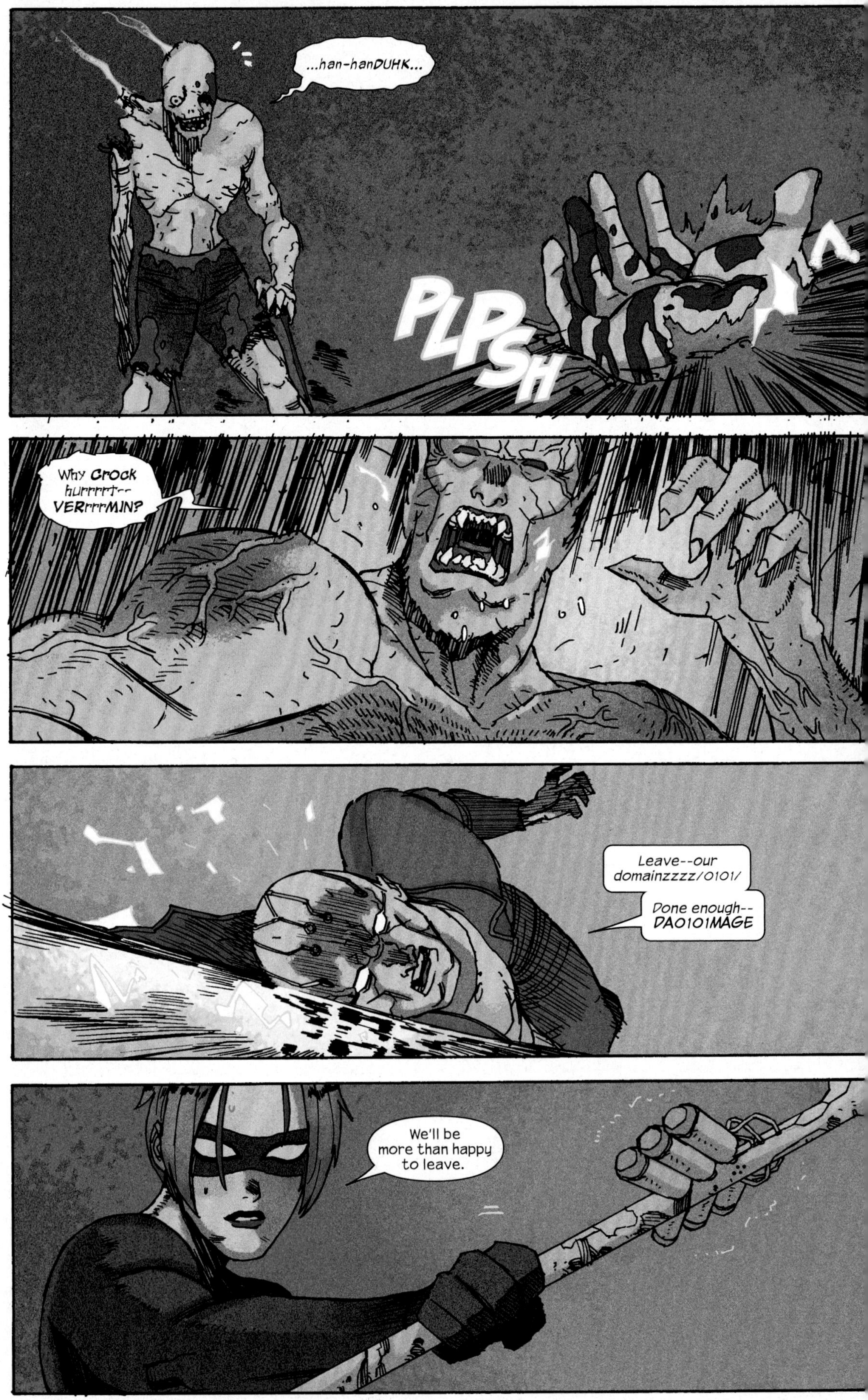
...han-hanDUHK...
PLPSH
Why Crock hurrrrrt-- VERrrrMIN?
Leave--our domainzzzz/0101/
Done enough-- DA0101MAGE
We'll be more than happy to leave.

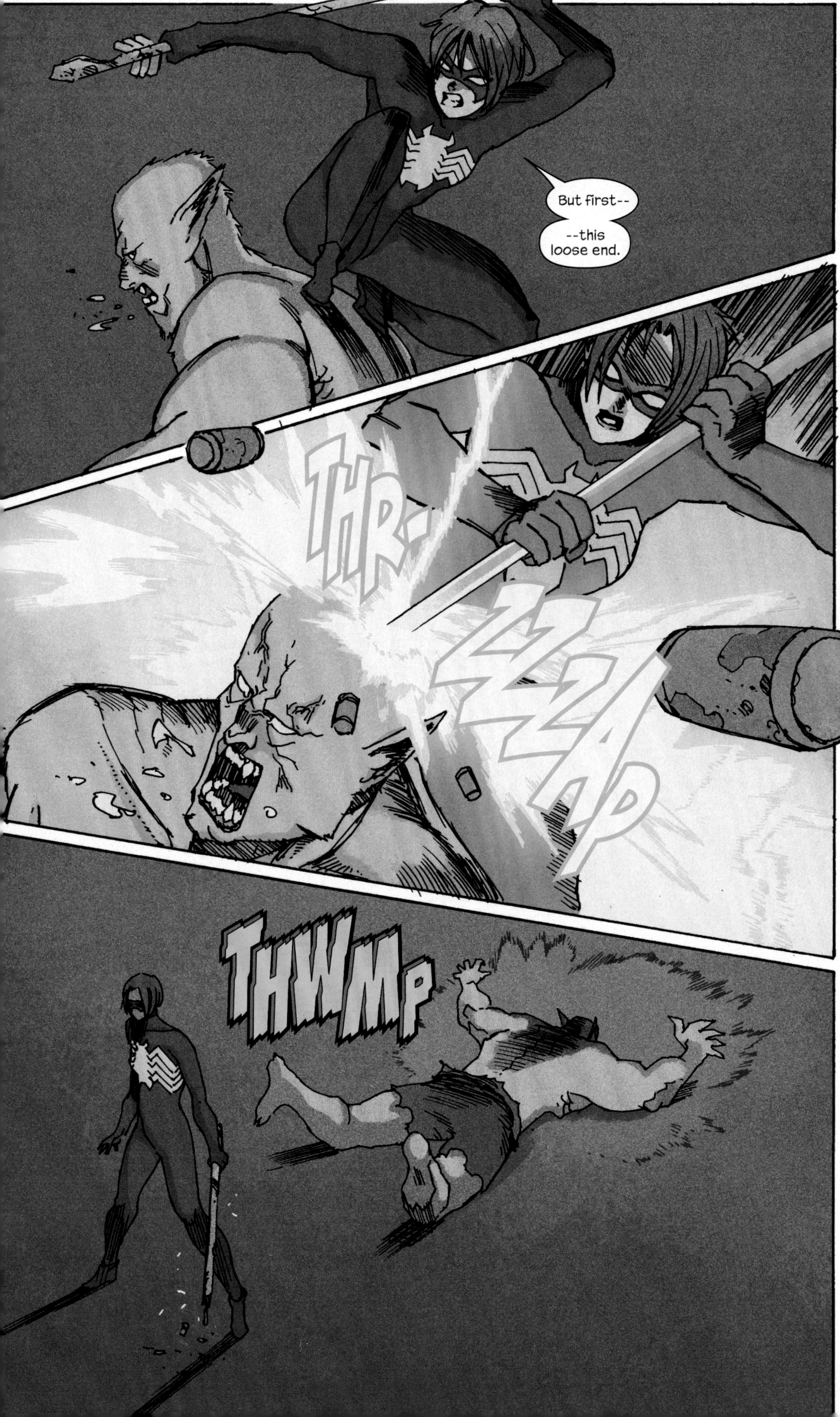
But first--
--this loose end.
THR-ZZAP
THWMP

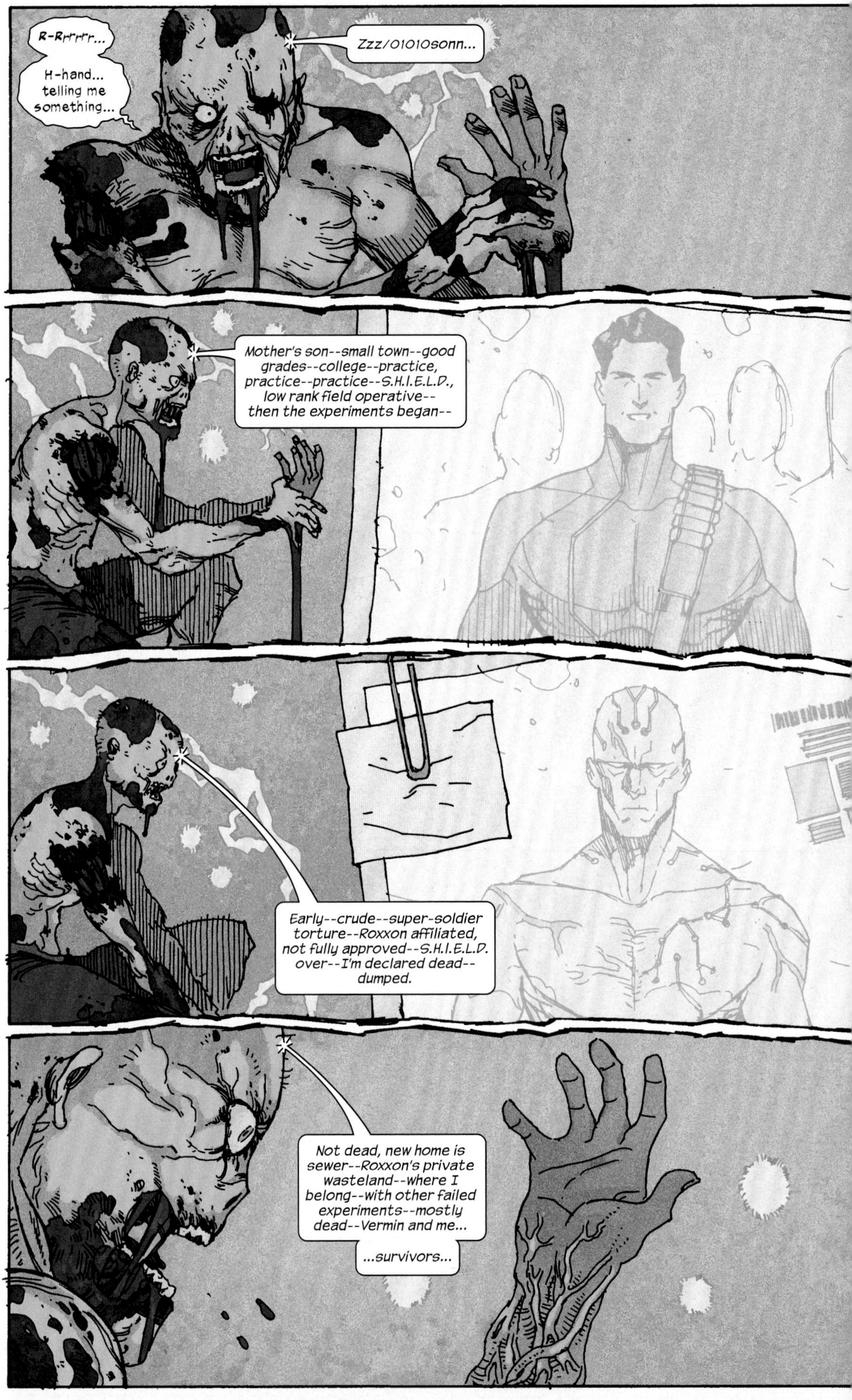
R-Rrrrrr...
H-hand... telling me something...
Zzz/01010sonn...
Mother's son--small town--good grades--college--practice, practice--practice--S.H.I.E.L.D., low rank field operative-- then the experiments began--
Early--crude--super-soldier torture--Roxxon affiliated, not fully approved--S.H.I.E.L.D. over--I'm declared dead-- dumped.
Not dead, new home is sewer--Roxxon's private wasteland--where I belong--with other failed experiments--mostly dead--Vermin and me...
...survivors...

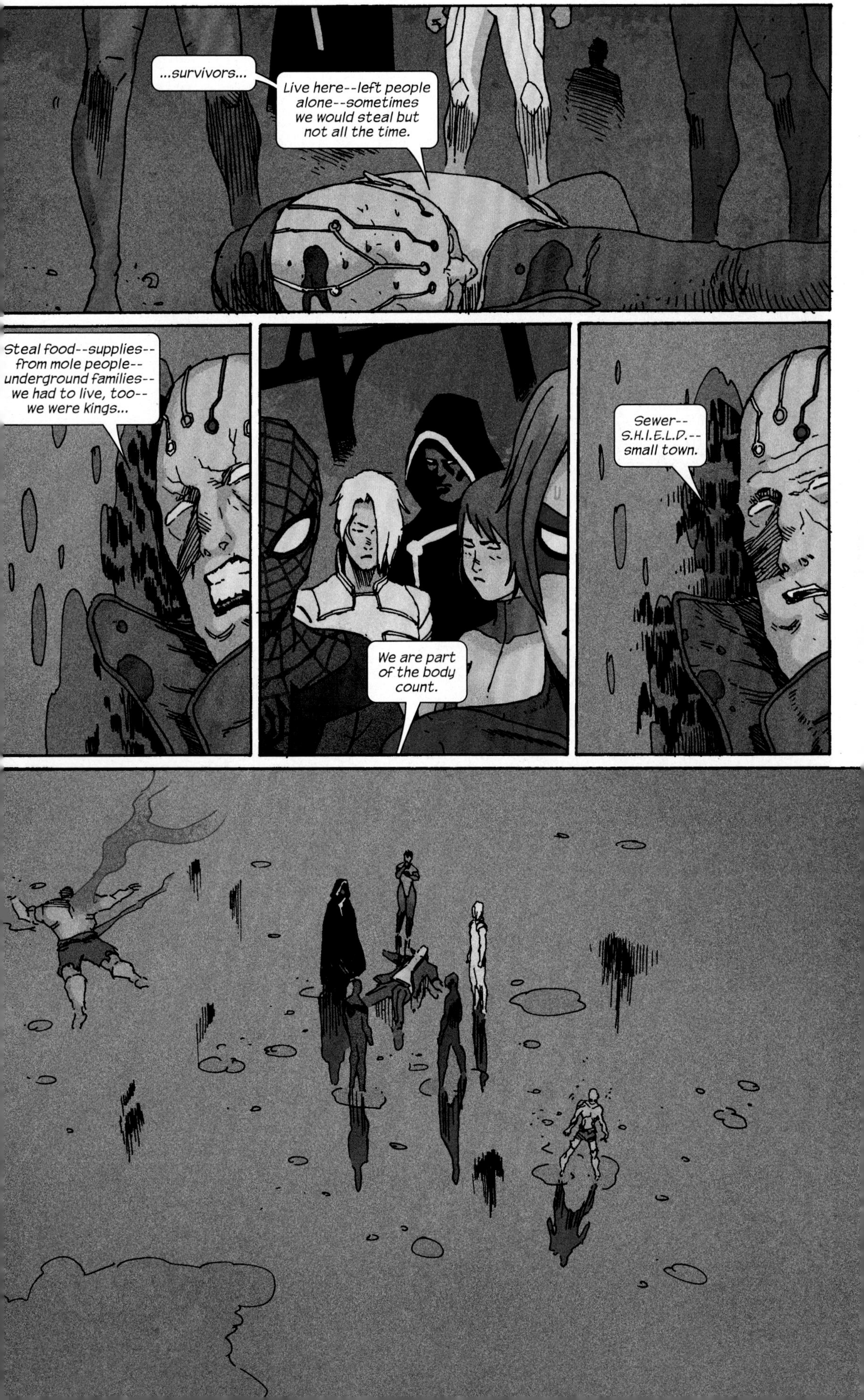
...survivors...
Live here--left people alone--sometimes we would steal but not all the time.
Steal food--supplies--from mole people--underground families--we had to live, too--we were kings...
We are part of the body count.
Sewer--S.H.I.E.L.D.--small town.

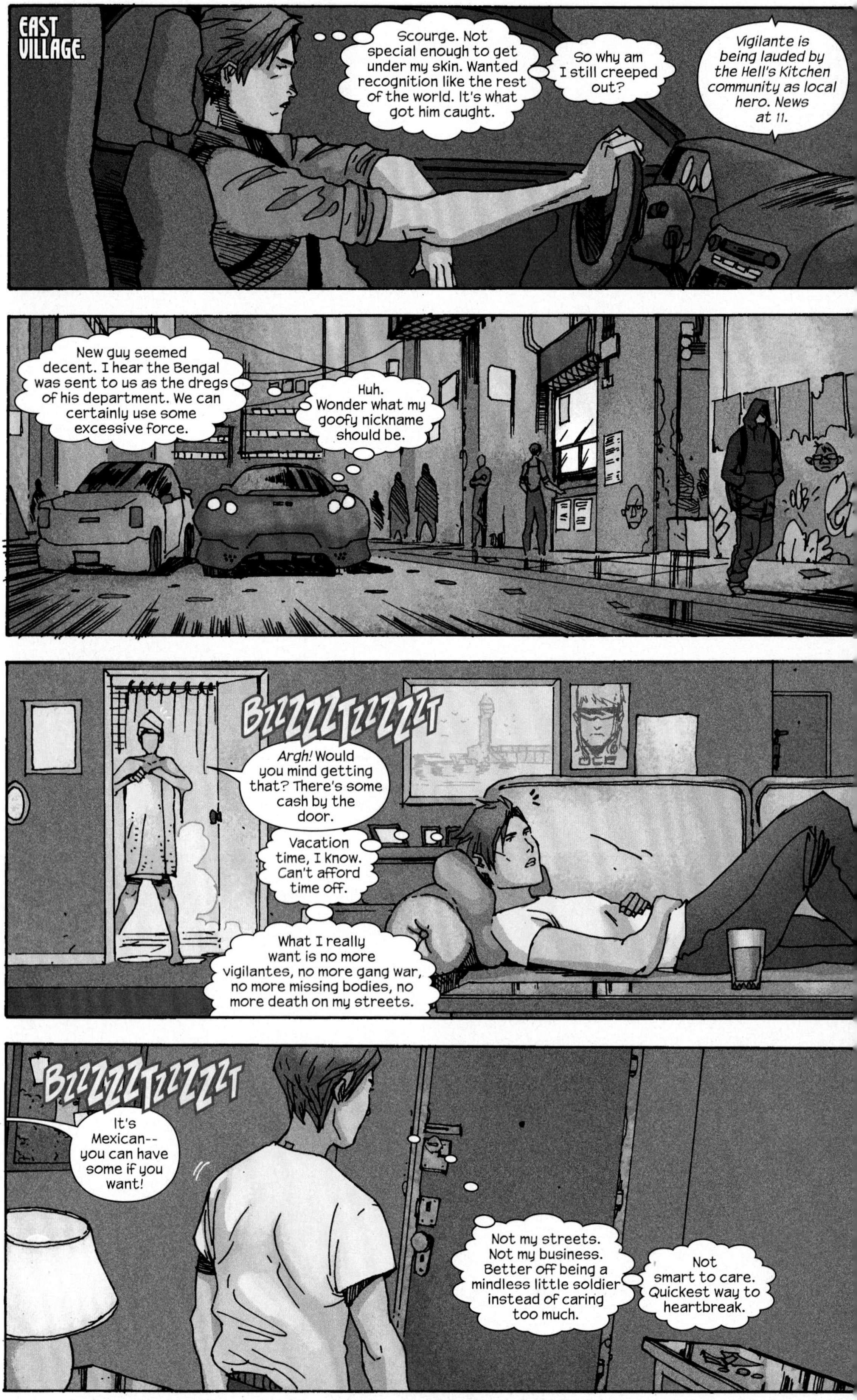
EAST VILLAGE.
Scourge. Not special enough to get under my skin. Wanted recognition like the rest of the world. It's what got him caught.
So why am I still creeped out?
Vigilante is being lauded by the Hell's Kitchen community as local hero. News at 11.
New guy seemed decent. I hear the Bengal was sent to us as the dregs of his department. We can certainly use some excessive force.
Huh. Wonder what my goofy nickname should be.
BZZZZZTZZZZZT
Argh! Would you mind getting that? There's some cash by the door.
Vacation time, I know. Can't afford time off.
What I really want is no more vigilantes, no more gang war, no more missing bodies, no more death on my streets.
BZZZZZTZZZZZT
It's Mexican--you can have some if you want!
Not my streets. Not my business. Better off being a mindless little soldier instead of caring too much.
Not smart to care. Quickest way to heartbreak.

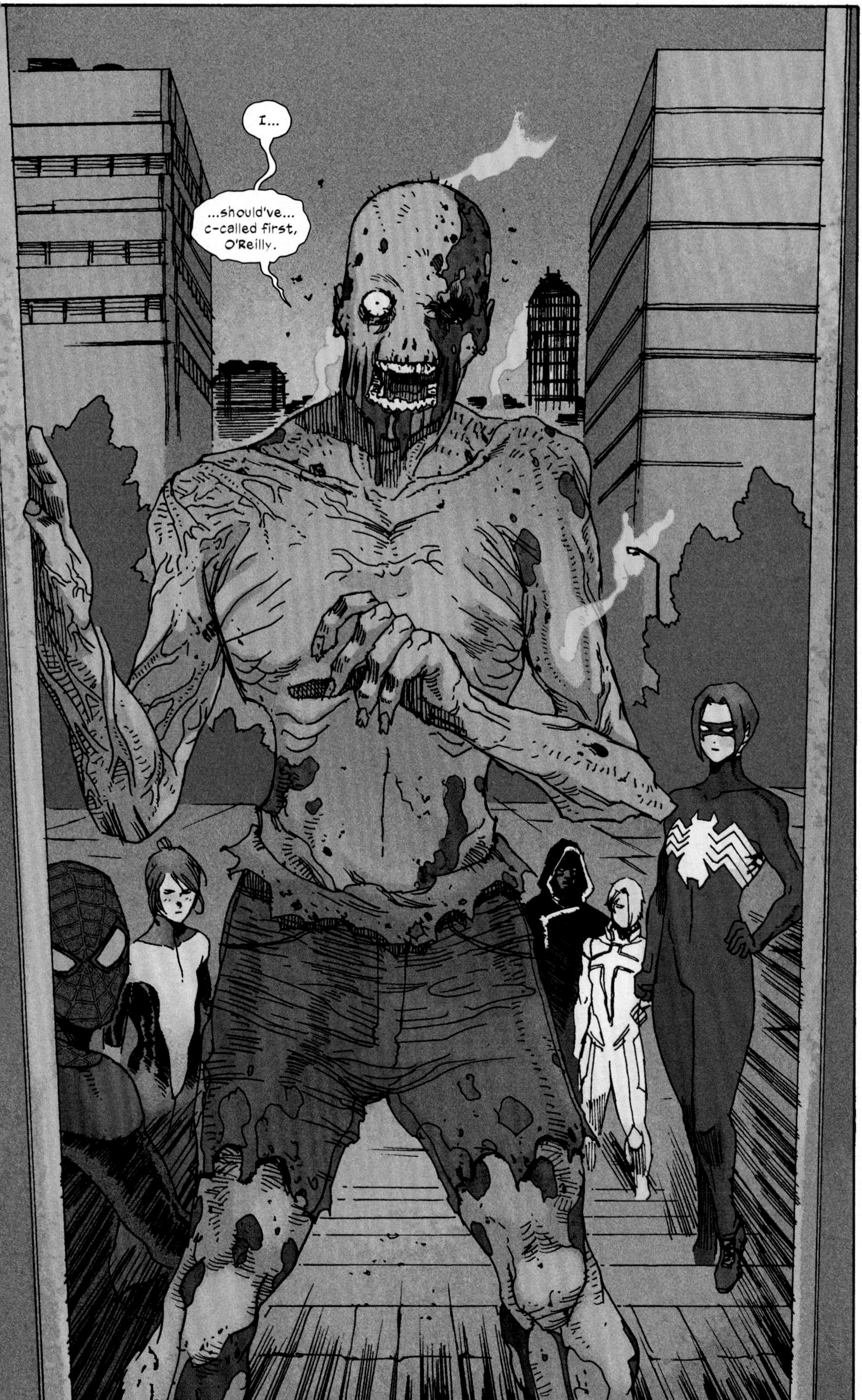
I...
...should've... c-called first, O'Reilly.

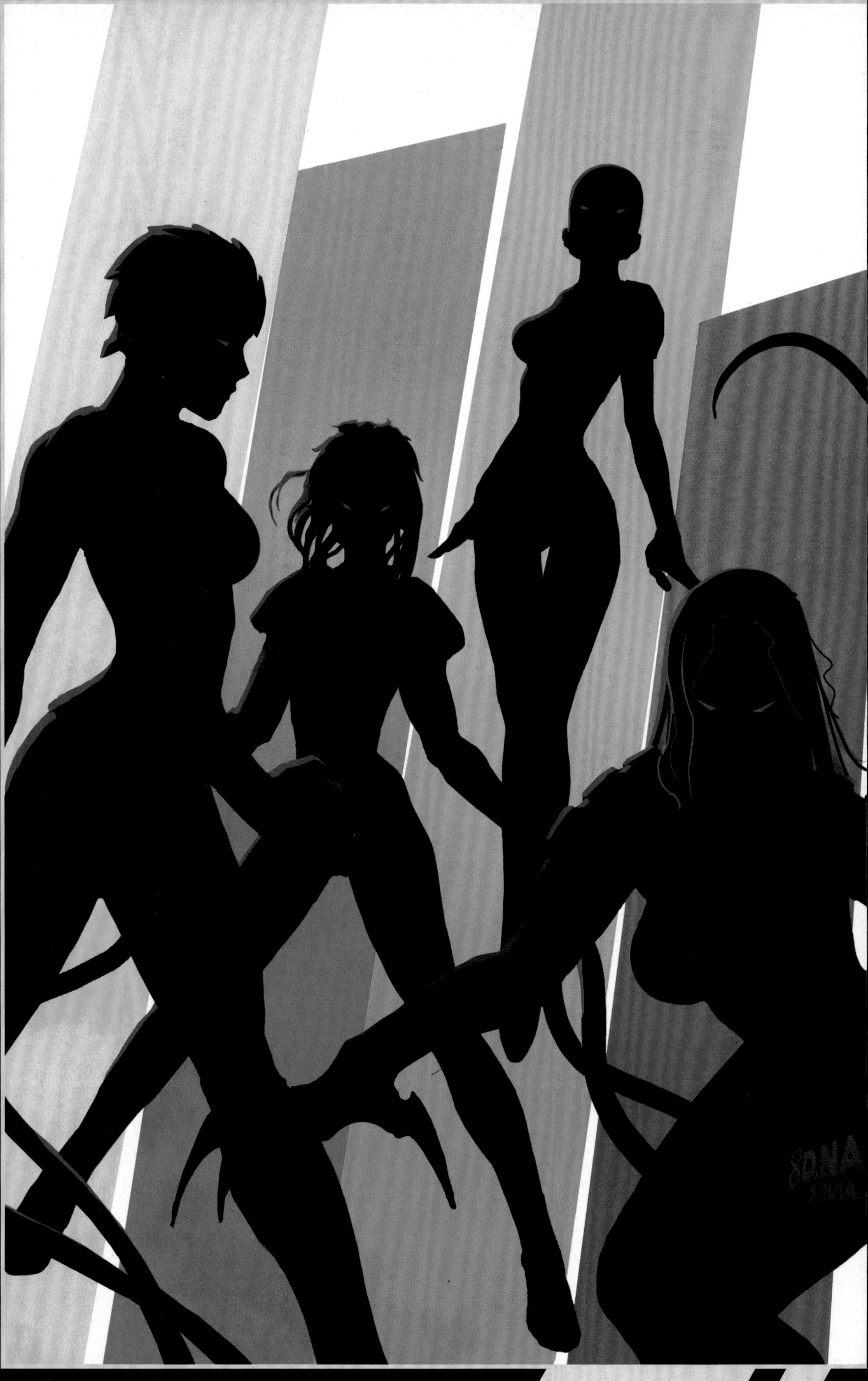

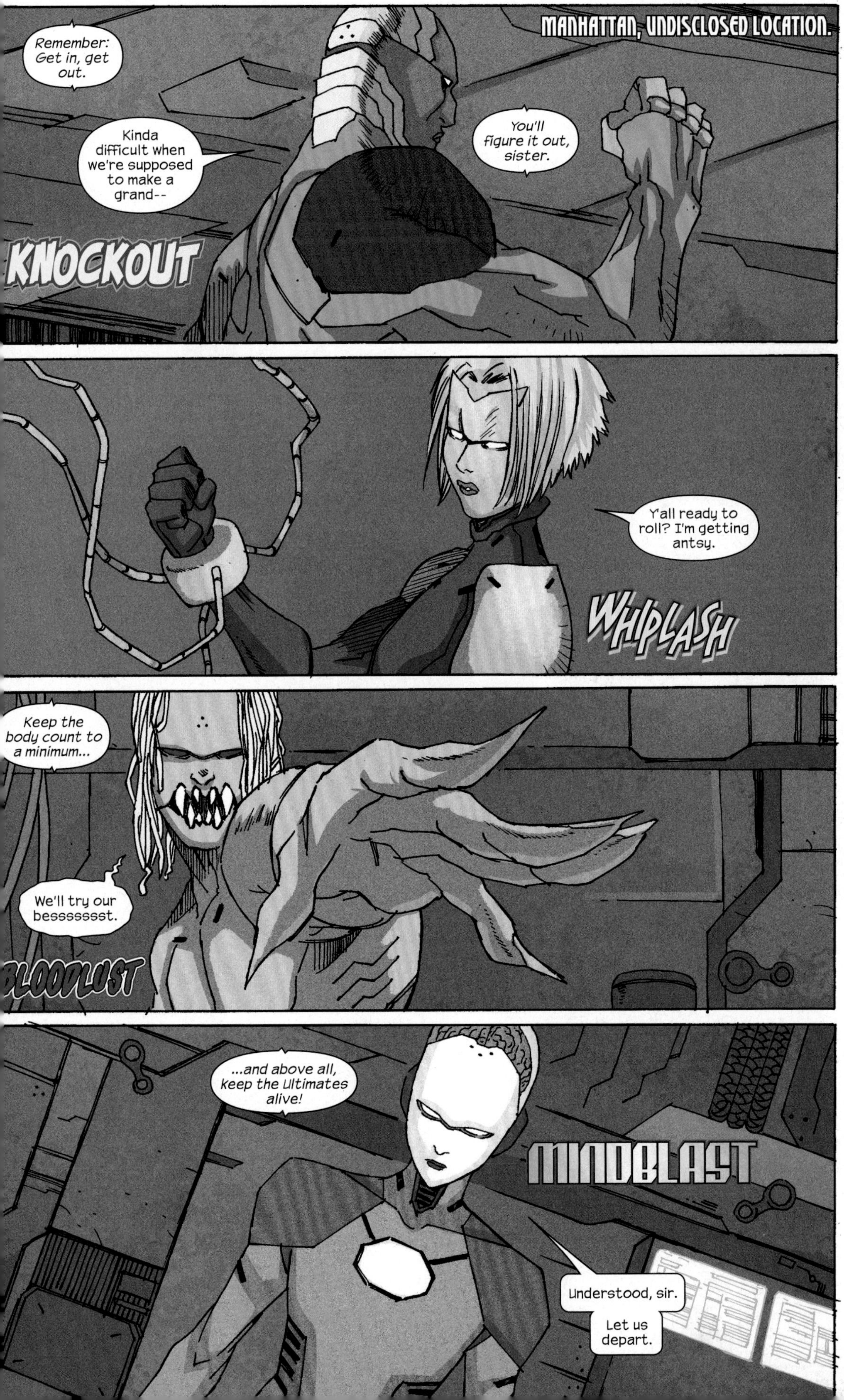
MANHATTAN, UNDISCLOSED LOCATION.
Remember: Get in, get out.
Kinda difficult when we're supposed to make a grand--
You'll figure it out, sister.
KNOCKOUT
Y'all ready to roll? I'm getting antsy.
WHIPLASH
Keep the body count to a minimum...
We'll try our besssssssst.
BLOODLUST
...and above all, keep the Ultimates alive!
MINDBLAST
Understood, sir.
Let us depart.

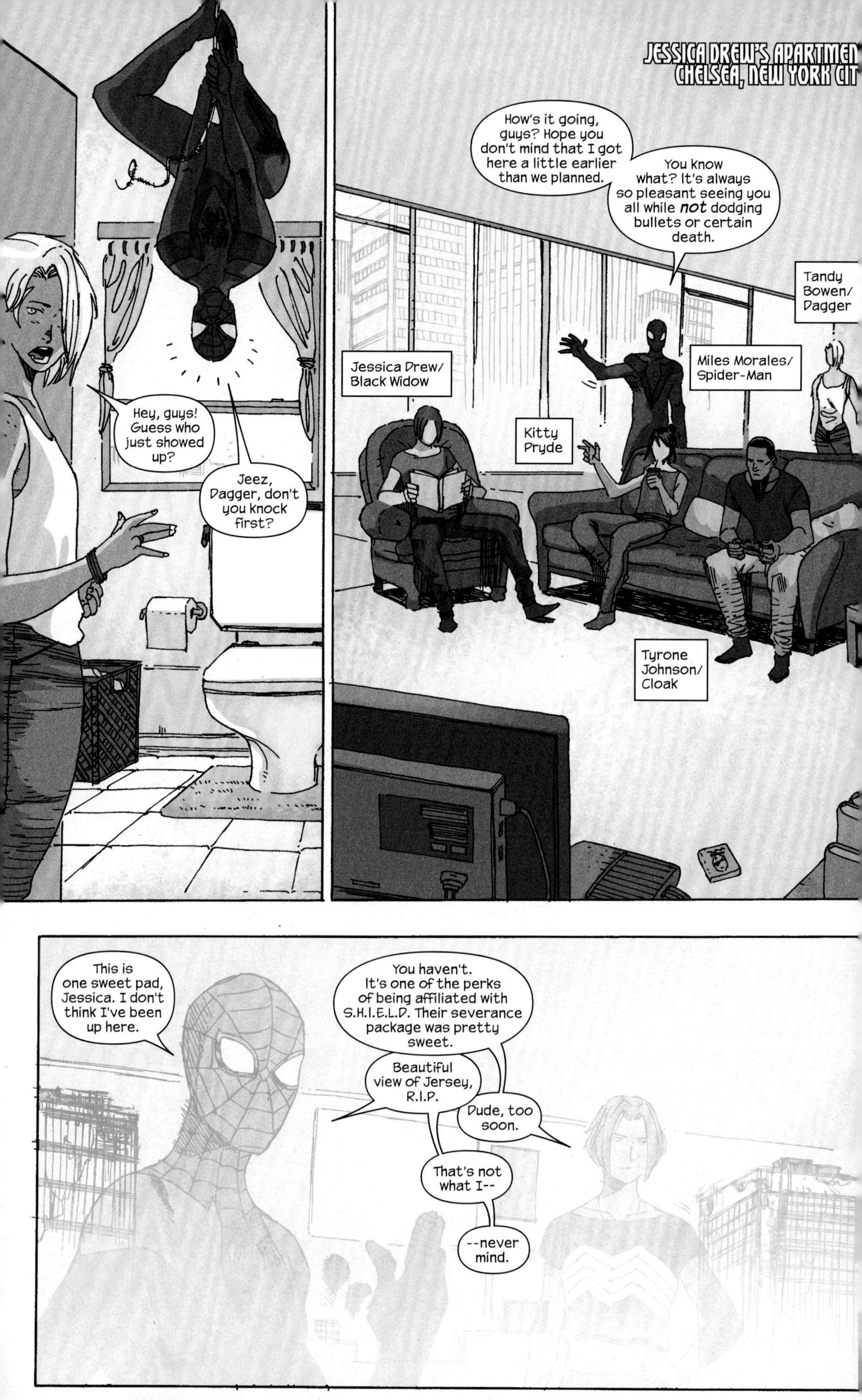
Hey, guys! Guess who just showed up?
Jeez, Dagger, don't you knock first?
JESSICA DREW'S APARTMEN
CHELSEA, NEW YORK CIT
How's it going, guys? Hope you don't mind that I got here a little earlier than we planned.
You know what? It's always so pleasant seeing you all while *not* dodging bullets or certain death.
Tandy Bowen/ Dagger
Jessica Drew/ Black Widow
Miles Morales/ Spider-Man
Kitty Pryde
Tyrone Johnson/ Cloak
This is one sweet pad, Jessica. I don't think I've been up here.
You haven't. It's one of the perks of being affiliated with S.H.I.E.L.D. Their severance package was pretty sweet.
Beautiful view of Jersey, R.I.P.
Dude, too soon.
That's not what I--
--never mind.

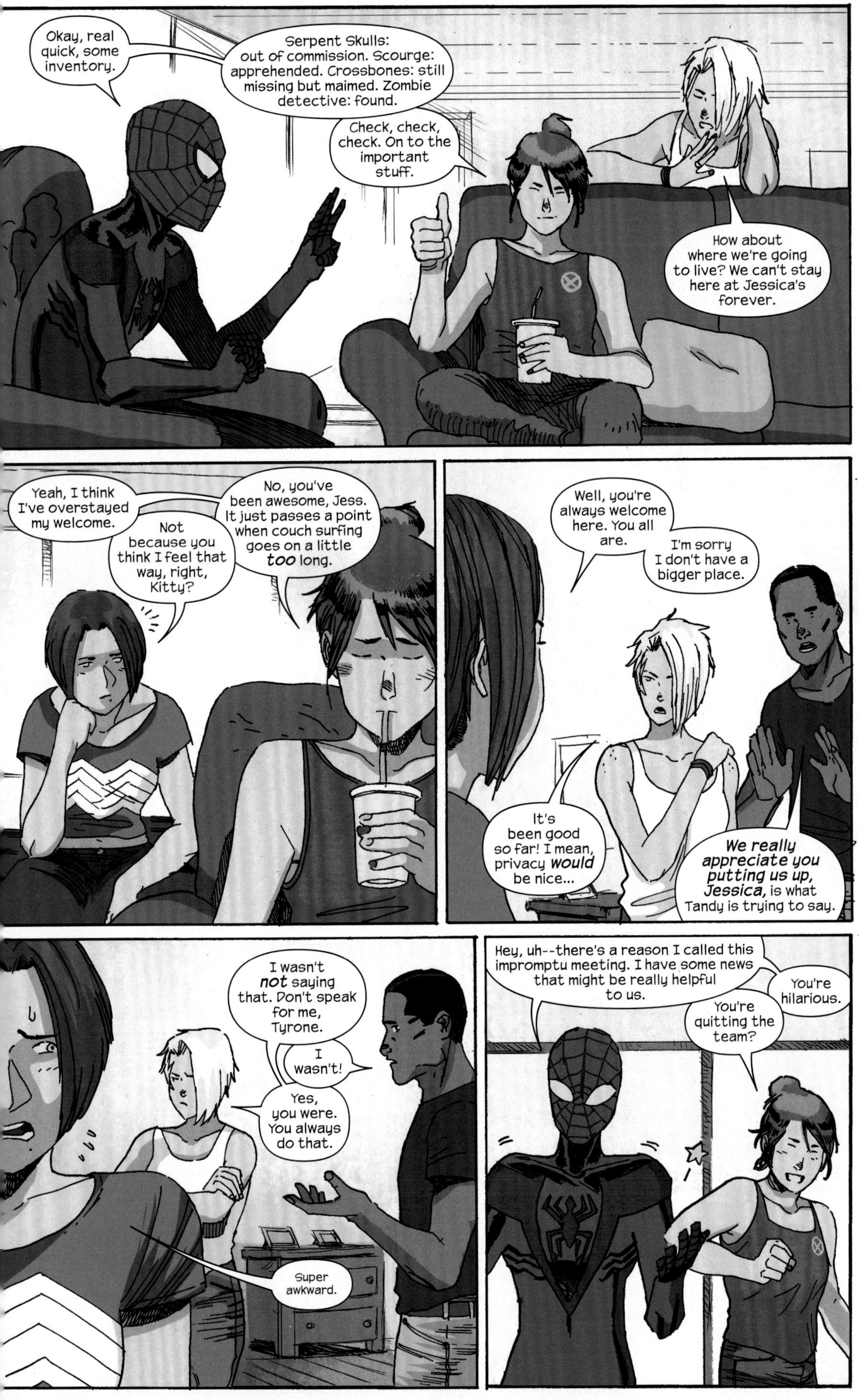

Okay, real quick, some inventory.
Serpent Skulls: out of commission. Scourge: apprehended. Crossbones: still missing but maimed. Zombie detective: found.
Check, check, check. On to the important stuff.
How about where we're going to live? We can't stay here at Jessica's forever.
Yeah, I think I've overstayed my welcome.
No, you've been awesome, Jess. It just passes a point when couch surfing goes on a little *too* long.
Not because you think I feel that way, right, Kitty?
Well, you're always welcome here. You all are.
I'm sorry I don't have a bigger place.
It's been good so far! I mean, privacy *would* be nice...
We really appreciate you putting us up, Jessica, is what Tandy is trying to say.
I wasn't *not* saying that. Don't speak for me, Tyrone.
I wasn't!
Yes, you were. You always do that.
Super awkward.
Hey, uh--there's a reason I called this impromptu meeting. I have some news that might be really helpful to us.
You're quitting the team?
You're hilarious.

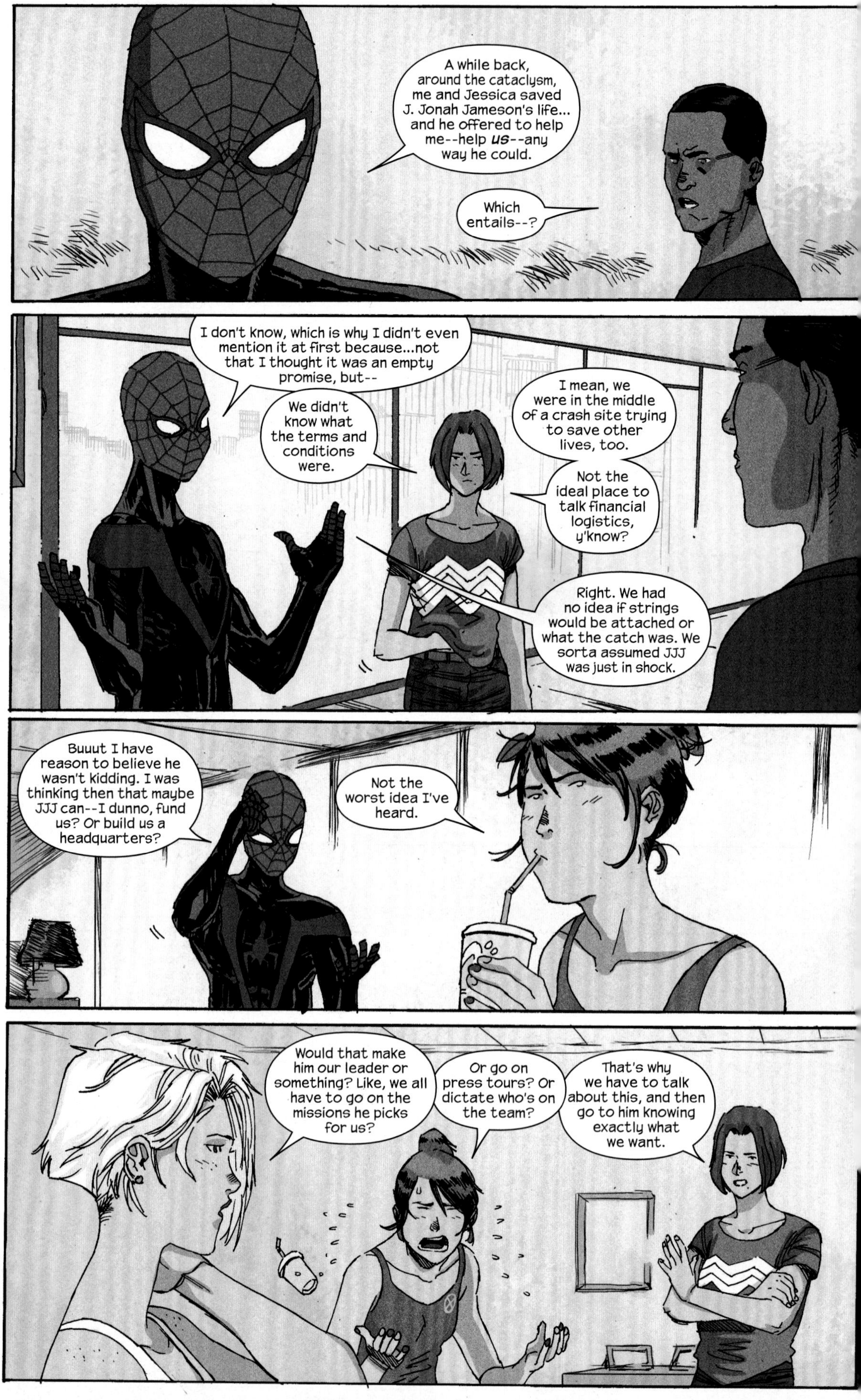
A while back, around the cataclysm, me and Jessica saved J. Jonah Jameson's life... and he offered to help me--help US--any way he could.
Which entails--?
I don't know, which is why I didn't even mention it at first because...not that I thought it was an empty promise, but--
We didn't know what the terms and conditions were.
I mean, we were in the middle of a crash site trying to save other lives, too.
Not the ideal place to talk financial logistics, y'know?
Right. We had no idea if strings would be attached or what the catch was. We sorta assumed JJJ was just in shock.
Buuut I have reason to believe he wasn't kidding. I was thinking then that maybe JJJ can--I dunno, fund us? Or build us a headquarters?
Not the worst idea I've heard.
Would that make him our leader or something? Like, we all have to go on the missions he picks for us?
Or go on press tours? Or dictate who's on the team?
That's why we have to talk about this, and then go to him knowing exactly what we want.

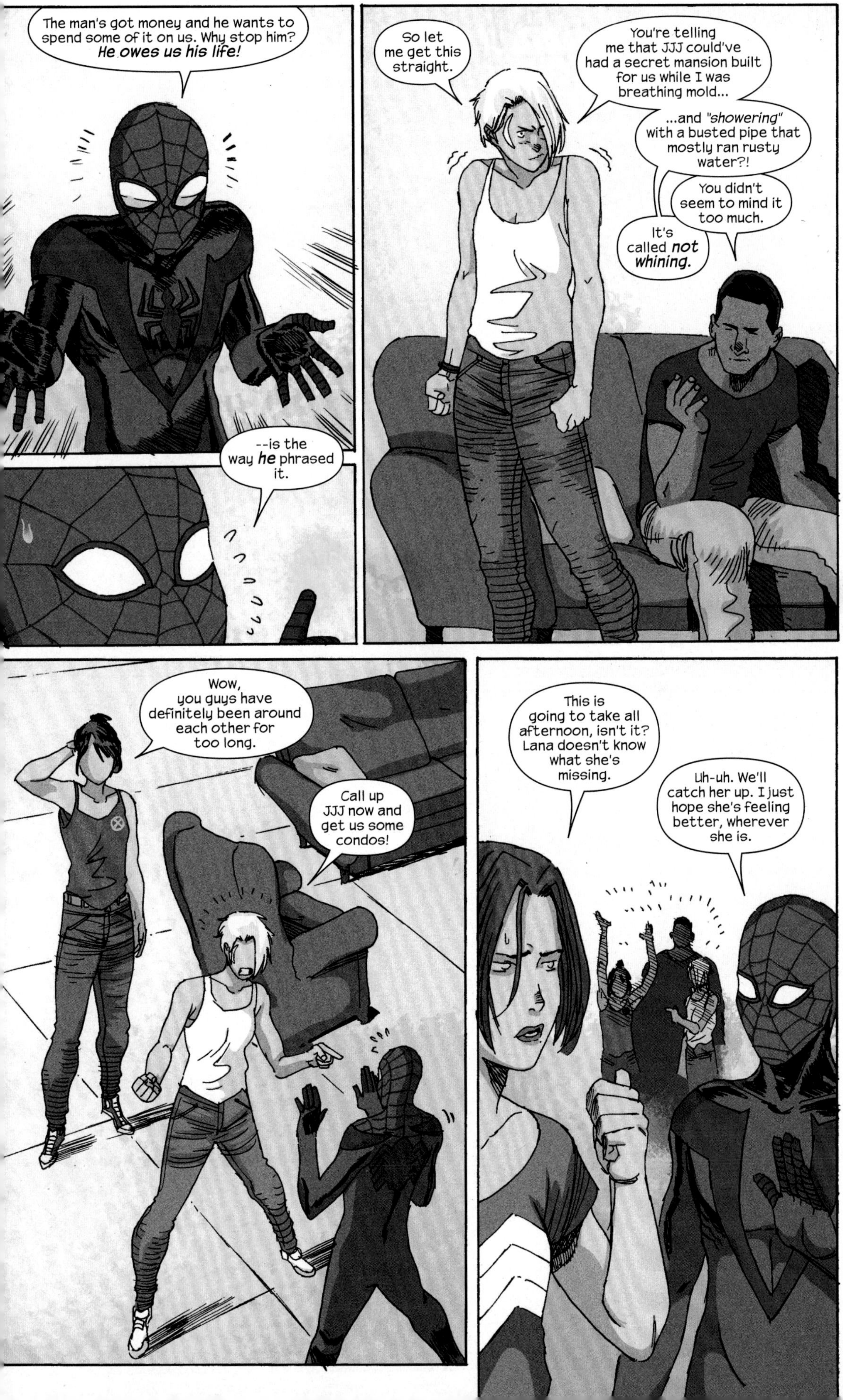
The man's got money and he wants to spend some of it on us. Why stop him? *He owes us his life!*
--is the way *he* phrased it.
So let me get this straight.
You're telling me that JJJ could've had a secret mansion built for us while I was breathing mold...
...and *"showering"* with a busted pipe that mostly ran rusty water?!
You didn't seem to mind it too much.
It's called *not whining.*
Wow, you guys have definitely been around each other for too long.
Call up JJJ now and get us some condos!
This is going to take all afternoon, isn't it? Lana doesn't know what she's missing.
Uh-uh. We'll catch her up. I just hope she's feeling better, wherever she is.

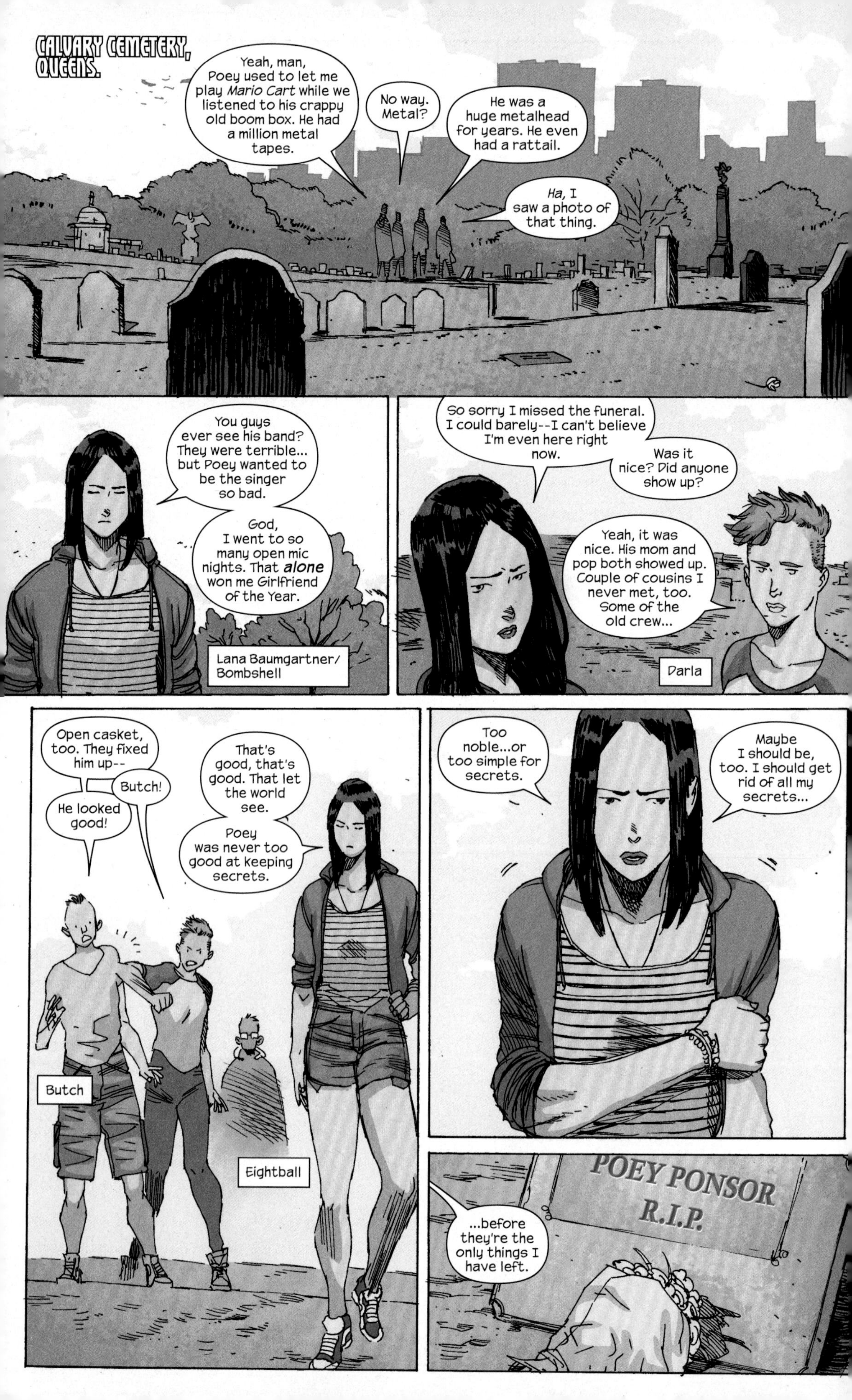
CALVARY CEMETERY, QUEENS.
Yeah, man, Poey used to let me play *Mario Cart* while we listened to his crappy old boom box. He had a million metal tapes.
No way. Metal?
He was a huge metalhead for years. He even had a rattail.
Ha, I saw a photo of that thing.
You guys ever see his band? They were terrible... but Poey wanted to be the singer so bad.
God, I went to so many open mic nights. That ***alone*** won me Girlfriend of the Year.
Lana Baumgartner/ Bombshell
So sorry I missed the funeral. I could barely--I can't believe I'm even here right now.
Was it nice? Did anyone show up?
Yeah, it was nice. His mom and pop both showed up. Couple of cousins I never met, too. Some of the old crew...
Darla
Open casket, too. They fixed him up--
Butch!
He looked good!
That's good, that's good. That let the world see.
Poey was never too good at keeping secrets.
Butch
Eightball
Too noble...or too simple for secrets.
Maybe I should be, too. I should get rid of all my secrets...
POEY PONSOR R.I.P.
...before they're the only things I have left.

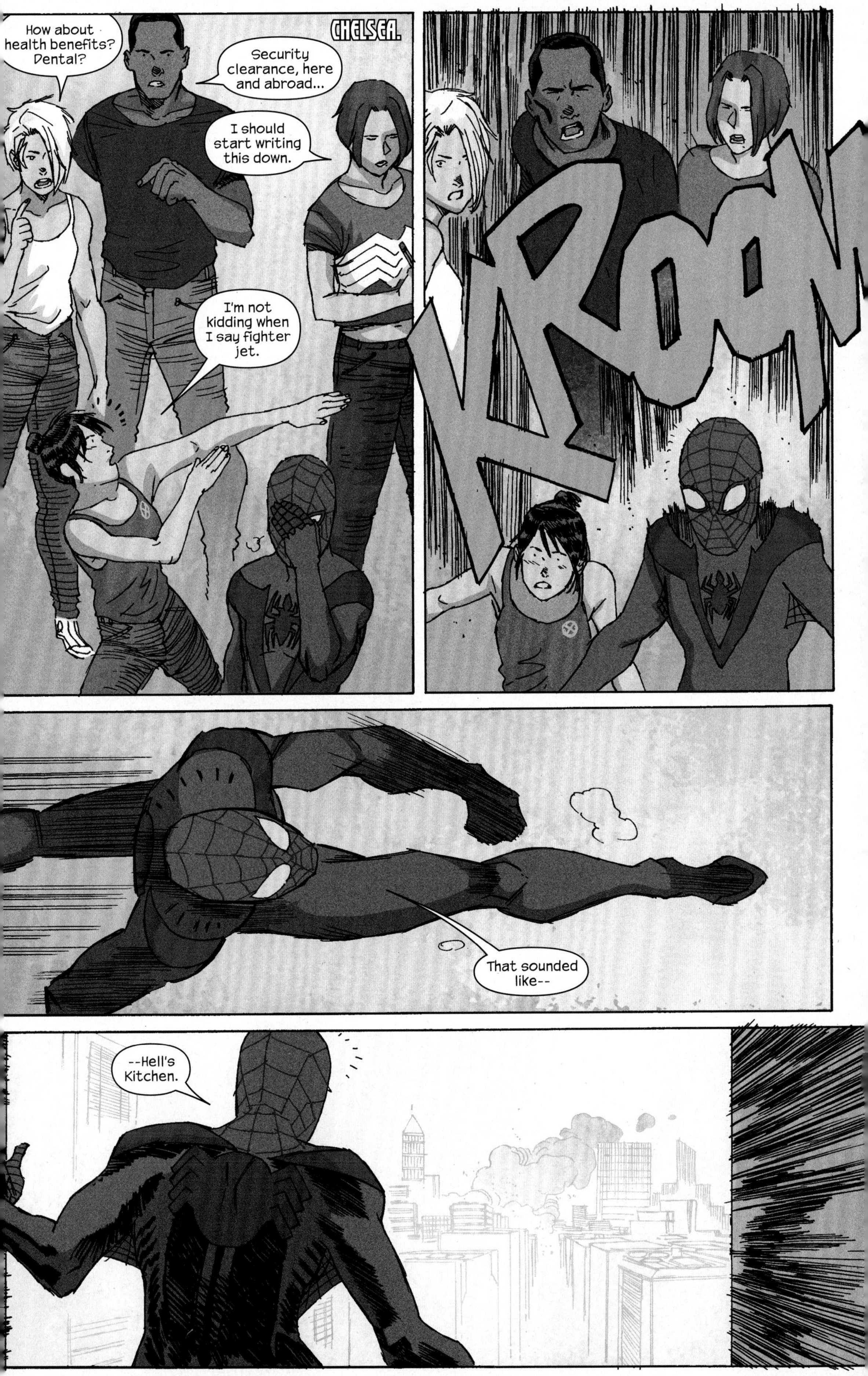
CHELSEA.
How about health benefits? Dental?
Security clearance, here and abroad...
I should start writing this down.
I'm not kidding when I say fighter jet.
KROOM
That sounded like--
--Hell's Kitchen.

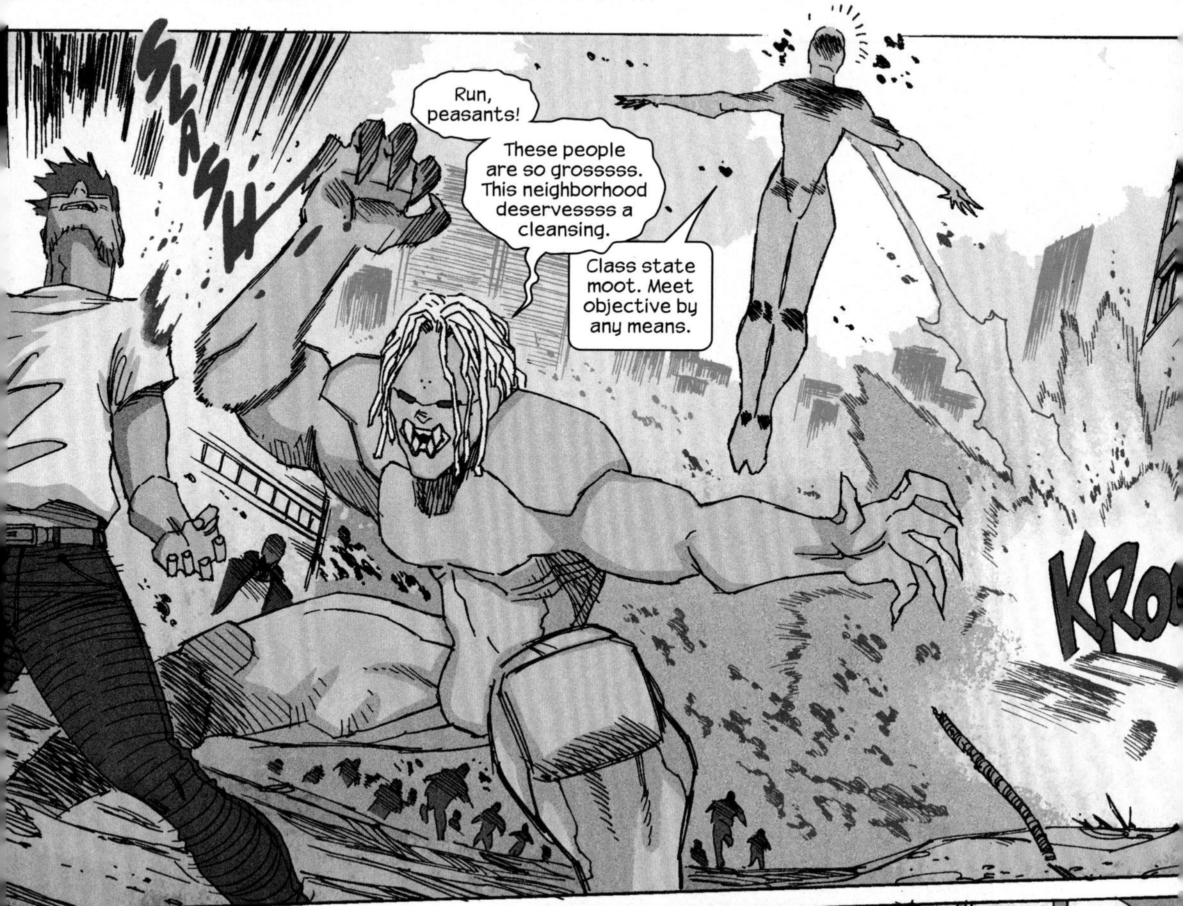
SLASH
Run, peasants!
These people are so grosssss. This neighborhood deservessss a cleansing.
Class state moot. Meet objective by any means.
KROO

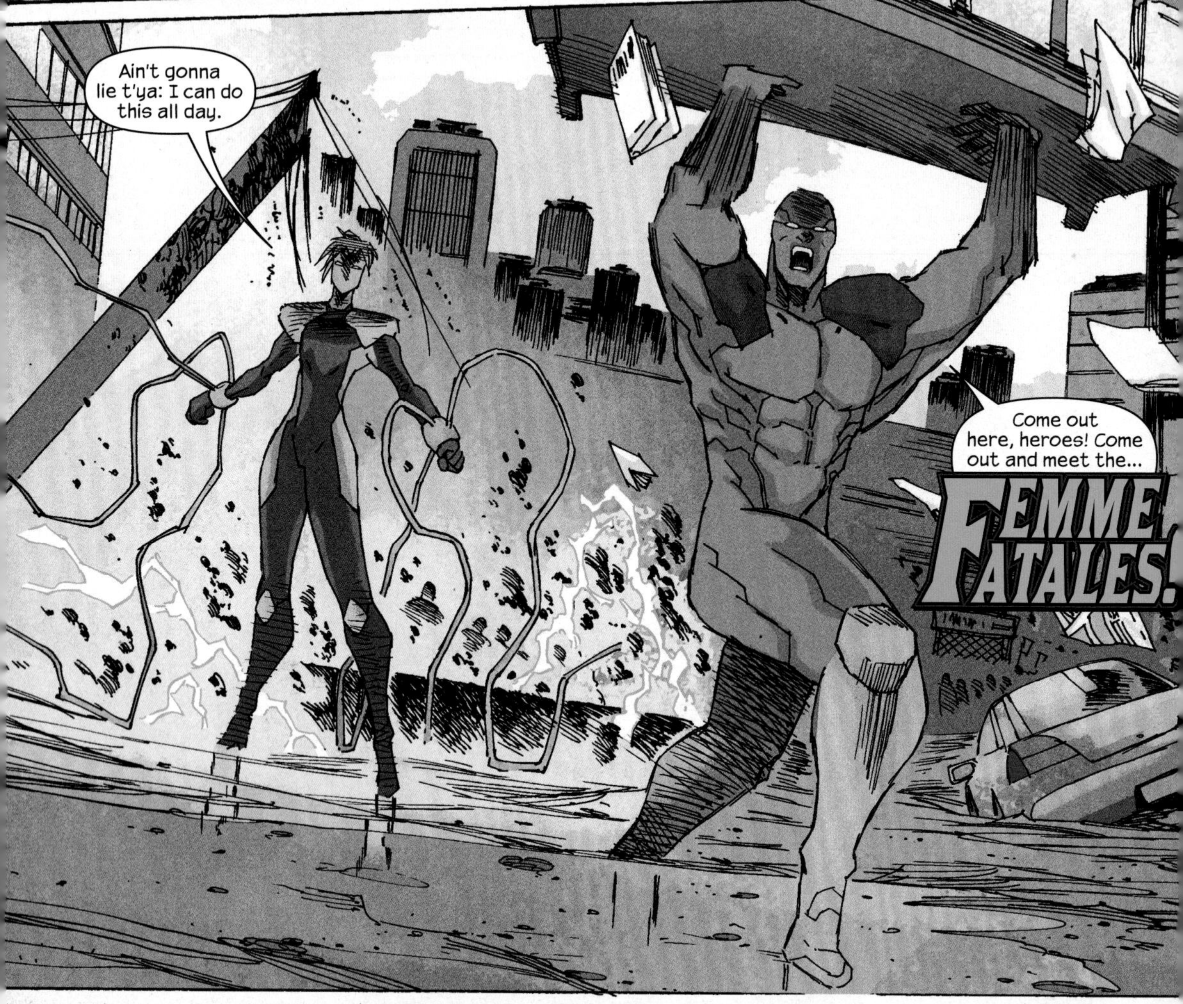
Ain't gonna lie t'ya: I can do this all day.
Come out here, heroes! Come out and meet the...
FEMME FATALES.

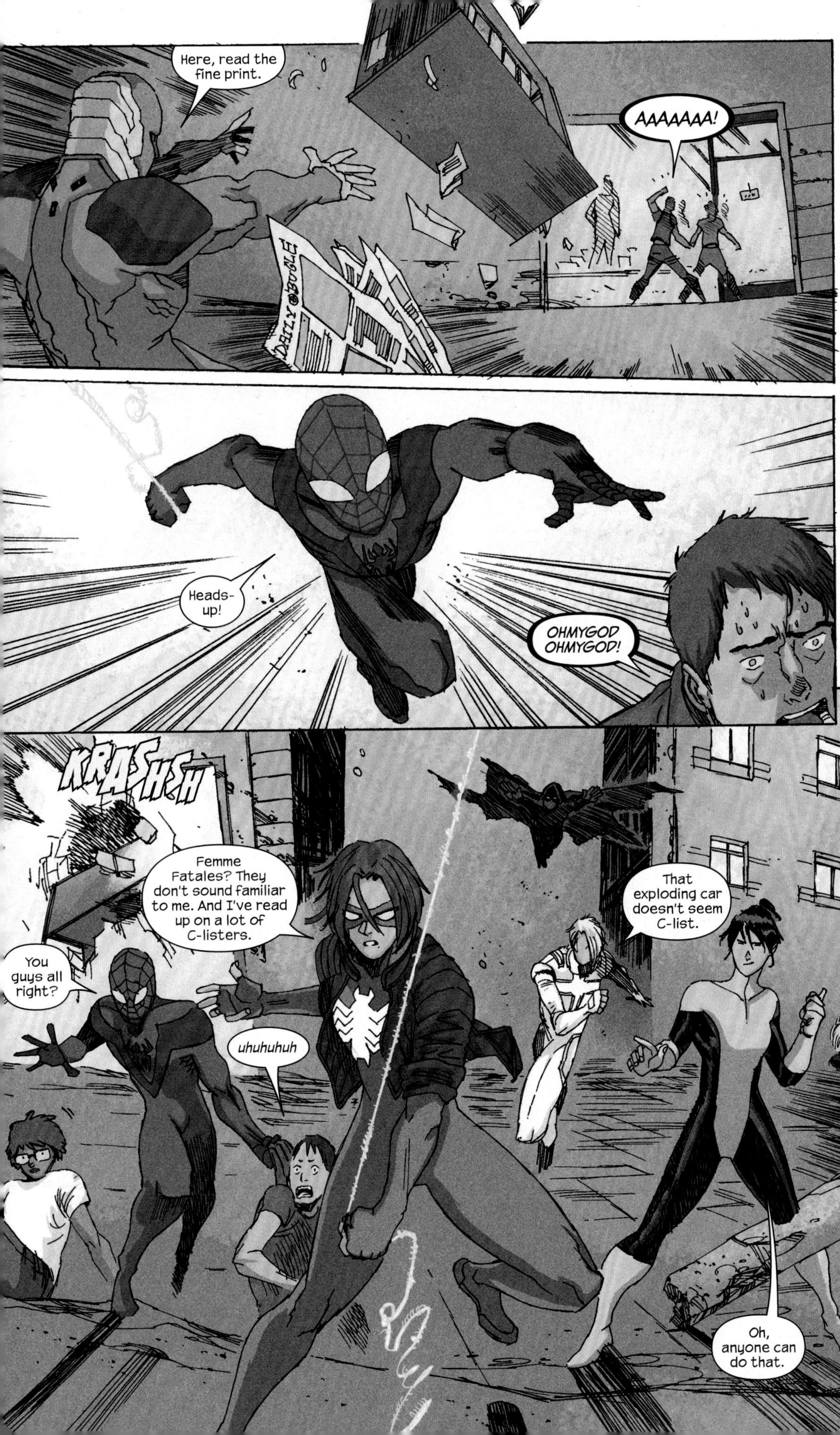
Here, read the fine print.
AAAAAAA!
DAILY BUGLE
Heads-up!
OHMYGOD OHMYGOD!
KRASHSH
Femme Fatales? They don't sound familiar to me. And I've read up on a lot of C-listers.
That exploding car doesn't seem C-list.
You guys all right?
uhuhuhuh
Oh, anyone can do that.

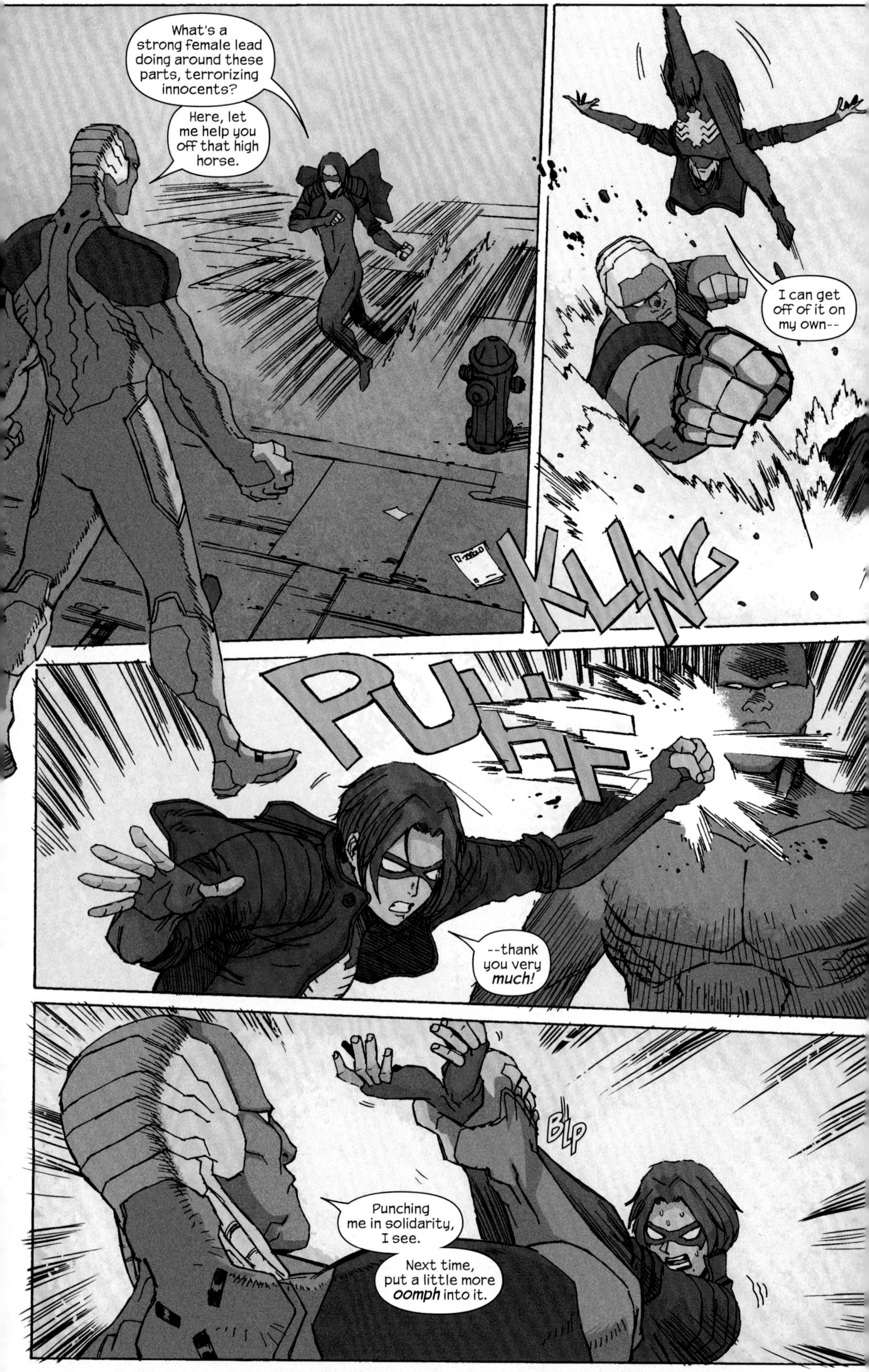
What's a strong female lead doing around these parts, terrorizing innocents?
Here, let me help you off that high horse.
I can get off of it on my own--
KLUNG
PUHFF
--thank you very *much!*
BLP
Punching me in solidarity, I see.
Next time, put a little more *oomph* into it.

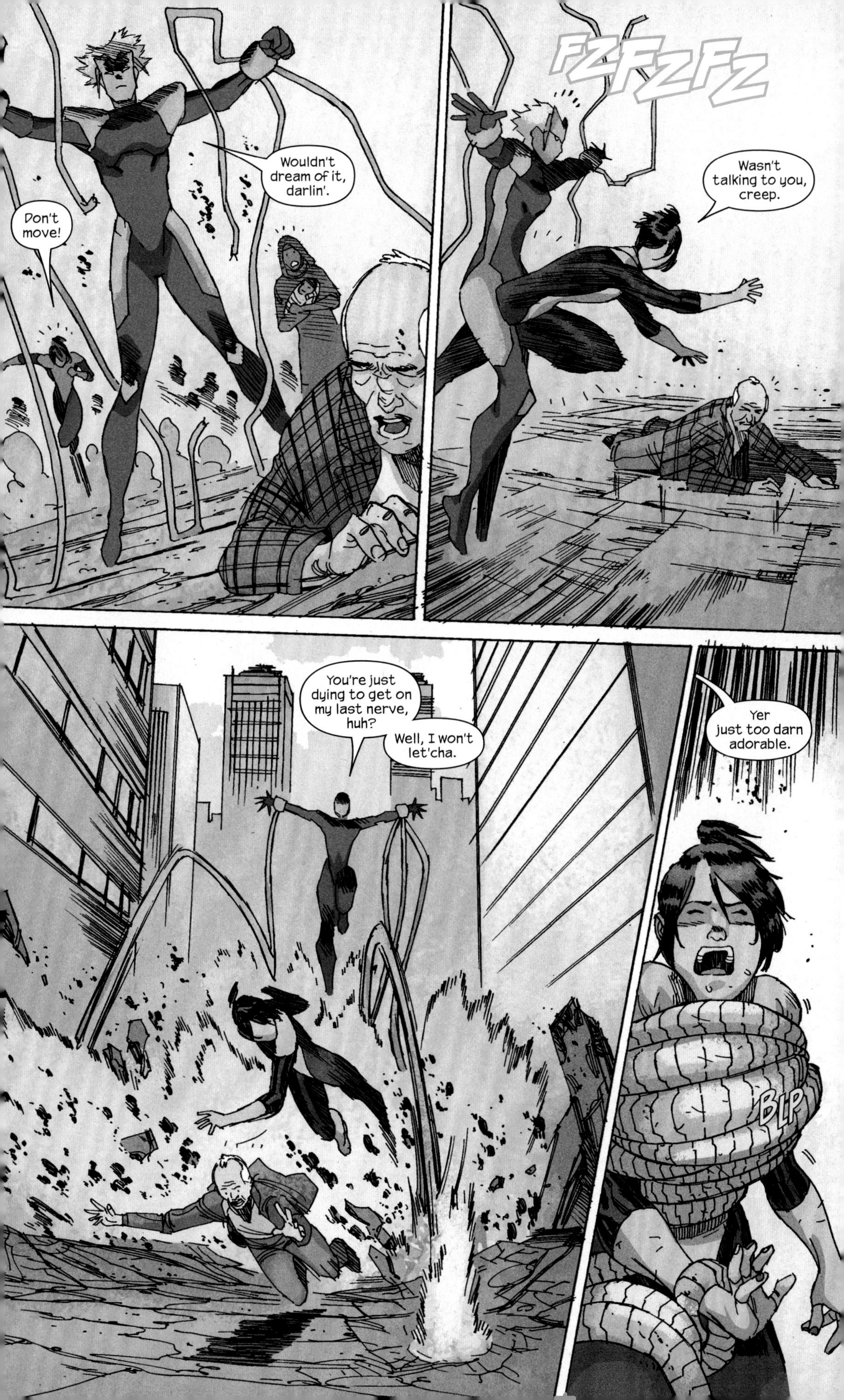
Don't move!
Wouldn't dream of it, darlin'.
FZFZFZ
Wasn't talking to you, creep.
You're just dying to get on my last nerve, huh?
Well, I won't let'cha.
Yer just too darn adorable.
BLP

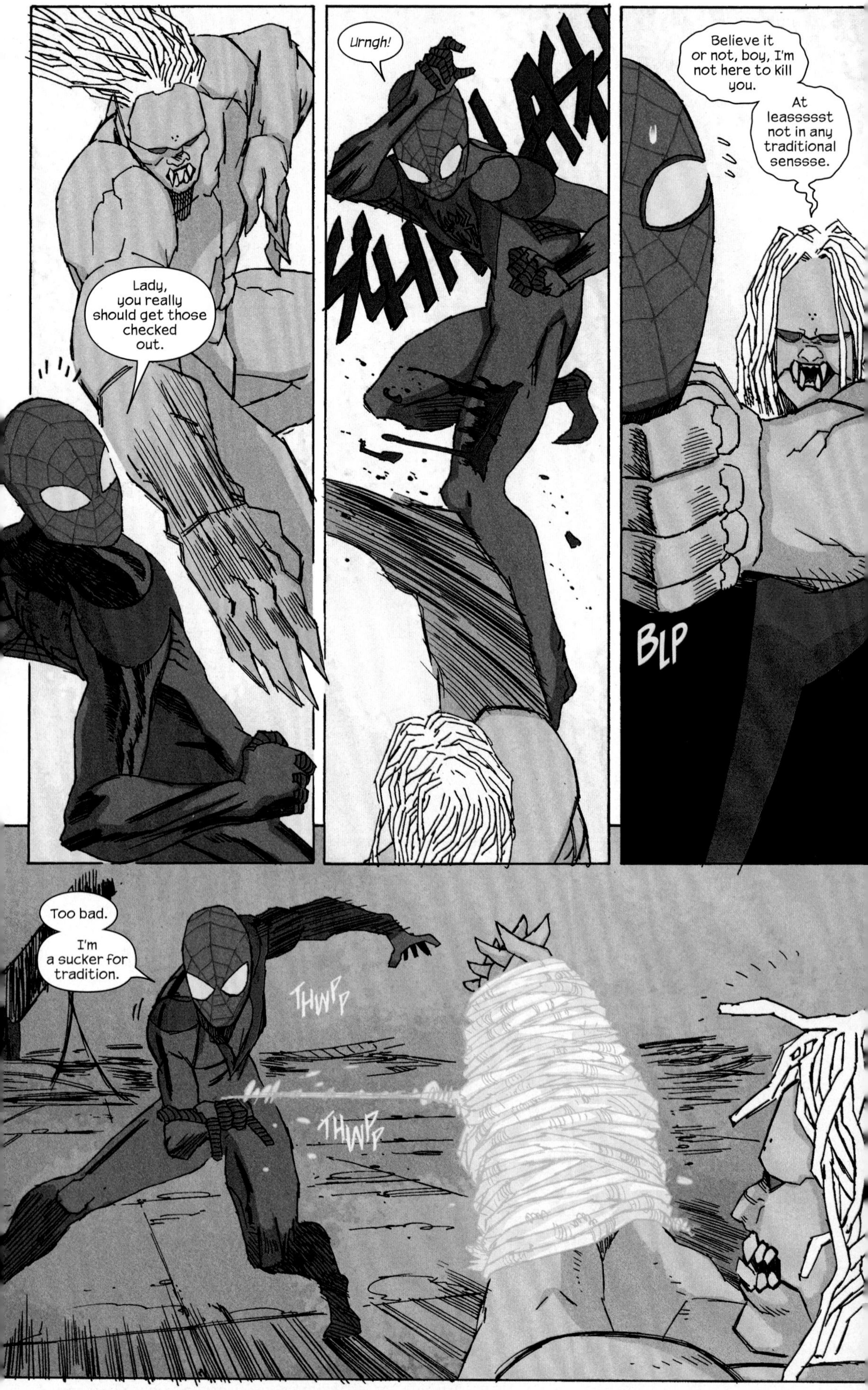
Lady, you really should get those checked out.
Urngh!
SHHHAKK
Believe it or not, boy, I'm not here to kill you.
At leassssst not in any traditional sensssse.
BLP
Too bad.
I'm a sucker for tradition.
THWPP
THWPP

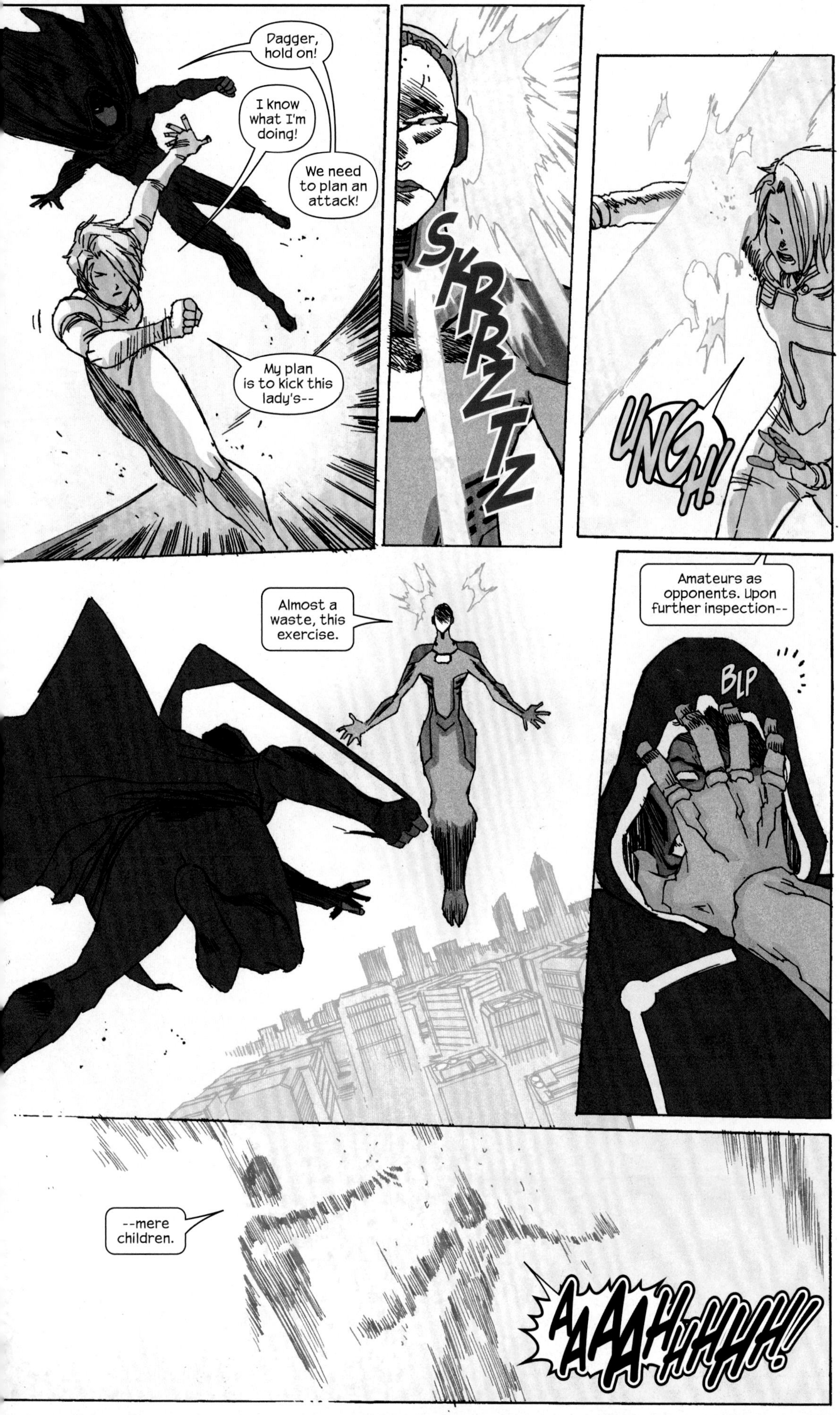
Dagger, hold on!
I know what I'm doing!
We need to plan an attack!
My plan is to kick this lady's--
SKRRZZTZ
UNGH!
Almost a waste, this exercise.
Amateurs as opponents. Upon further inspection--
BLP
--mere children.
AAAAHHHHHH!

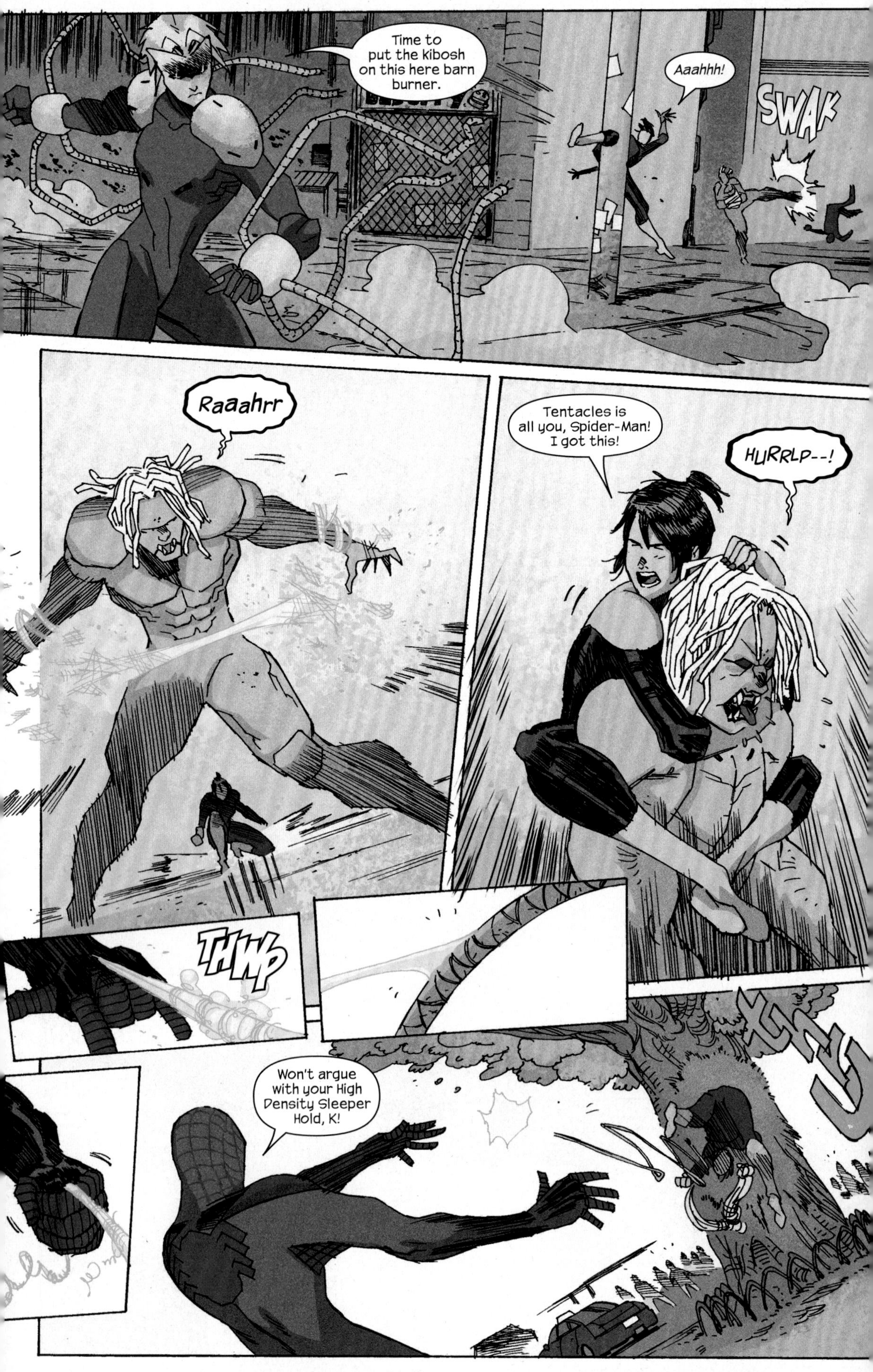
Time to put the kibosh on this here barn burner.
Aaahhh!
SWAK
Raaahrr
Tentacles is all you, Spider-Man! I got this!
HURRLP--!
THWP
Won't argue with your High Density Sleeper Hold, K!

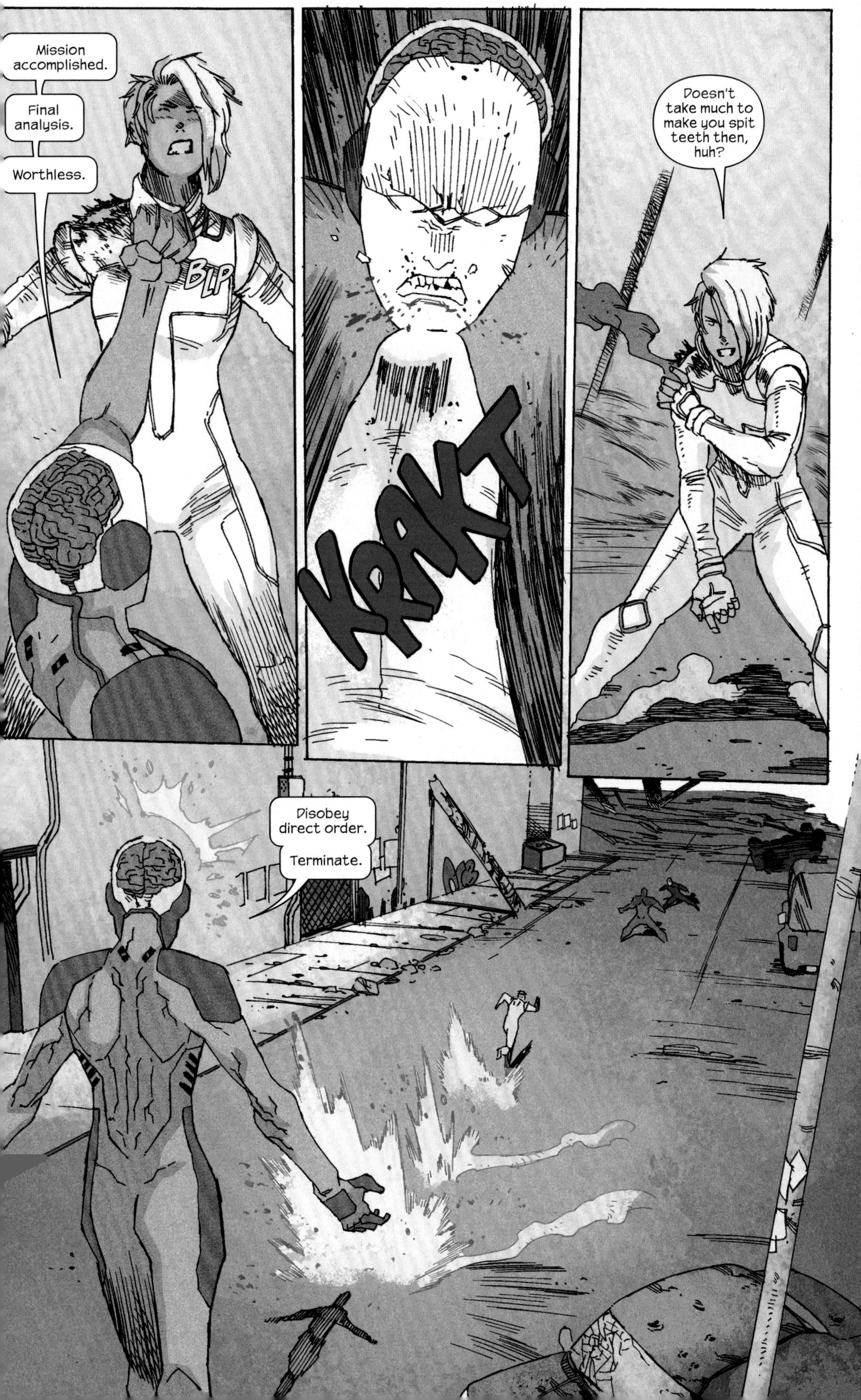
Mission accomplished.
Final analysis.
Worthless.
BLIP
KRAKT
Doesn't take much to make you spit teeth then, huh?
Disobey direct order.
Terminate.

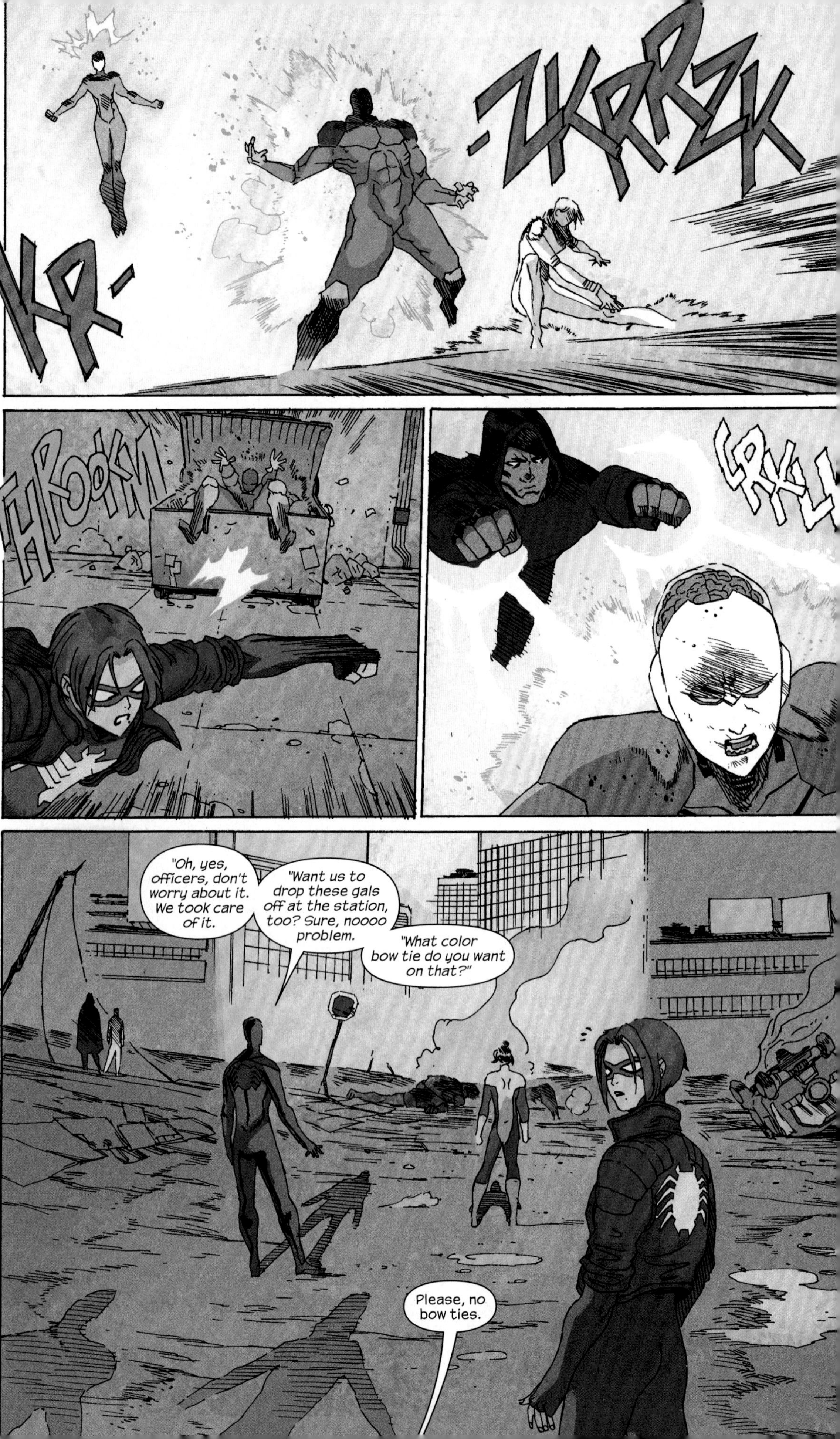

-ZKRRZK
KR-
THROOKM
"Oh, yes, officers, don't worry about it. We took care of it.
"Want us to drop these gals off at the station, too? Sure, noooo problem.
"What color bow tie do you want on that?"
Please, no bow ties.

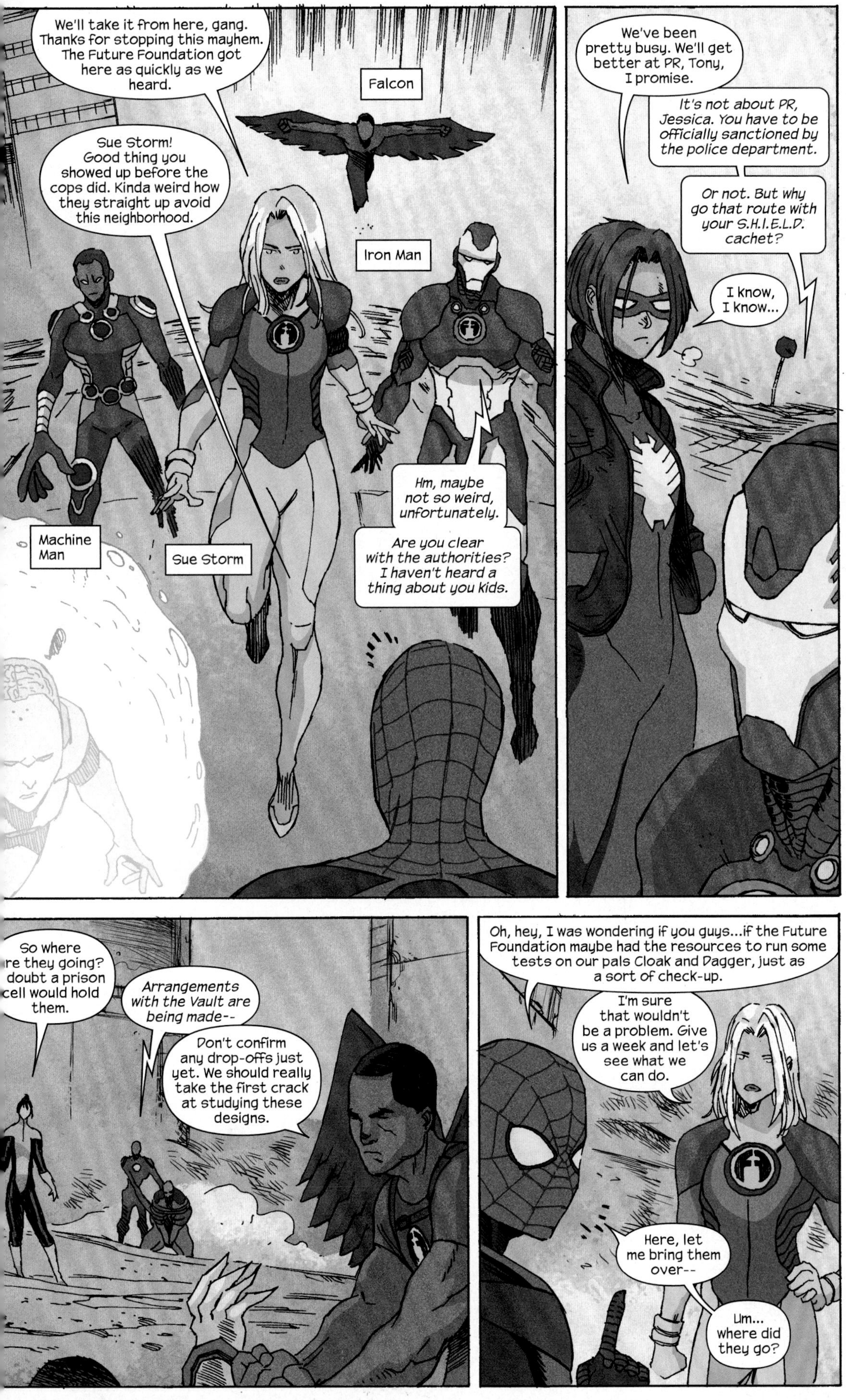
We'll take it from here, gang. Thanks for stopping this mayhem. The Future Foundation got here as quickly as we heard.
Falcon
Sue Storm! Good thing you showed up before the cops did. Kinda weird how they straight up avoid this neighborhood.
Iron Man
Hm, maybe not so weird, unfortunately.
Are you clear with the authorities? I haven't heard a thing about you kids.
Machine Man
Sue Storm
We've been pretty busy. We'll get better at PR, Tony, I promise.
It's not about PR, Jessica. You have to be officially sanctioned by the police department.
Or not. But why go that route with your S.H.I.E.L.D. cachet?
I know, I know...
So where re they going? doubt a prison cell would hold them.
Arrangements with the Vault are being made--
Don't confirm any drop-offs just yet. We should really take the first crack at studying these designs.
Oh, hey, I was wondering if you guys...if the Future Foundation maybe had the resources to run some tests on our pals Cloak and Dagger, just as a sort of check-up.
I'm sure that wouldn't be a problem. Give us a week and let's see what we can do.
Here, let me bring them over--
Um... where did they go?

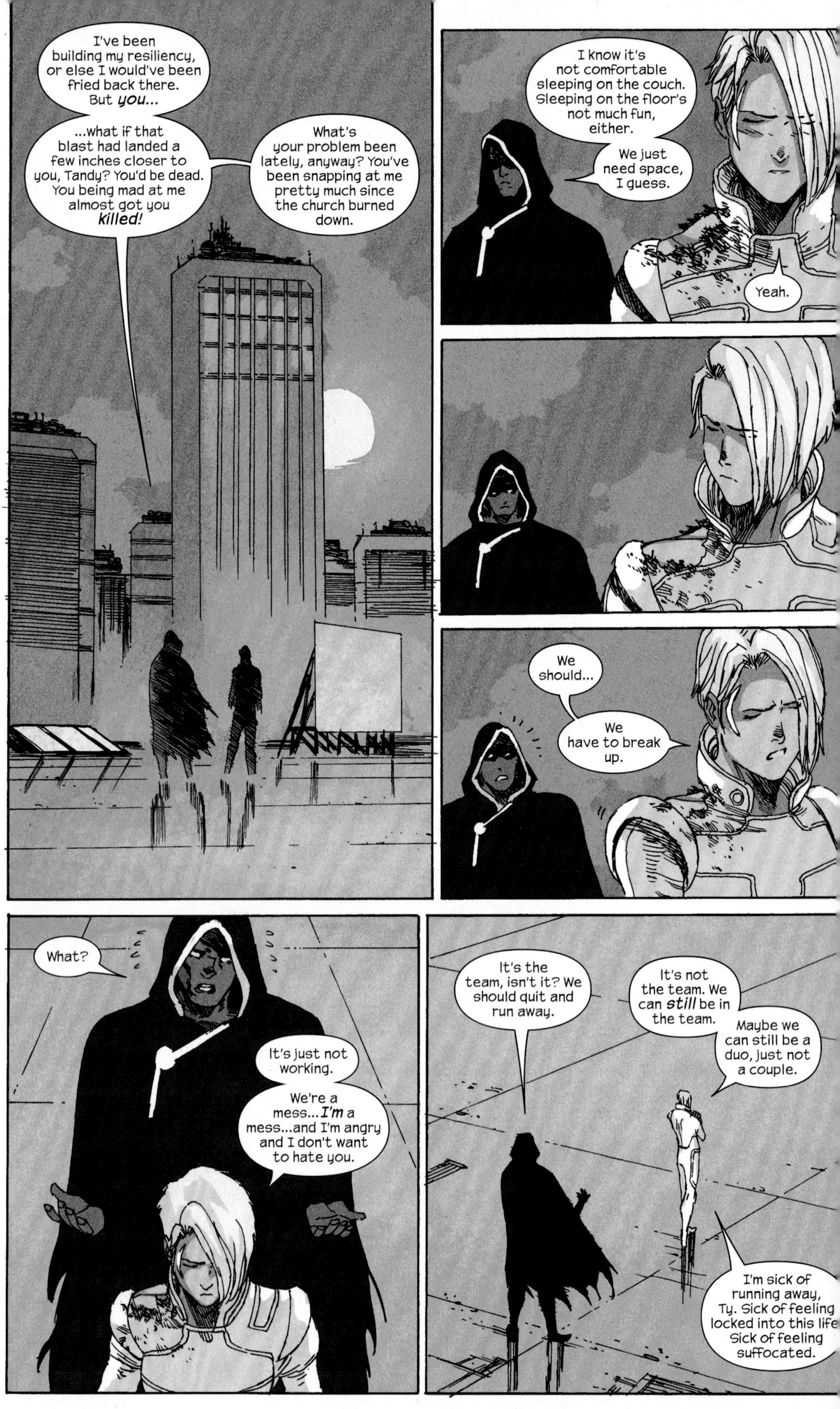
I've been building my resiliency, or else I would've been fried back there. But *you*...
What's your problem been lately, anyway? You've been snapping at me pretty much since the church burned down.
...what if that blast had landed a few inches closer to you, Tandy? You'd be dead. You being mad at me almost got you *killed!*
I know it's not comfortable sleeping on the couch. Sleeping on the floor's not much fun, either.
We just need space, I guess.
Yeah.
We should...
We have to break up.
What?
It's just not working.
We're a mess... *I'm* a mess...and I'm angry and I don't want to hate you.
It's the team, isn't it? We should quit and run away.
It's not the team. We can *still* be in the team.
Maybe we can still be a duo, just not a couple.
I'm sick of running away, Ty. Sick of feeling locked into this life. Sick of feeling suffocated.

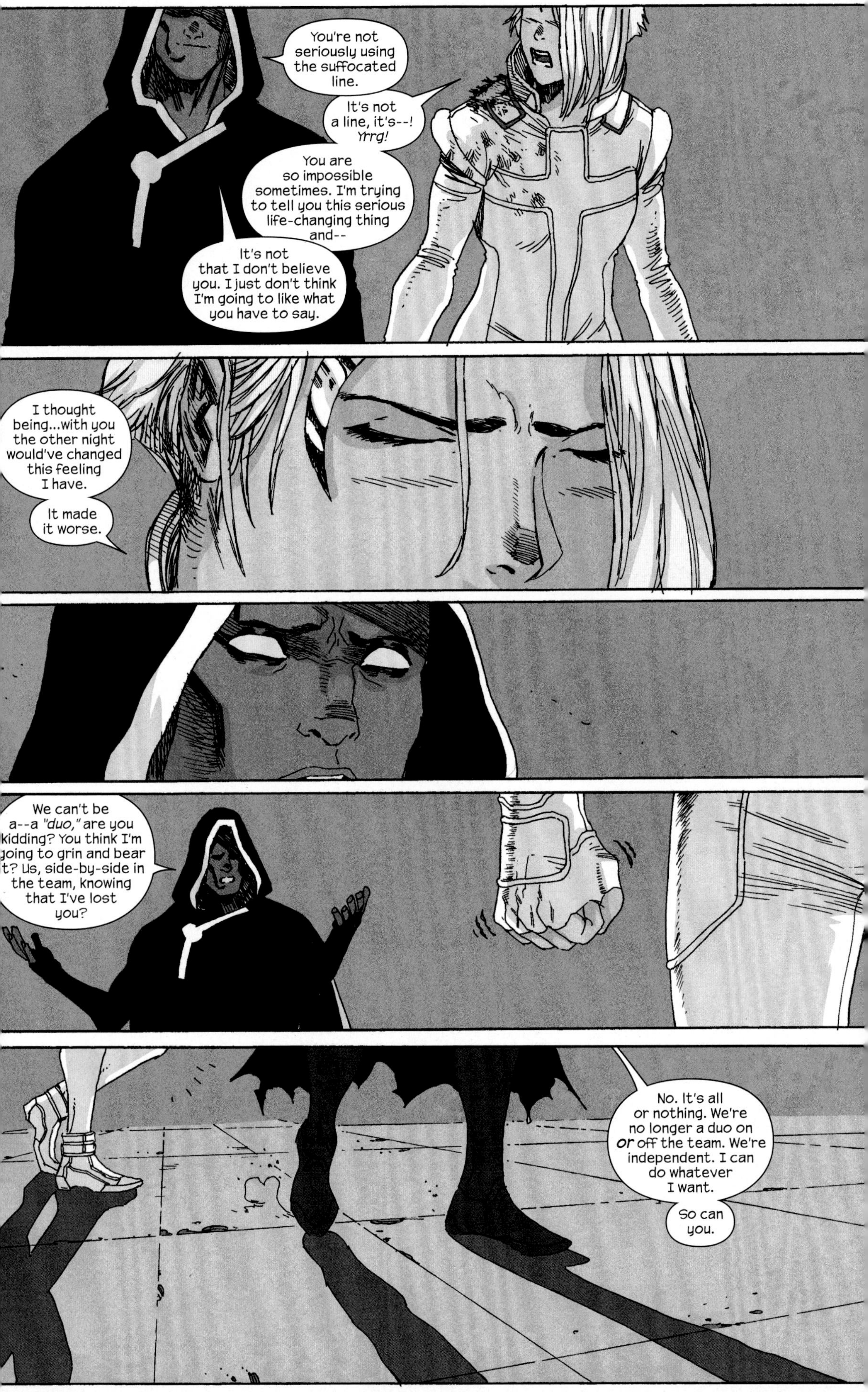
You're not seriously using the suffocated line.
It's not a line, it's--! *Yrrg!*
You are so impossible sometimes. I'm trying to tell you this serious life-changing thing and--
It's not that I don't believe you. I just don't think I'm going to like what you have to say.
I thought being...with you the other night would've changed this feeling I have.
It made it worse.
We can't be a--a *"duo,"* are you kidding? You think I'm going to grin and bear it? Us, side-by-side in the team, knowing that I've lost you?
No. It's all or nothing. We're no longer a duo on *or* off the team. We're independent. I can do whatever I want.
So can you.

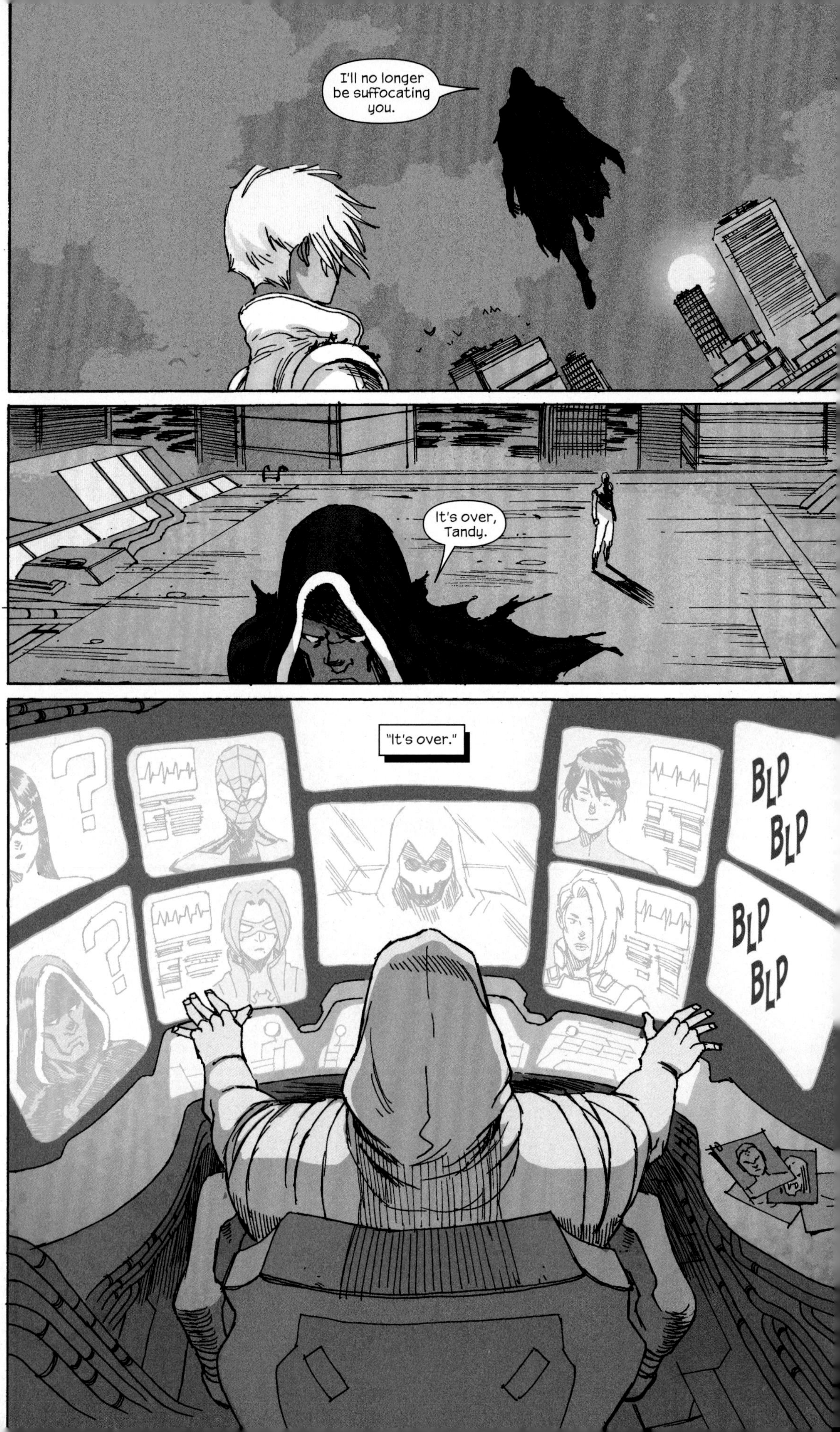

I'll no longer be suffocating you.
It's over, Tandy.
"It's over."
BLP BLP
BLP BLP

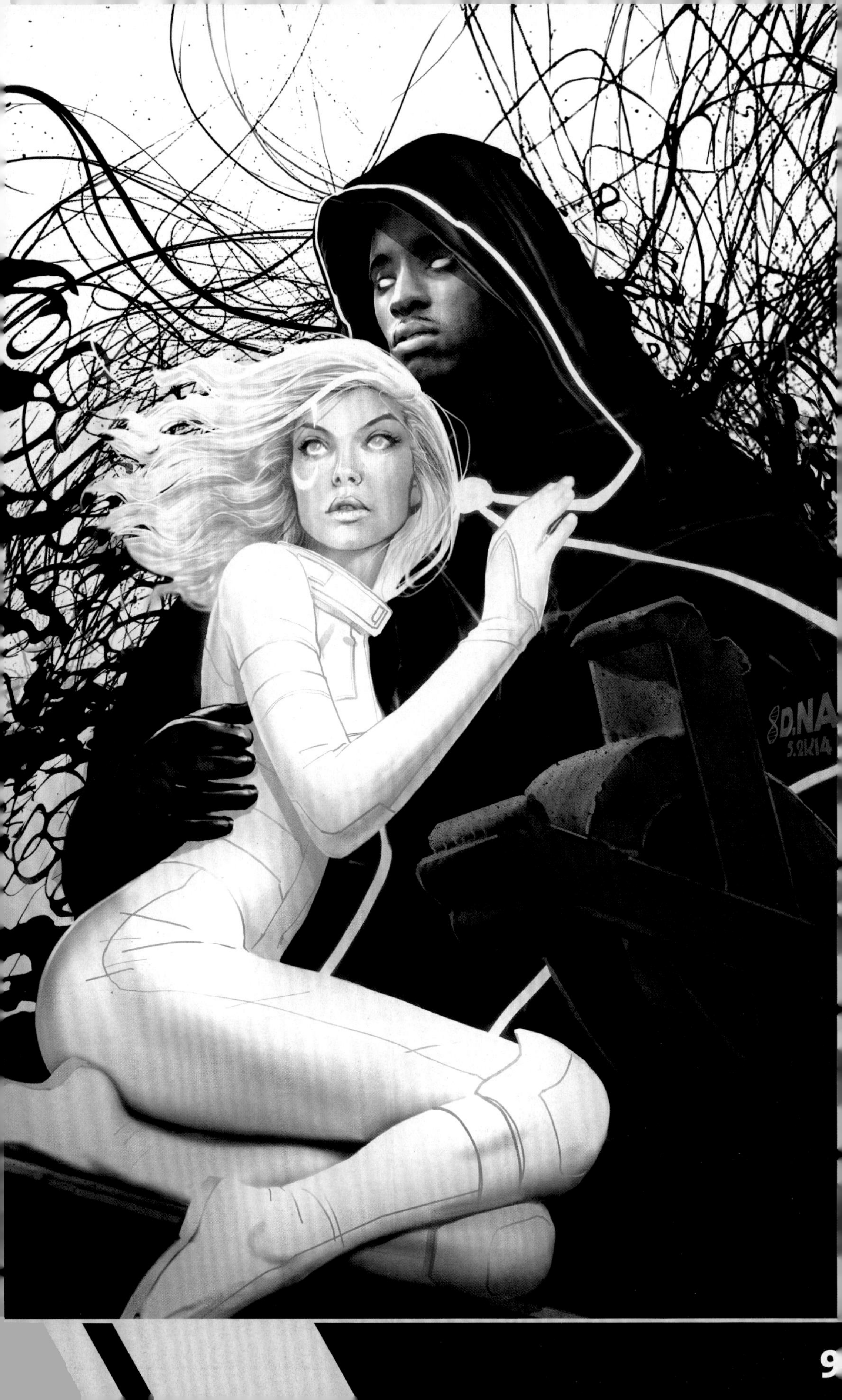
D.NA
5.2K14

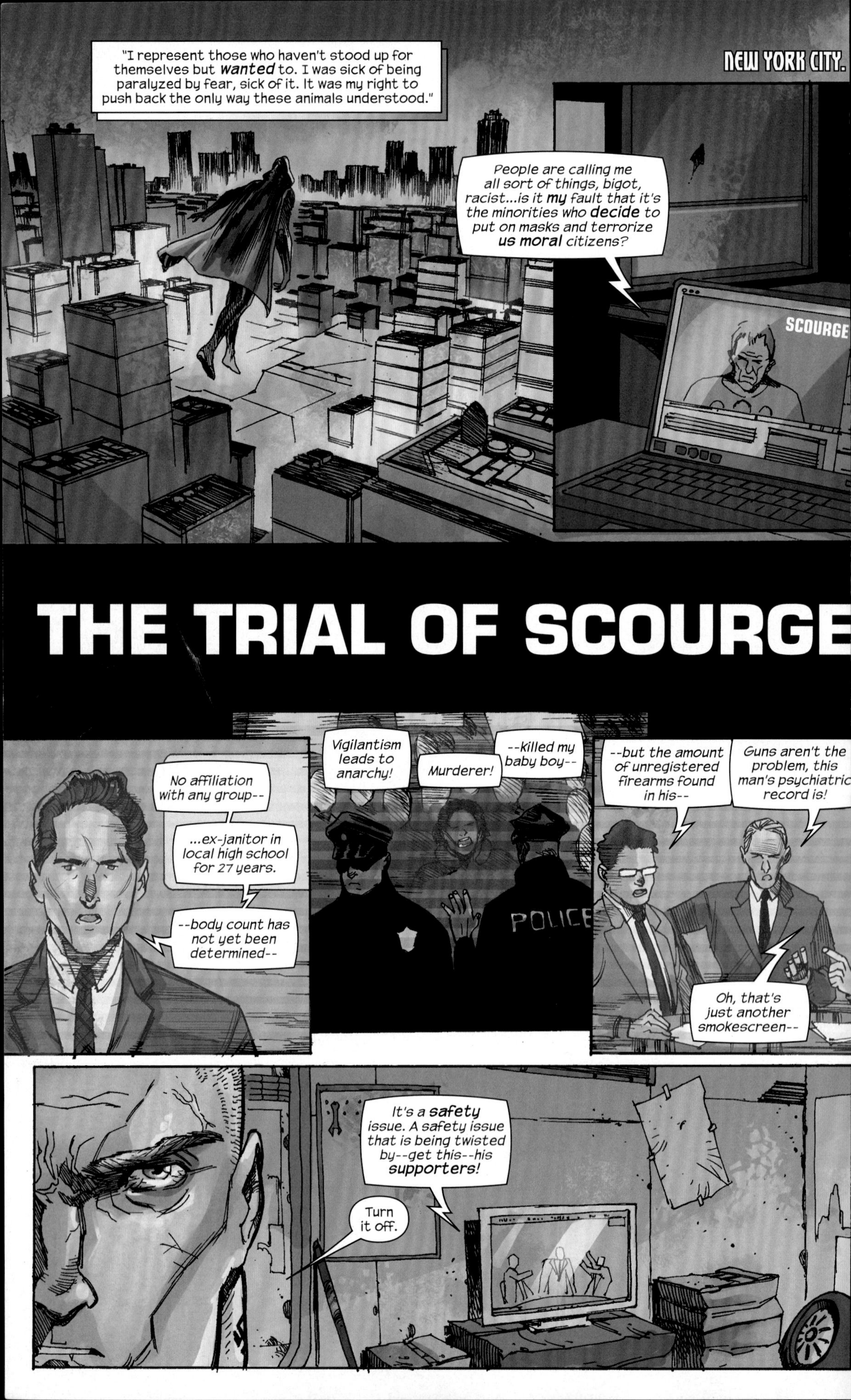

"I represent those who haven't stood up for themselves but wanted to. I was sick of being paralyzed by fear, sick of it. It was my right to push back the only way these animals understood."
NEW YORK CITY.
People are calling me all sort of things, bigot, racist...is it my fault that it's the minorities who decide to put on masks and terrorize us moral citizens?
SCOURGE
THE TRIAL OF SCOURGE
No affiliation with any group--
...ex-janitor in local high school for 27 years.
--body count has not yet been determined--
Vigilantism leads to anarchy!
Murderer!
--killed my baby boy--
POLICE
--but the amount of unregistered firearms found in his--
Guns aren't the problem, this man's psychiatric record is!
Oh, that's just another smokescreen--
It's a safety issue. A safety issue that is being twisted by--get this--his supporters!
Turn it off.

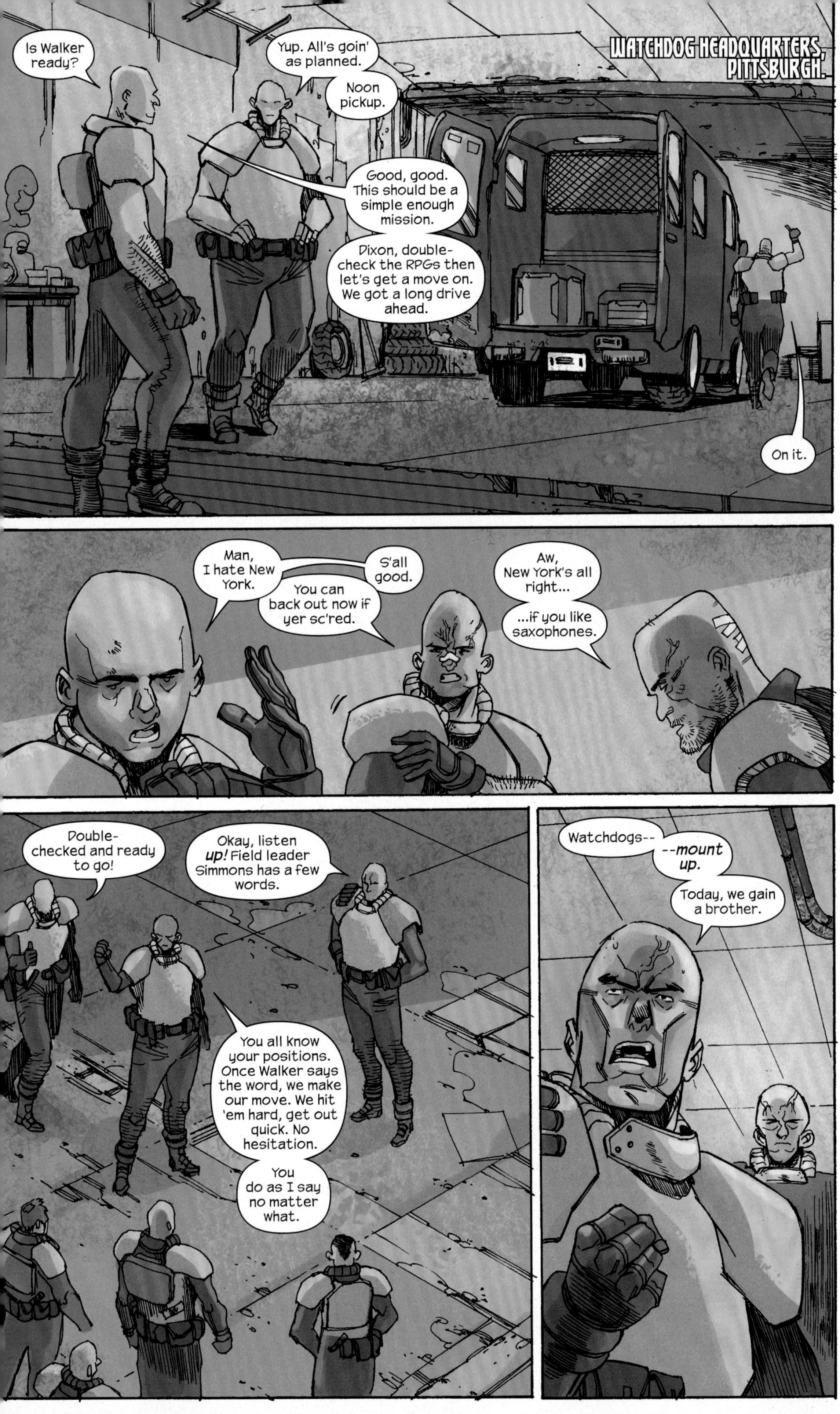
WATCHDOG HEADQUARTERS, PITTSBURGH.
Is Walker ready?
Yup. All's goin' as planned.
Noon pickup.
Good, good. This should be a simple enough mission.
Dixon, double-check the RPGs then let's get a move on. We got a long drive ahead.
On it.
Man, I hate New York.
S'all good.
You can back out now if yer sc'red.
Aw, New York's all right...
...if you like saxophones.
Double-checked and ready to go!
Okay, listen *up!* Field leader Simmons has a few words.
You all know your positions. Once Walker says the word, we make our move. We hit 'em hard, get out quick. No hesitation.
You do as I say no matter what.
Watchdogs--
--*mount up.*
Today, we gain a brother.

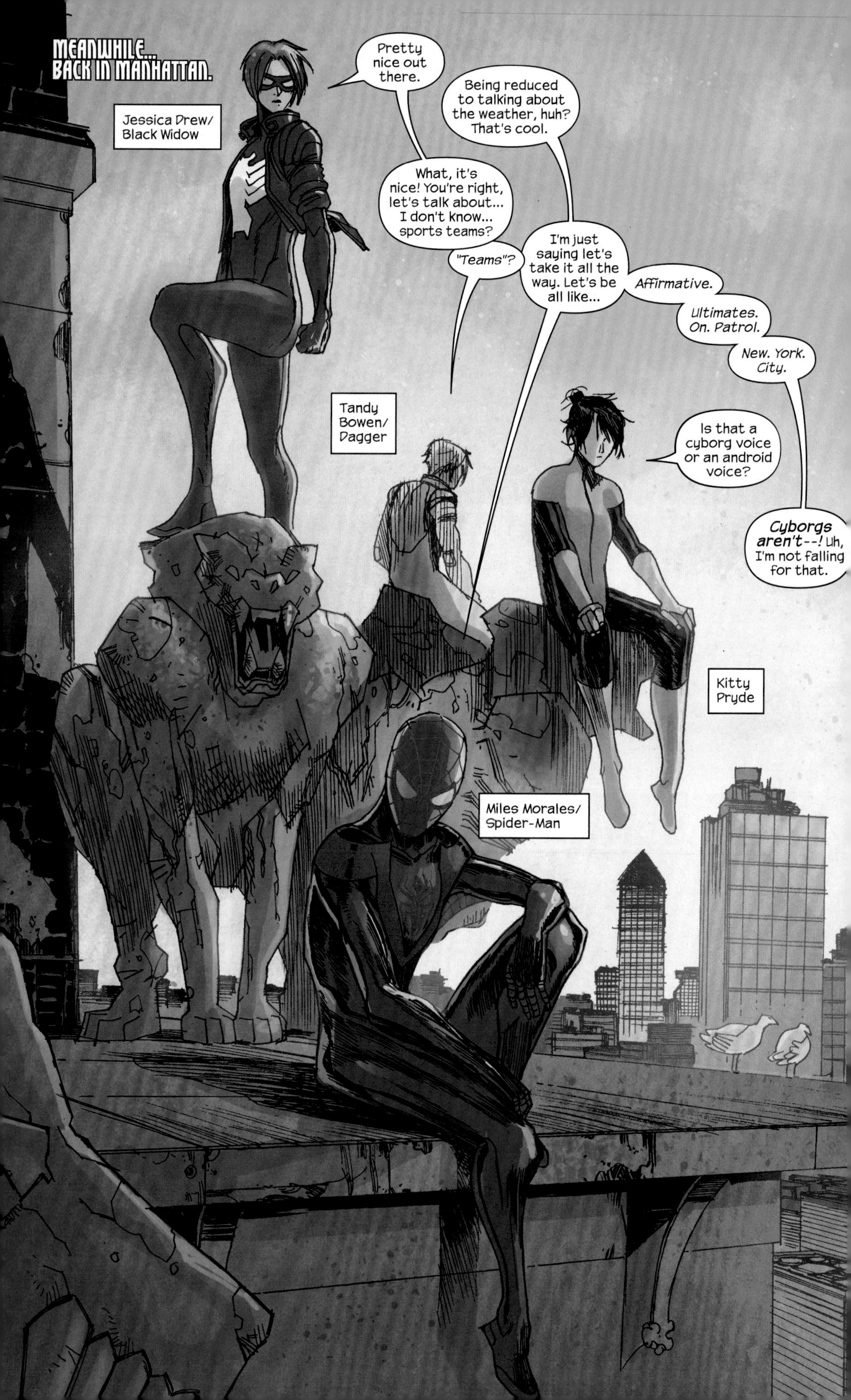
MEANWHILE... BACK IN MANHATTAN.
Jessica Drew/ Black Widow
Pretty nice out there.
Being reduced to talking about the weather, huh? That's cool.
What, it's nice! You're right, let's talk about... I don't know... sports teams?
"Teams"?
I'm just saying let's take it all the way. Let's be all like...
Affirmative.
Ultimates. On. Patrol.
New. York. City.
Tandy Bowen/ Dagger
Is that a cyborg voice or an android voice?
Cyborgs aren't--! Uh, I'm not falling for that.
Kitty Pryde
Miles Morales/ Spider-Man

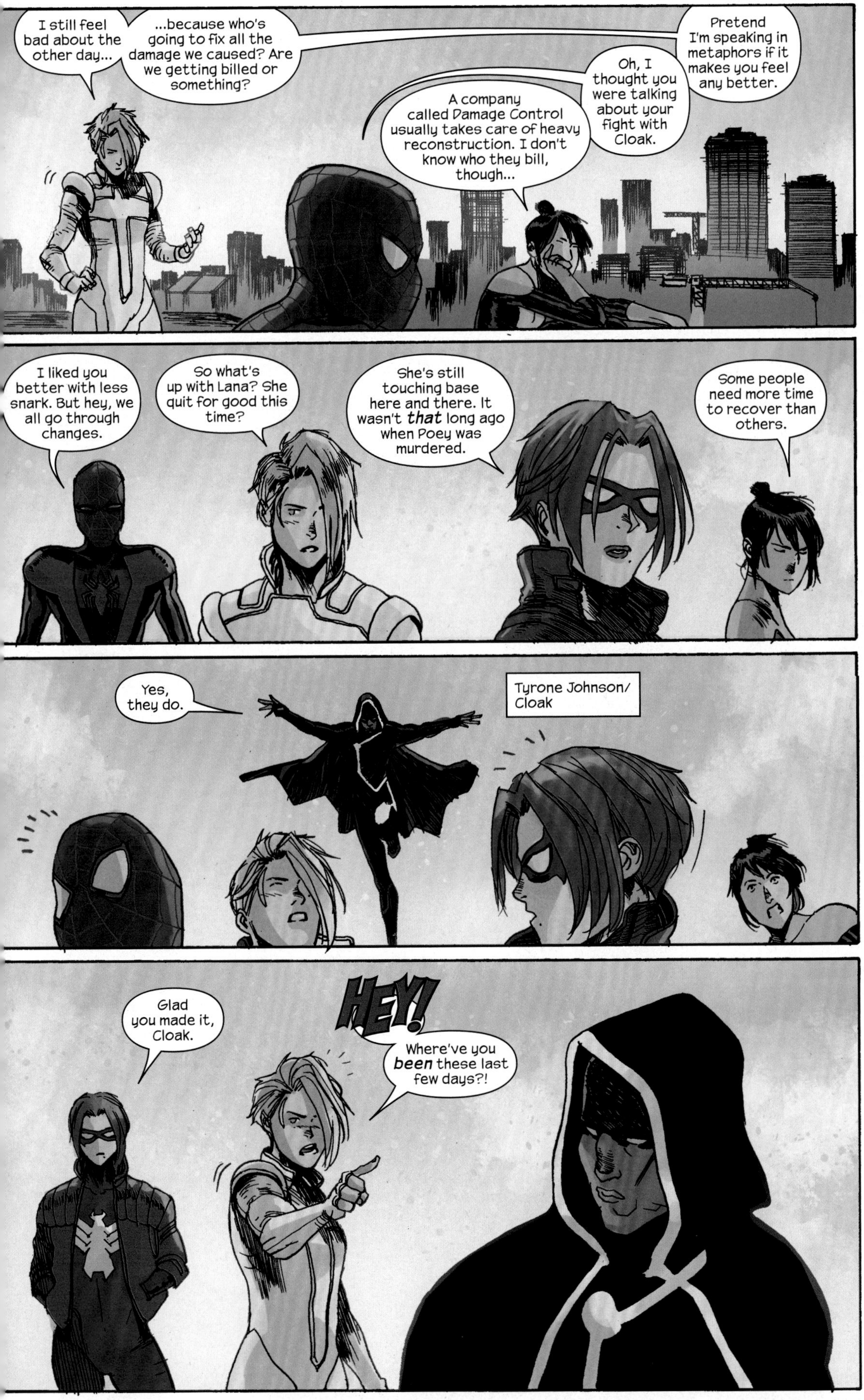

I still feel bad about the other day...
...because who's going to fix all the damage we caused? Are we getting billed or something?
A company called Damage Control usually takes care of heavy reconstruction. I don't know who they bill, though...
Oh, I thought you were talking about your fight with Cloak.
Pretend I'm speaking in metaphors if it makes you feel any better.
I liked you better with less snark. But hey, we all go through changes.
So what's up with Lana? She quit for good this time?
She's still touching base here and there. It wasn't that long ago when Poey was murdered.
Some people need more time to recover than others.
Yes, they do.
Tyrone Johnson/ Cloak
Glad you made it, Cloak.
HEY!
Where've you been these last few days?!

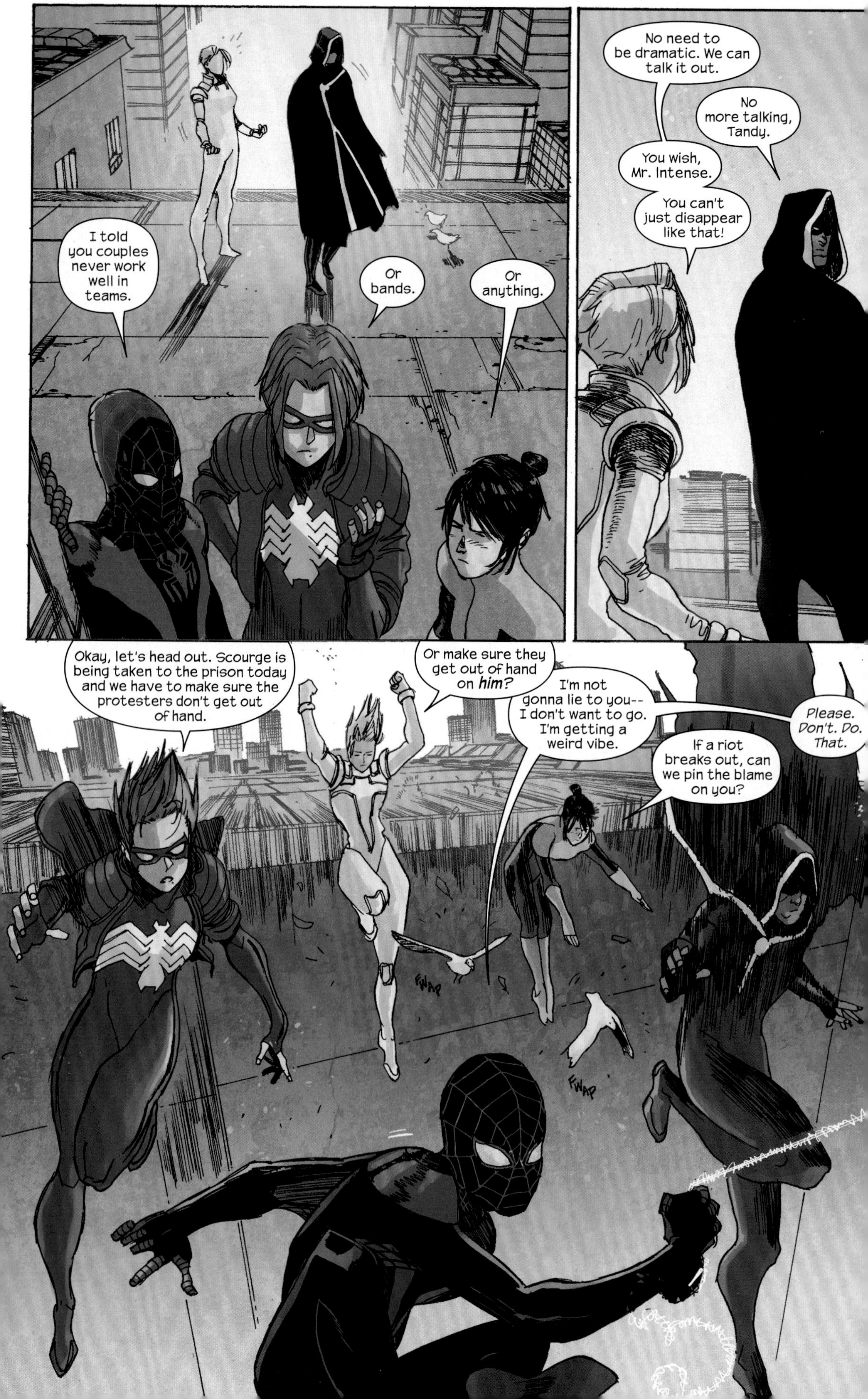
I told you couples never work well in teams.
Or bands.
Or anything.
No need to be dramatic. We can talk it out.
No more talking, Tandy.
You wish, Mr. Intense.
You can't just disappear like that!
Okay, let's head out. Scourge is being taken to the prison today and we have to make sure the protesters don't get out of hand.
Or make sure they get out of hand on *him*?
I'm not gonna lie to you-- I don't want to go. I'm getting a weird vibe.
Please. Don't. Do. That.
If a riot breaks out, can we pin the blame on you?
FWAP
FWAP

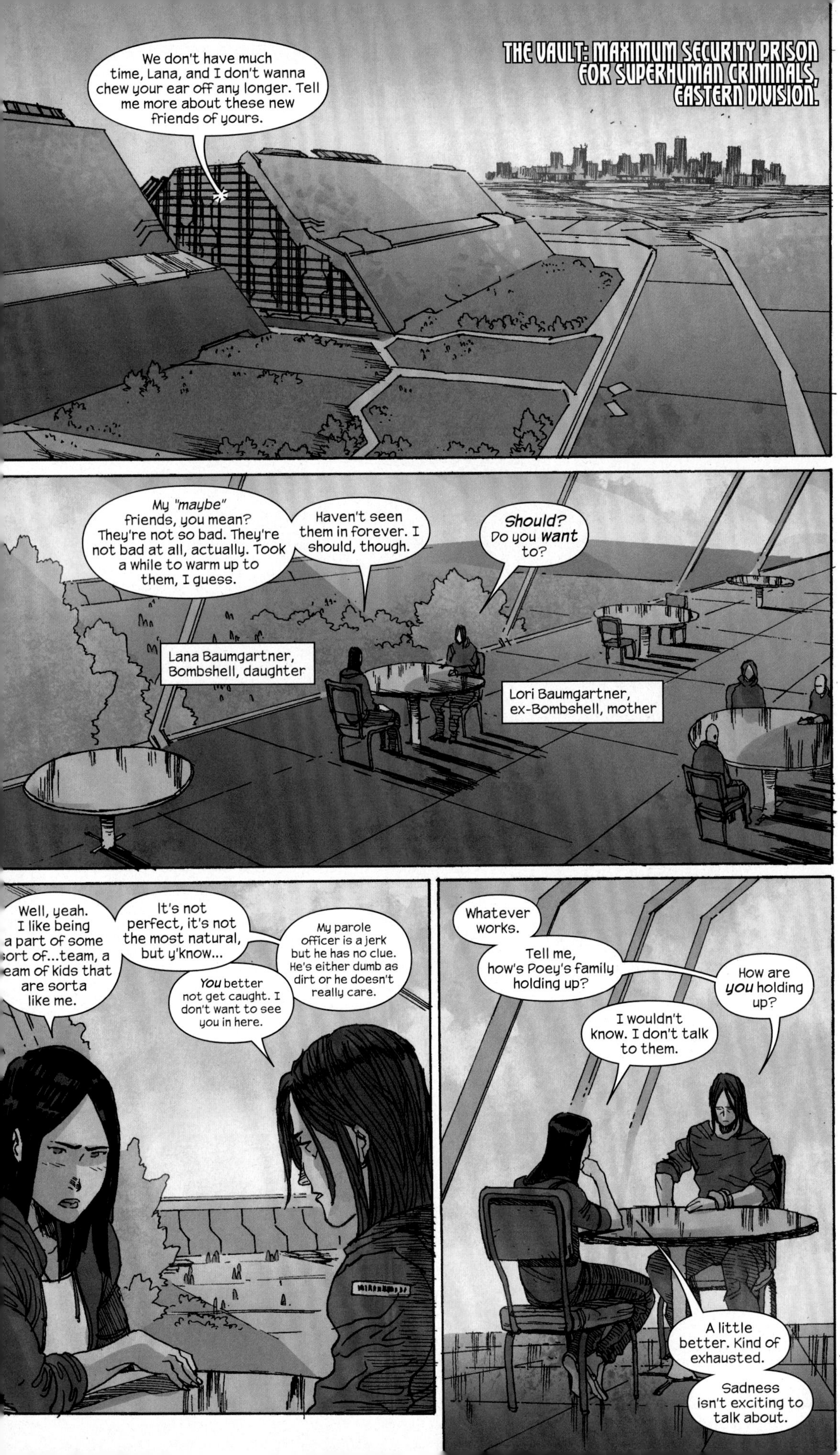
THE VAULT: MAXIMUM SECURITY PRISON FOR SUPERHUMAN CRIMINALS, EASTERN DIVISION.
We don't have much time, Lana, and I don't wanna chew your ear off any longer. Tell me more about these new friends of yours.
My "maybe" friends, you mean? They're not so bad. They're not bad at all, actually. Took a while to warm up to them, I guess.
Haven't seen them in forever. I should, though.
Should? Do you want to?
Lana Baumgartner, Bombshell, daughter
Lori Baumgartner, ex-Bombshell, mother
Well, yeah. I like being a part of some sort of...team, a team of kids that are sorta like me.
It's not perfect, it's not the most natural, but y'know...
You better not get caught. I don't want to see you in here.
My parole officer is a jerk but he has no clue. He's either dumb as dirt or he doesn't really care.
Whatever works.
Tell me, how's Poey's family holding up?
I wouldn't know. I don't talk to them.
How are you holding up?
A little better. Kind of exhausted.
Sadness isn't exciting to talk about.

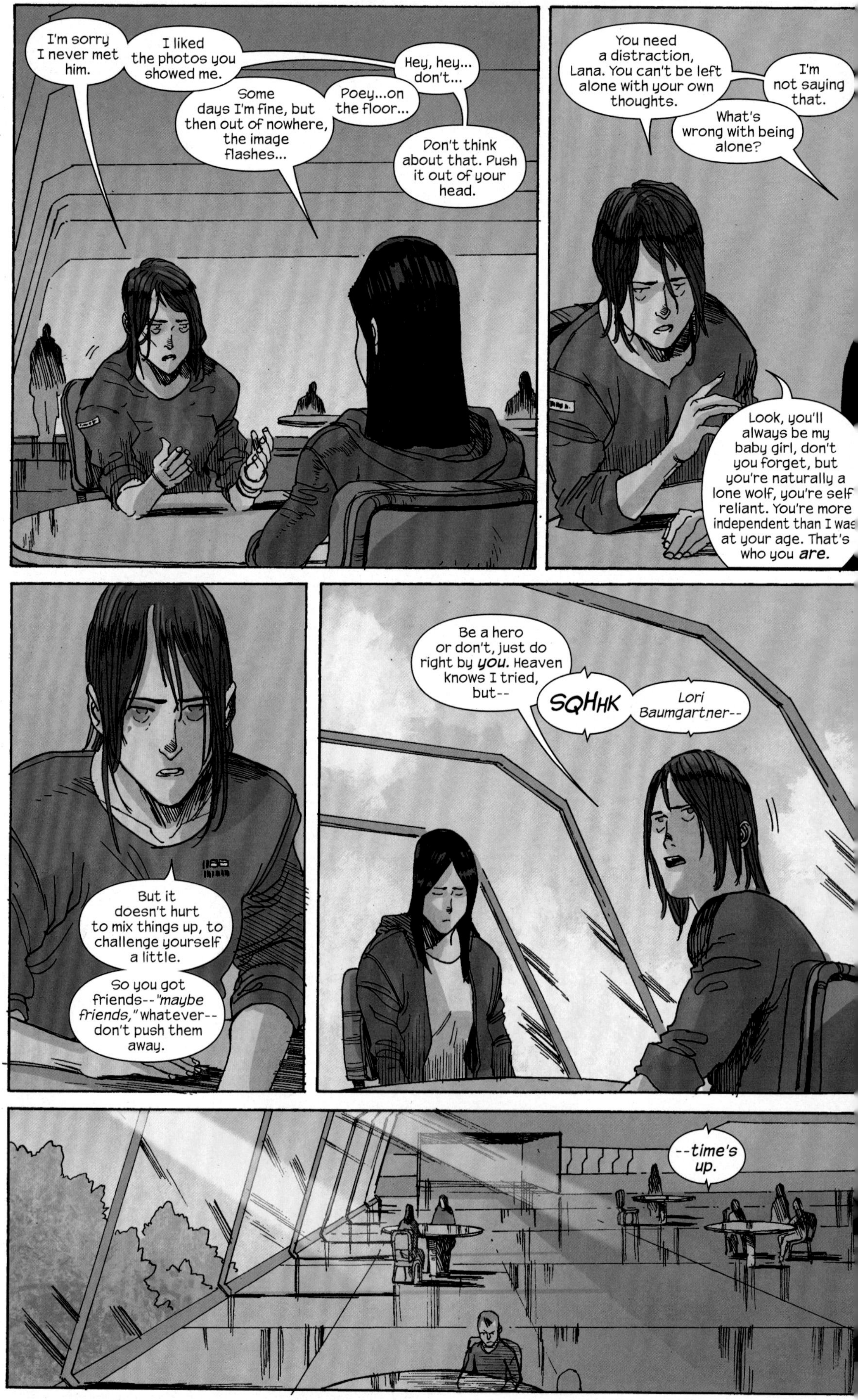
I'm sorry I never met him.
I liked the photos you showed me.
Hey, hey... don't...
Some days I'm fine, but then out of nowhere, the image flashes...
Poey...on the floor...
Don't think about that. Push it out of your head.
You need a distraction, Lana. You can't be left alone with your own thoughts.
I'm not saying that.
What's wrong with being alone?
Look, you'll always be my baby girl, don't you forget, but you're naturally a lone wolf, you're self reliant. You're more independent than I was at your age. That's who you *are.*
But it doesn't hurt to mix things up, to challenge yourself a little.
So you got friends--*"maybe friends,"* whatever--don't push them away.
Be a hero or don't, just do right by *you.* Heaven knows I tried, but--
SQHHK
Lori Baumgartner--
--time's up.

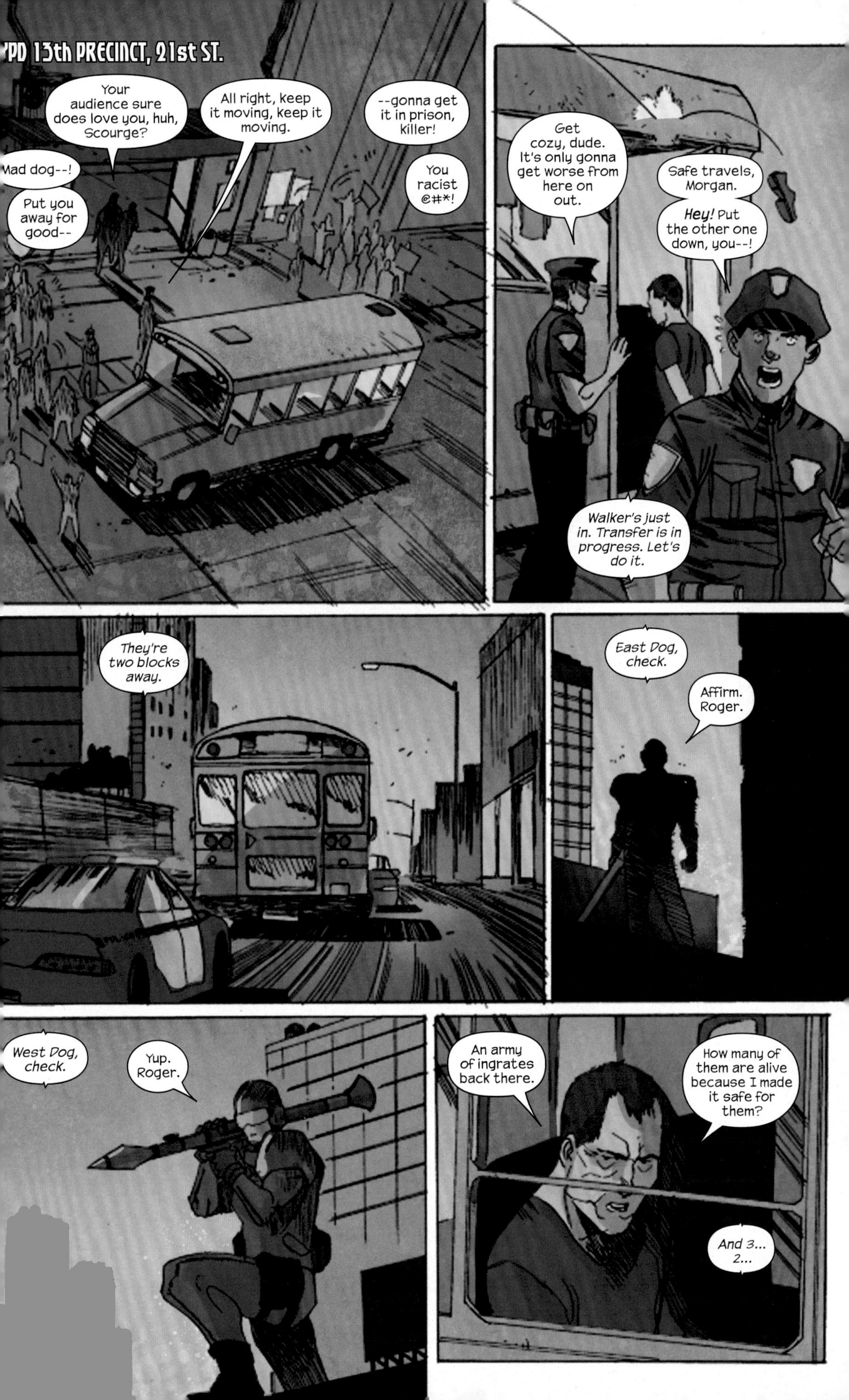
PD 13th PRECINCT, 21st ST.
Your audience sure does love you, huh, Scourge?
All right, keep it moving, keep it moving.
--gonna get it in prison, killer!
Mad dog--!
Put you away for good--
You racist @#*!
Get cozy, dude. It's only gonna get worse from here on out.
Safe travels, Morgan.
Hey! Put the other one down, you--!
Walker's just in. Transfer is in progress. Let's do it.
They're two blocks away.
East Dog, check.
Affirm. Roger.
West Dog, check.
Yup. Roger.
An army of ingrates back there.
How many of them are alive because I made it safe for them?
And 3... 2...

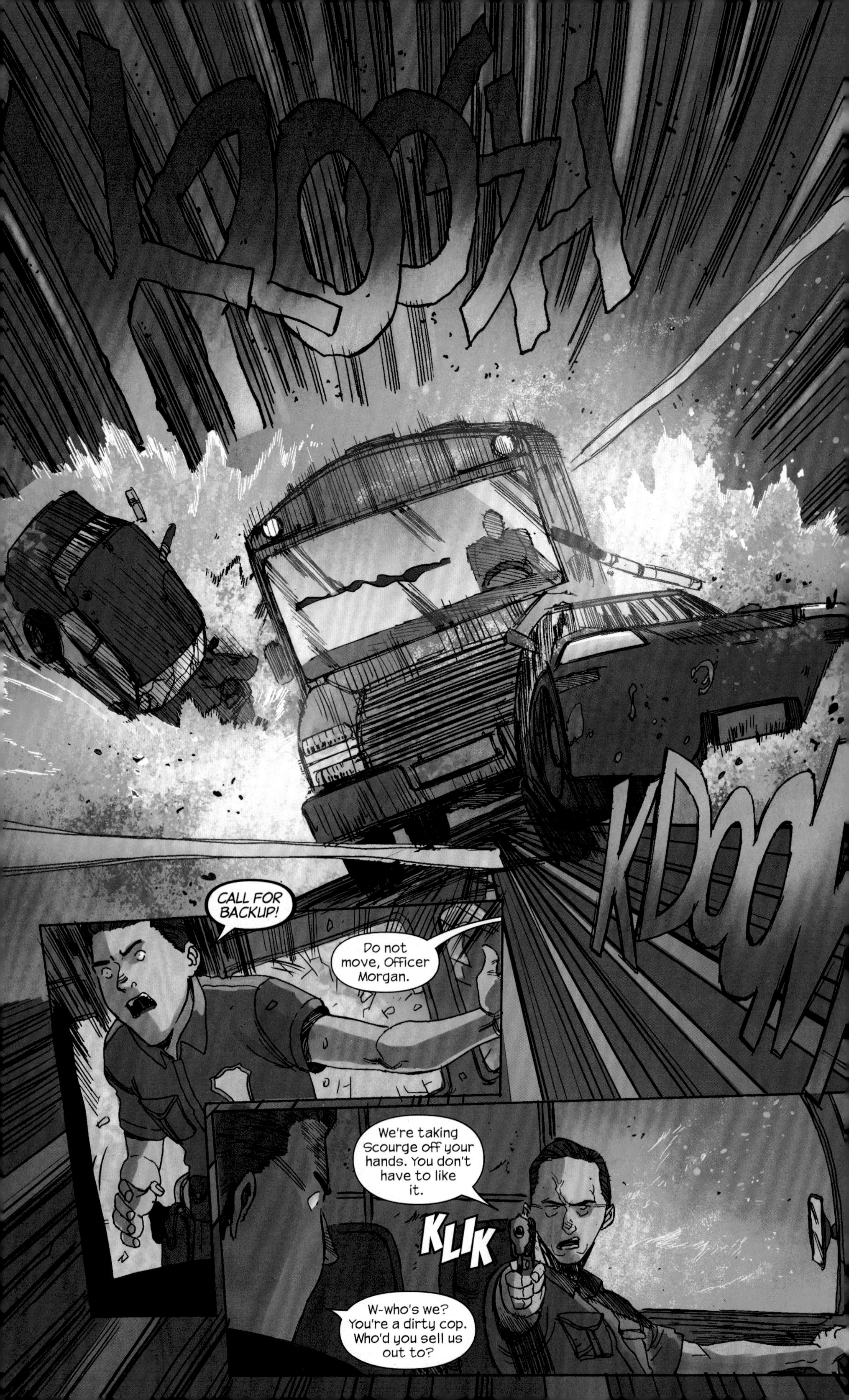
KDOOOM
CALL FOR BACKUP!
Do not move, Officer Morgan.
We're taking Scourge off your hands. You don't have to like it.
KLIK
W-who's we? You're a dirty cop. Who'd you sell us out to?

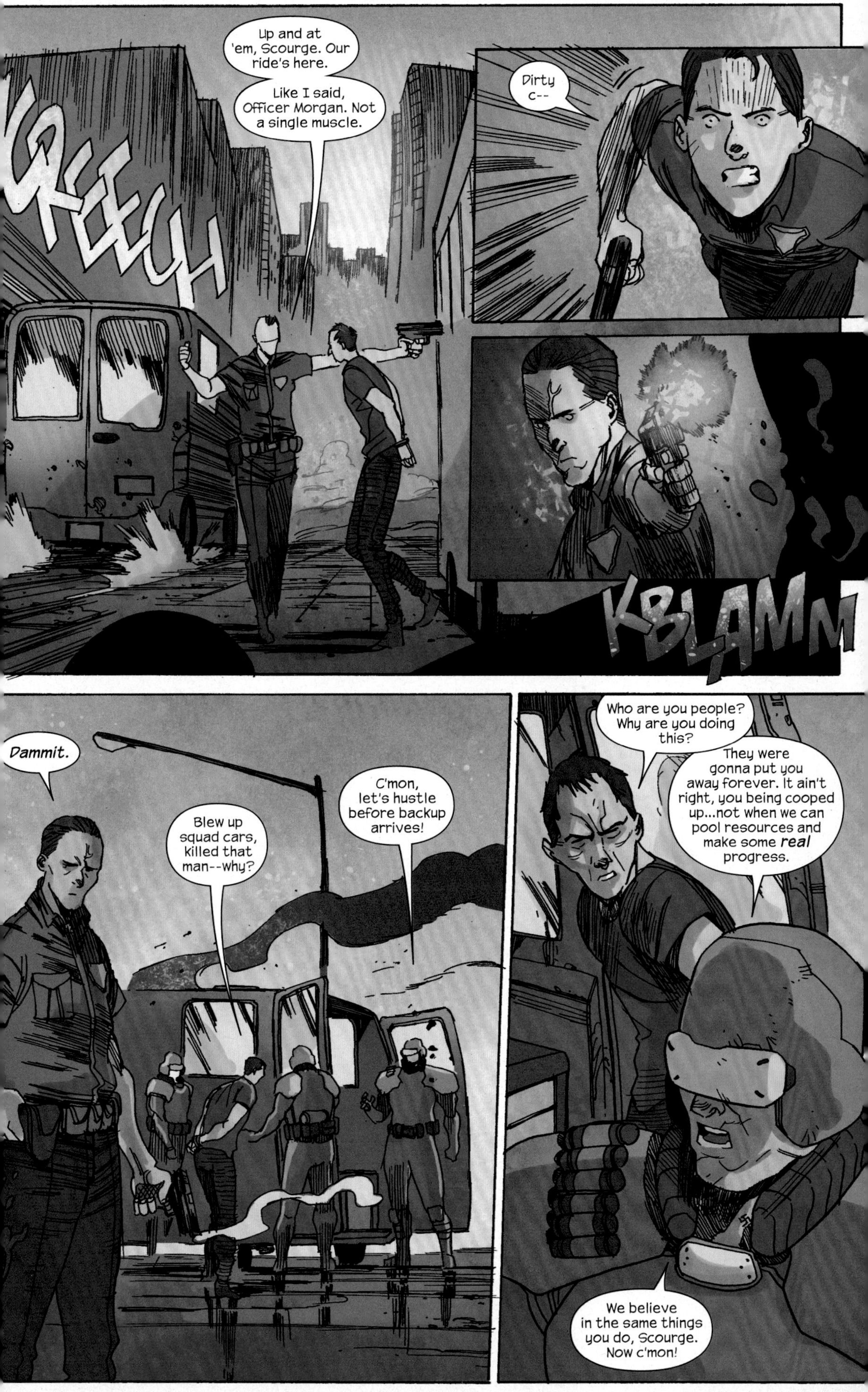
Up and at 'em, Scourge. Our ride's here.
Like I said, Officer Morgan. Not a single muscle.
SKREEECH
Dirty c--
KBLAMM
Dammit.
Blew up squad cars, killed that man--why?
C'mon, let's hustle before backup arrives!
Who are you people? Why are you doing this?
They were gonna put you away forever. It ain't right, you being cooped up...not when we can pool resources and make some *real* progress.
We believe in the same things you do, Scourge. Now c'mon!

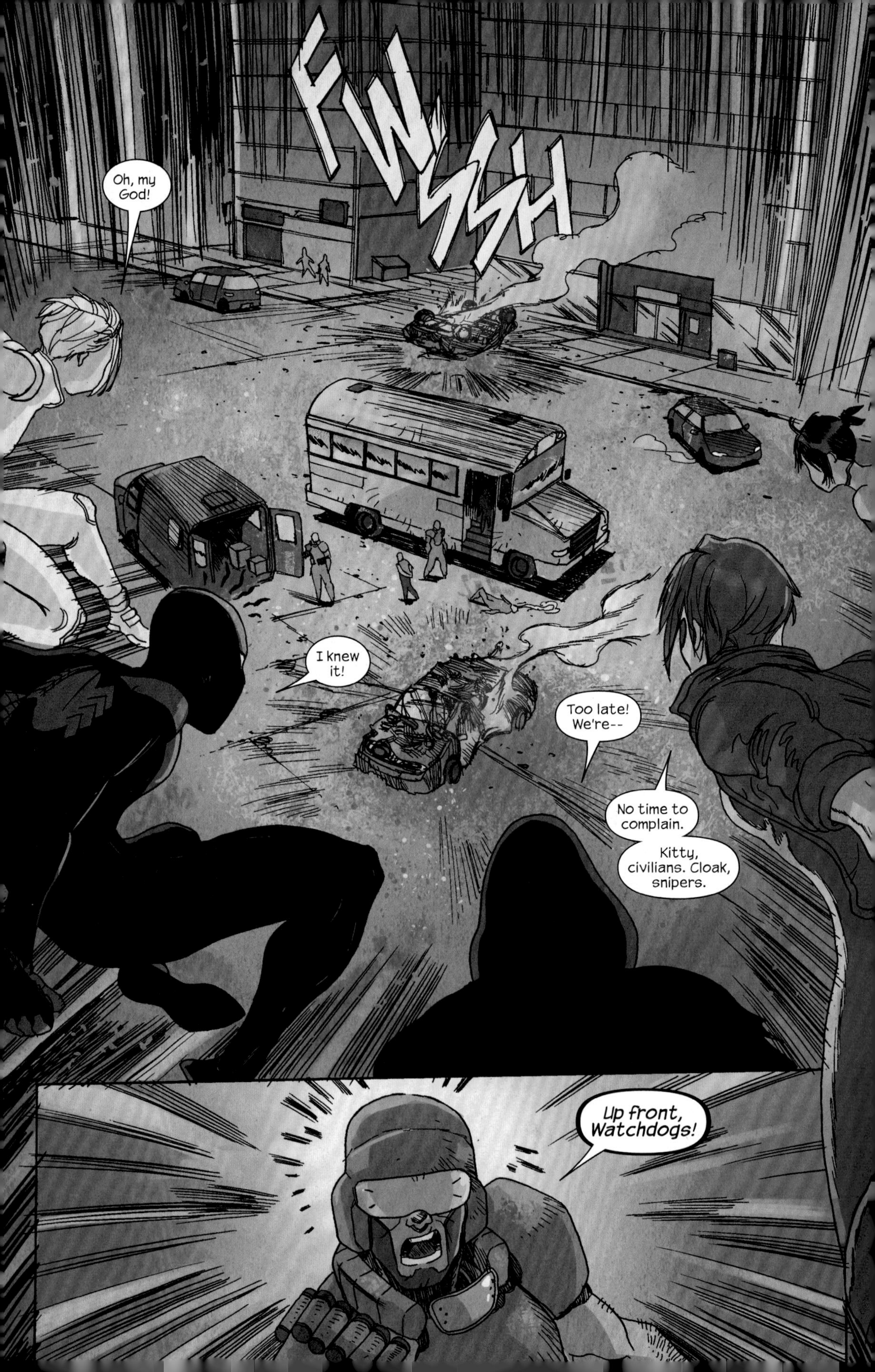
FWSSH
Oh, my God!
I knew it!
Too late! We're--
No time to complain.
Kitty, civilians. Cloak, snipers.
Up front, Watchdogs!

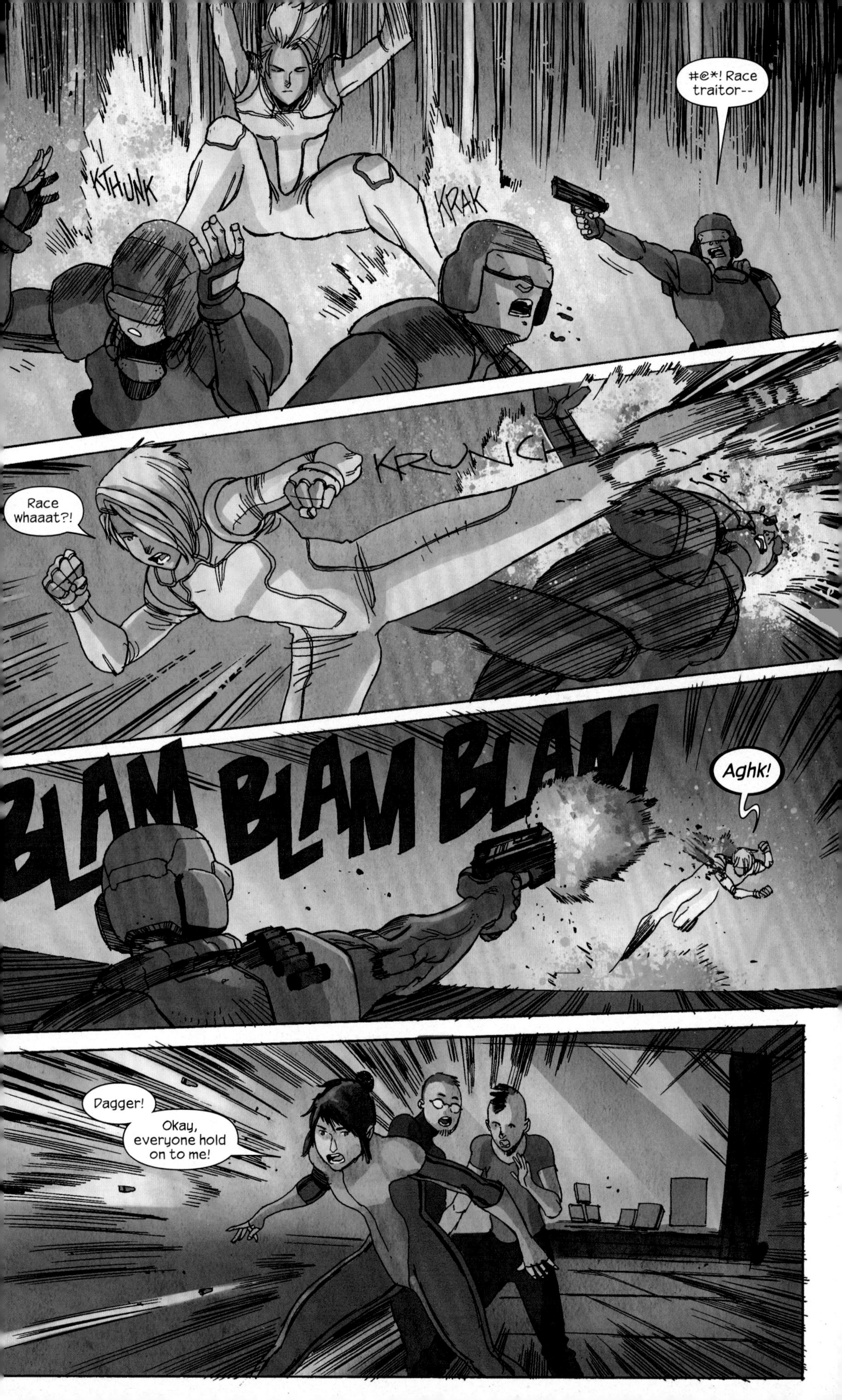
KTHUNK
KRAK
#@*! Race traitor--
KRUNCH
Race whaaat?!
BLAM BLAM BLAM
Aghk!
Dagger!
Okay, everyone hold on to me!

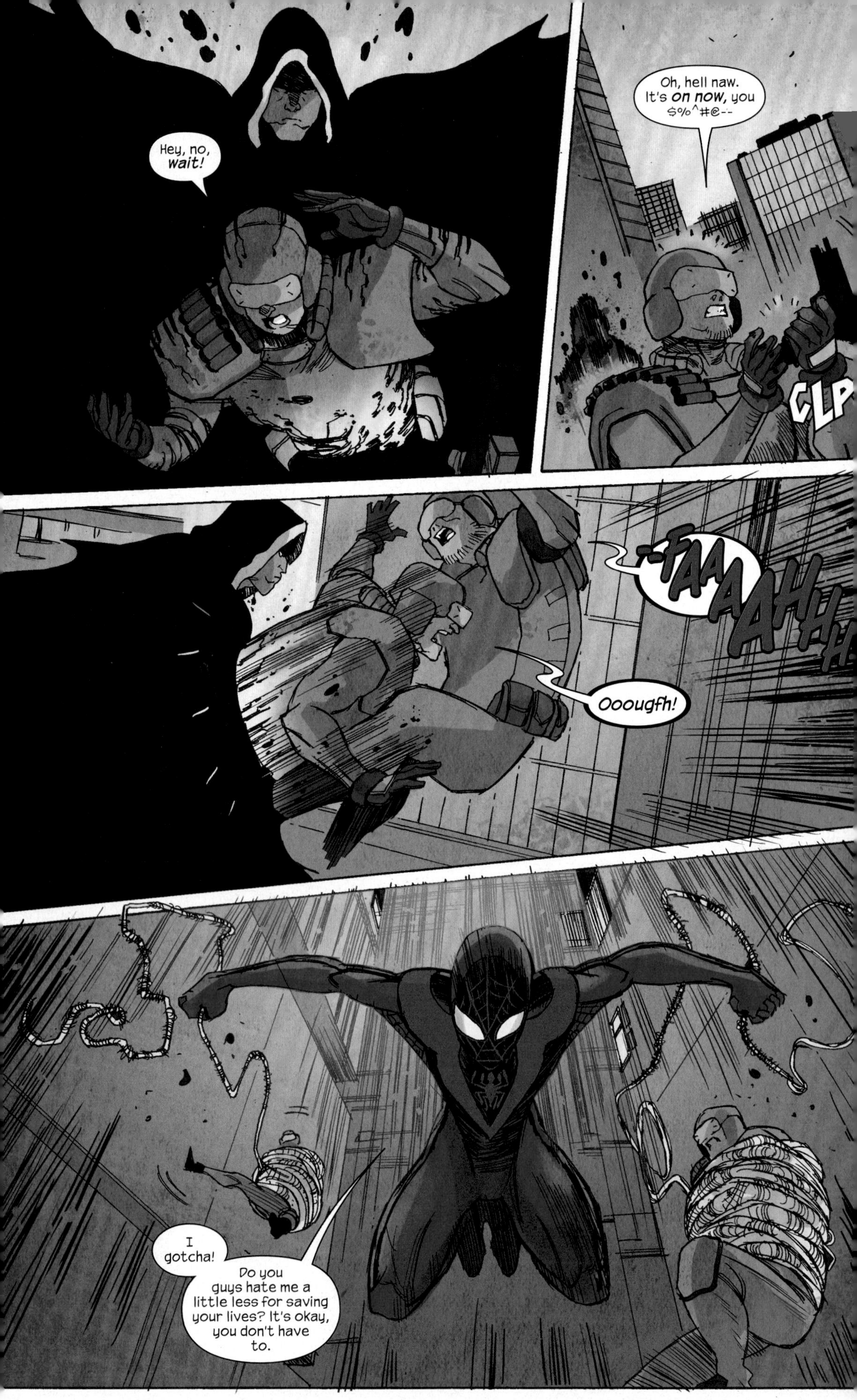

Hey, no, wait!
Oh, hell naw. It's on now, you $%^#@--
CLP
--FAAAAAHHHH
Ooougfh!
I gotcha!
Do you guys hate me a little less for saving your lives? It's okay, you don't have to.

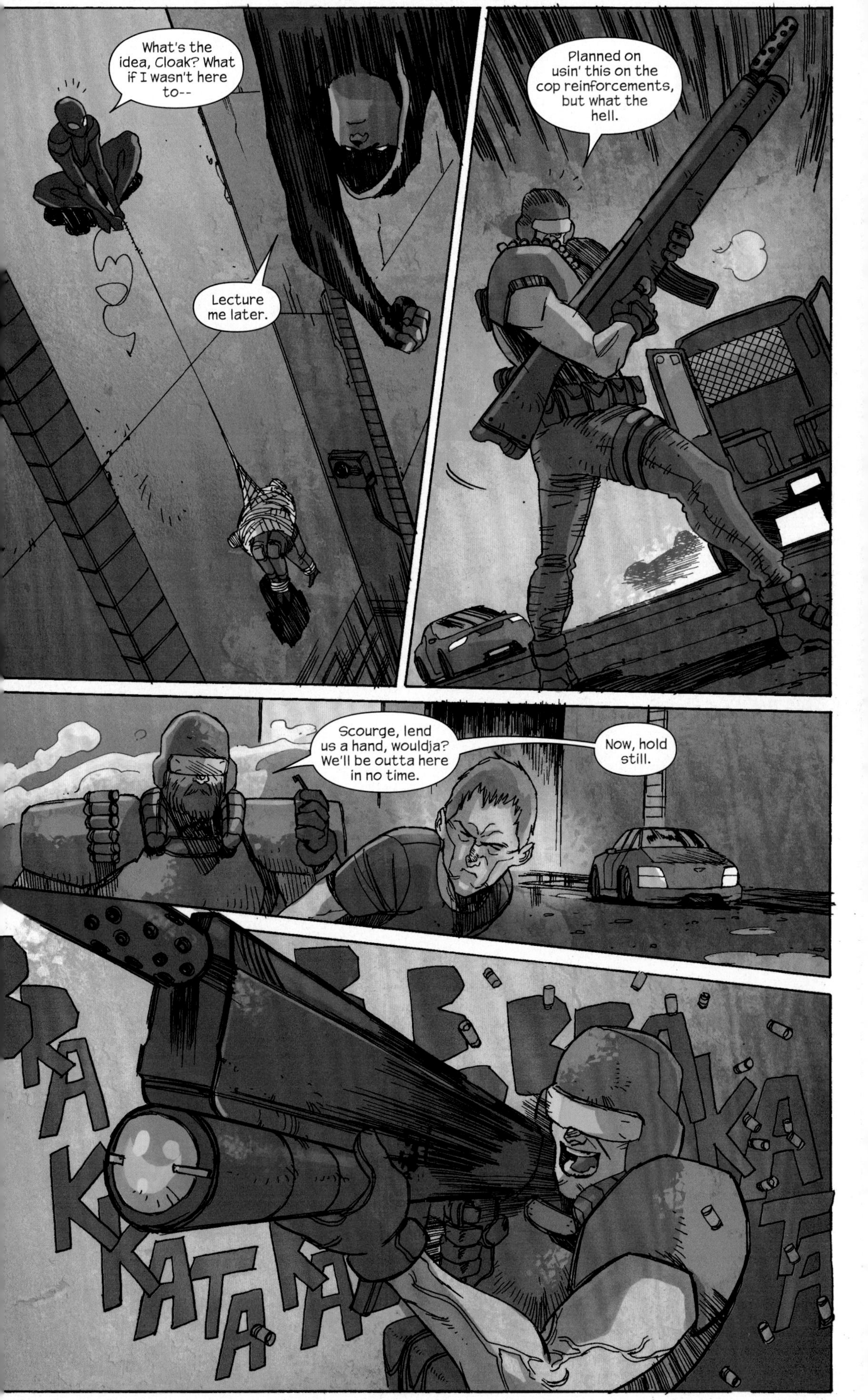
What's the idea, Cloak? What if I wasn't here to--
Lecture me later.
Planned on usin' this on the cop reinforcements, but what the hell.
Scourge, lend us a hand, wouldja? We'll be outta here in no time.
Now, hold still.
KRAKAKATATATA
KAKAKATA

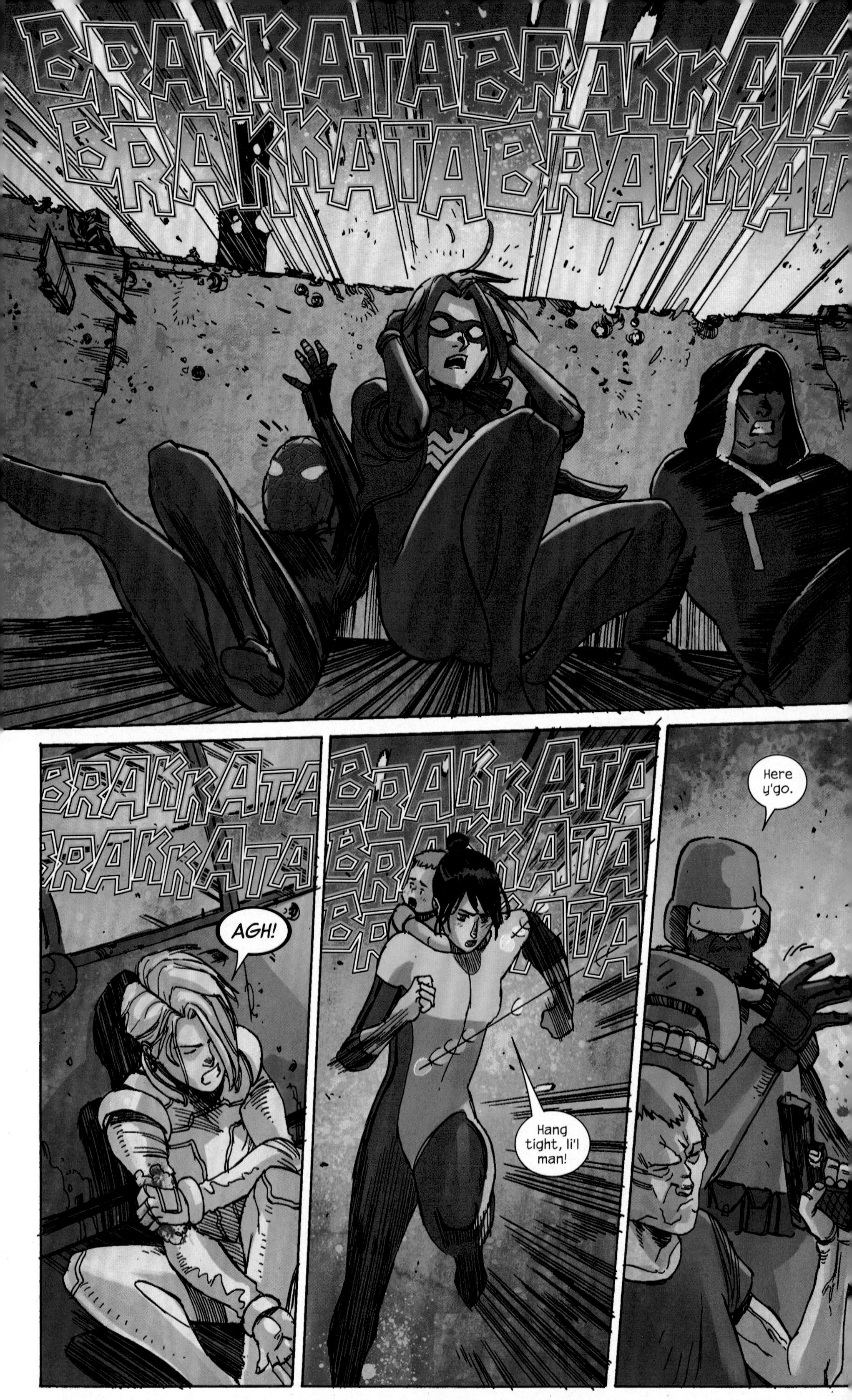
BRAKKATABRAKKATA
BRAKKATABRAKKAT
BRAKKATA
RAKKATA
AGH!
BRAKKATA
BRAKKATA
BRAKKATA
Hang tight, li'l man!
Here y'go.

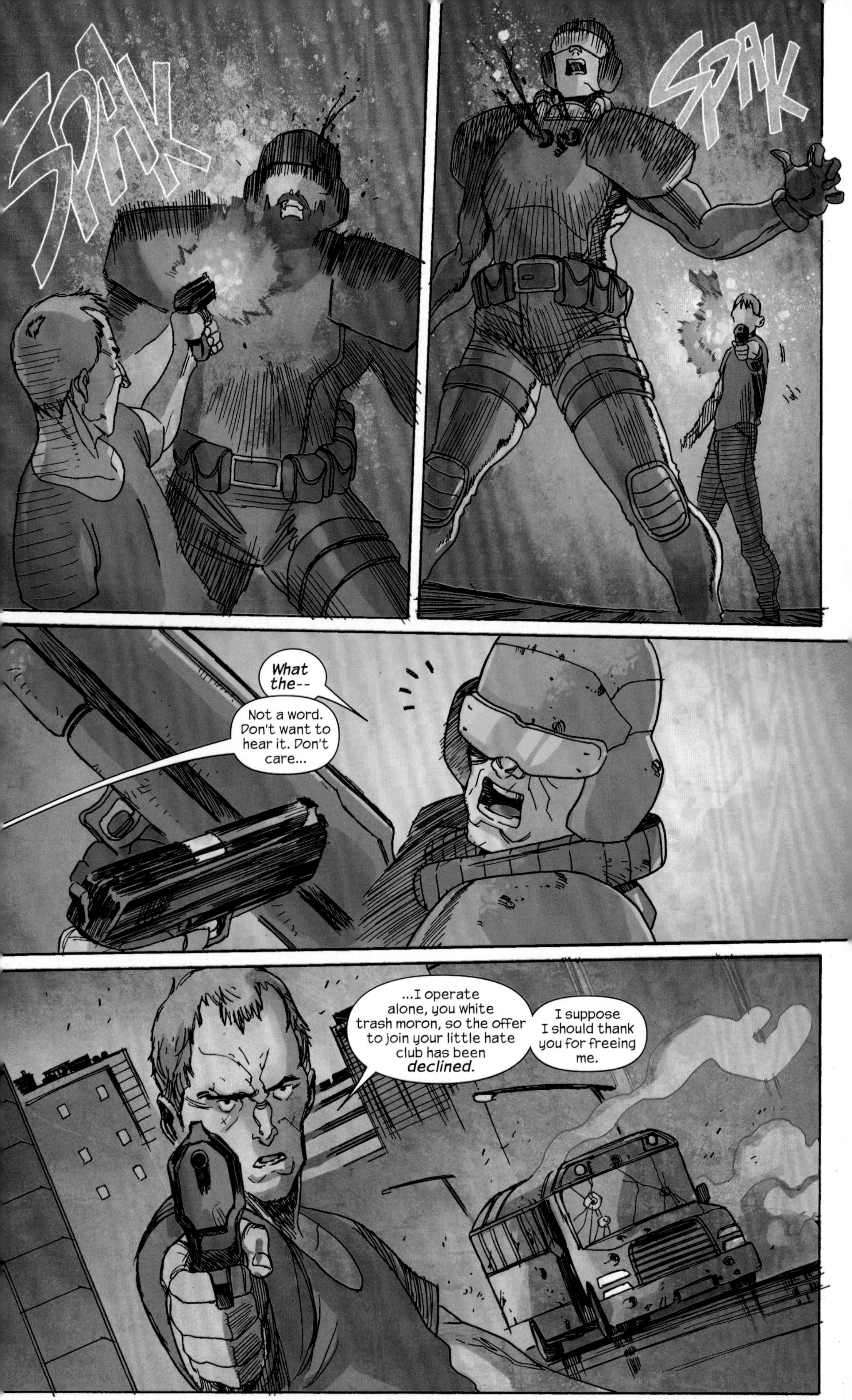
SPAK
SPAK
What the--
Not a word. Don't want to hear it. Don't care...
...I operate alone, you white trash moron, so the offer to join your little hate club has been *declined.*
I suppose I should thank you for freeing me.

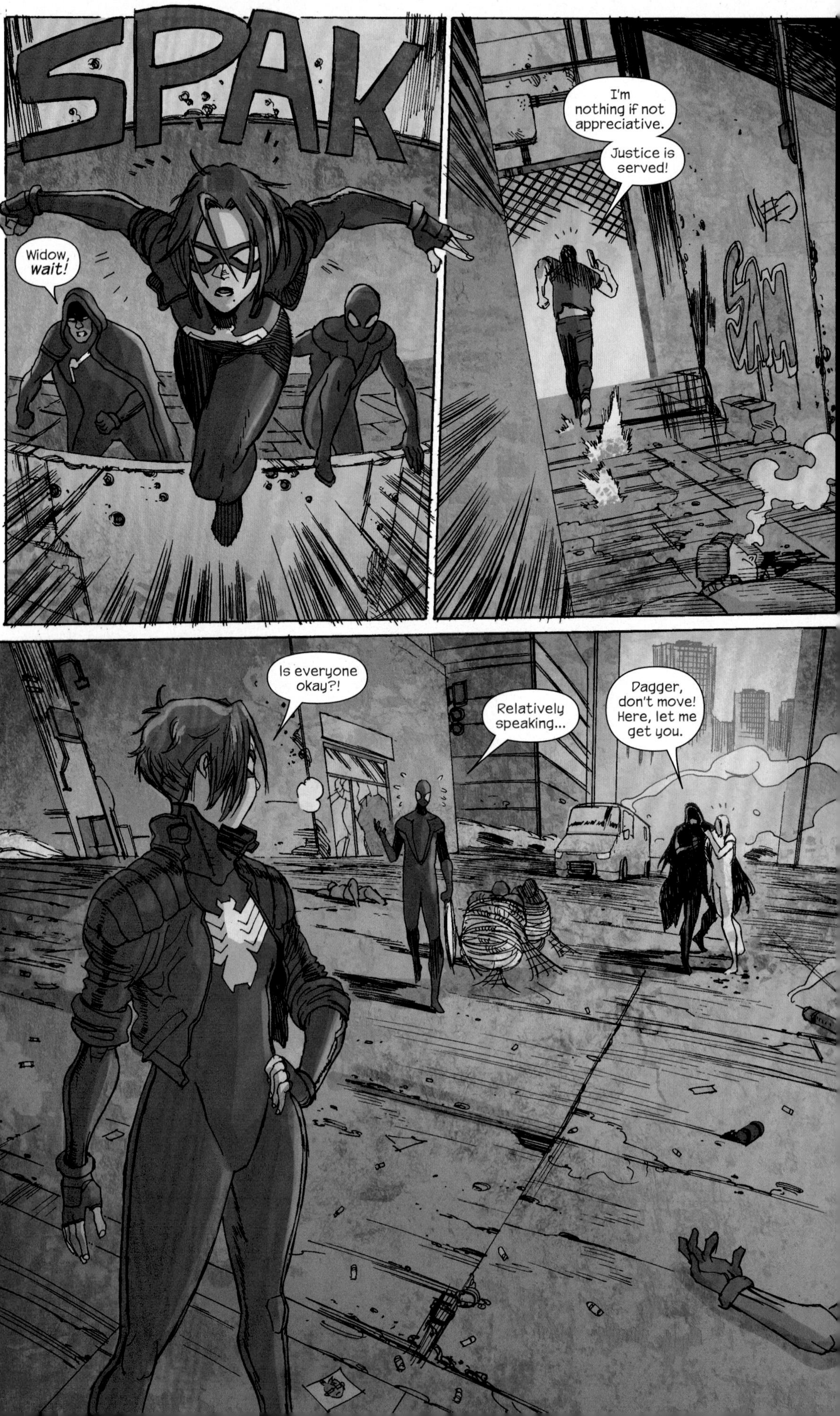
SPAK
Widow, wait!
I'm nothing if not appreciative.
Justice is served!
Is everyone okay?!
Relatively speaking...
Dagger, don't move! Here, let me get you.

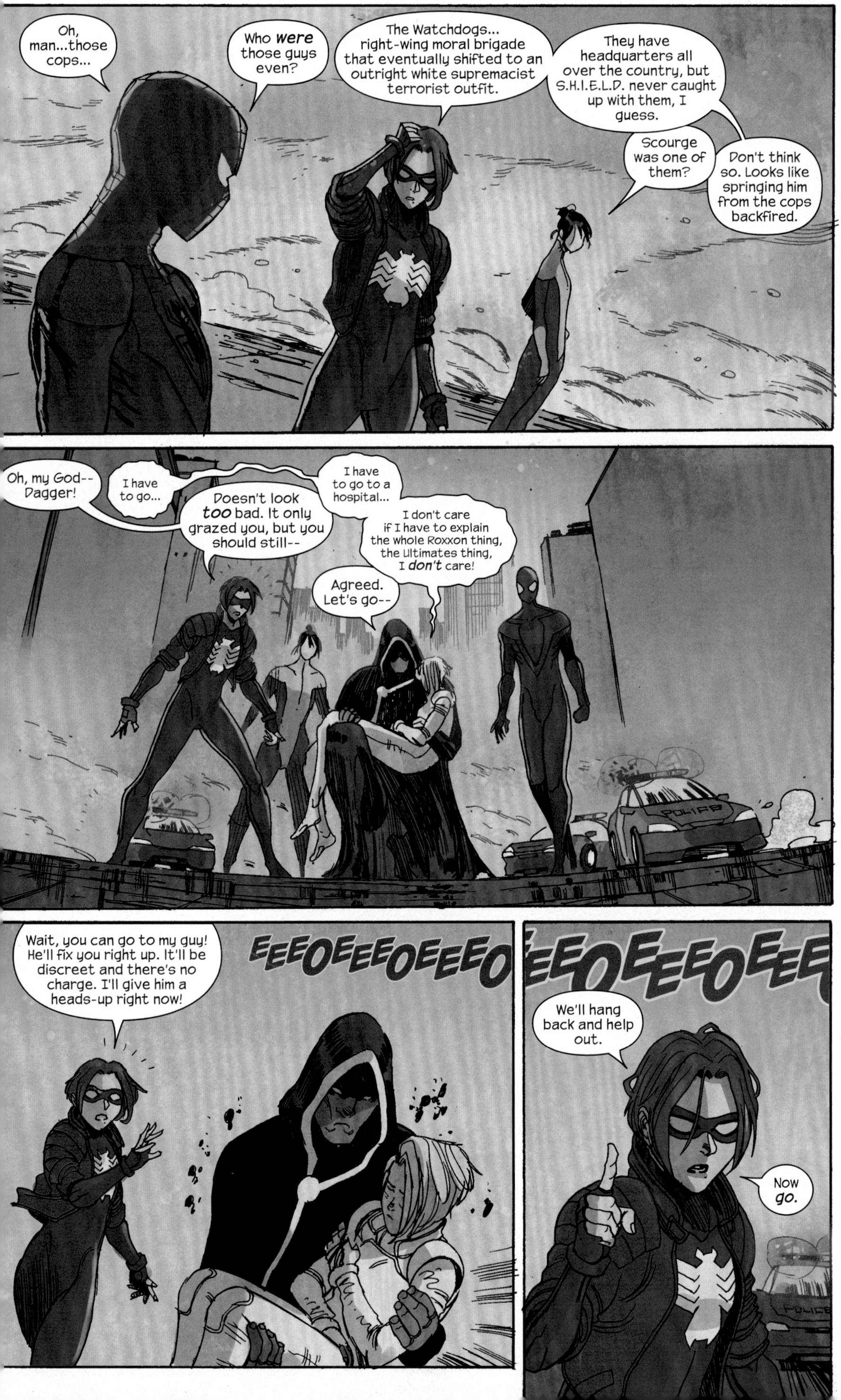
Oh, man...those cops...
Who *were* those guys even?
The Watchdogs... right-wing moral brigade that eventually shifted to an outright white supremacist terrorist outfit.
They have headquarters all over the country, but S.H.I.E.L.D. never caught up with them, I guess.
Scourge was one of them?
Don't think so. Looks like springing him from the cops backfired.
Oh, my God-- Dagger!
I have to go...
I have to go to a hospital...
Doesn't look *too* bad. It only grazed you, but you should still--
I don't care if I have to explain the whole Roxxon thing, the Ultimates thing, I *don't* care!
Agreed. Let's go--
POLICE
Wait, you can go to my guy! He'll fix you right up. It'll be discreet and there's no charge. I'll give him a heads-up right now!
EEEOEEEOEEEO
EEEOEEEOEE
We'll hang back and help out.
Now *go.*

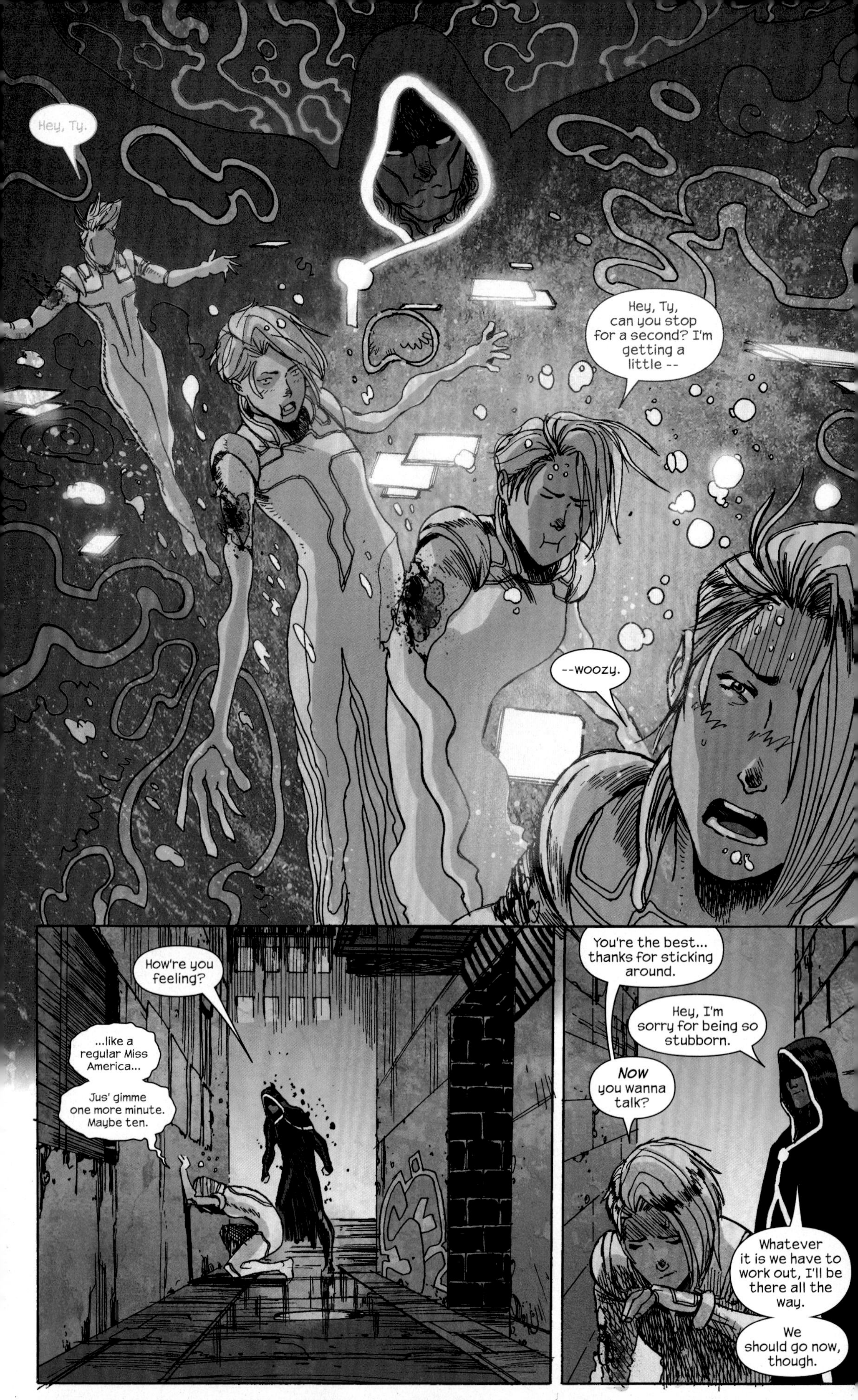

Hey, Ty.
Hey, Ty, can you stop for a second? I'm getting a little --
--woozy.
How're you feeling?
...like a regular Miss America...
Jus' gimme one more minute. Maybe ten.
You're the best... thanks for sticking around.
Hey, I'm sorry for being so stubborn.
NOW you wanna talk?
Whatever it is we have to work out, I'll be there all the way.
We should go now, though.

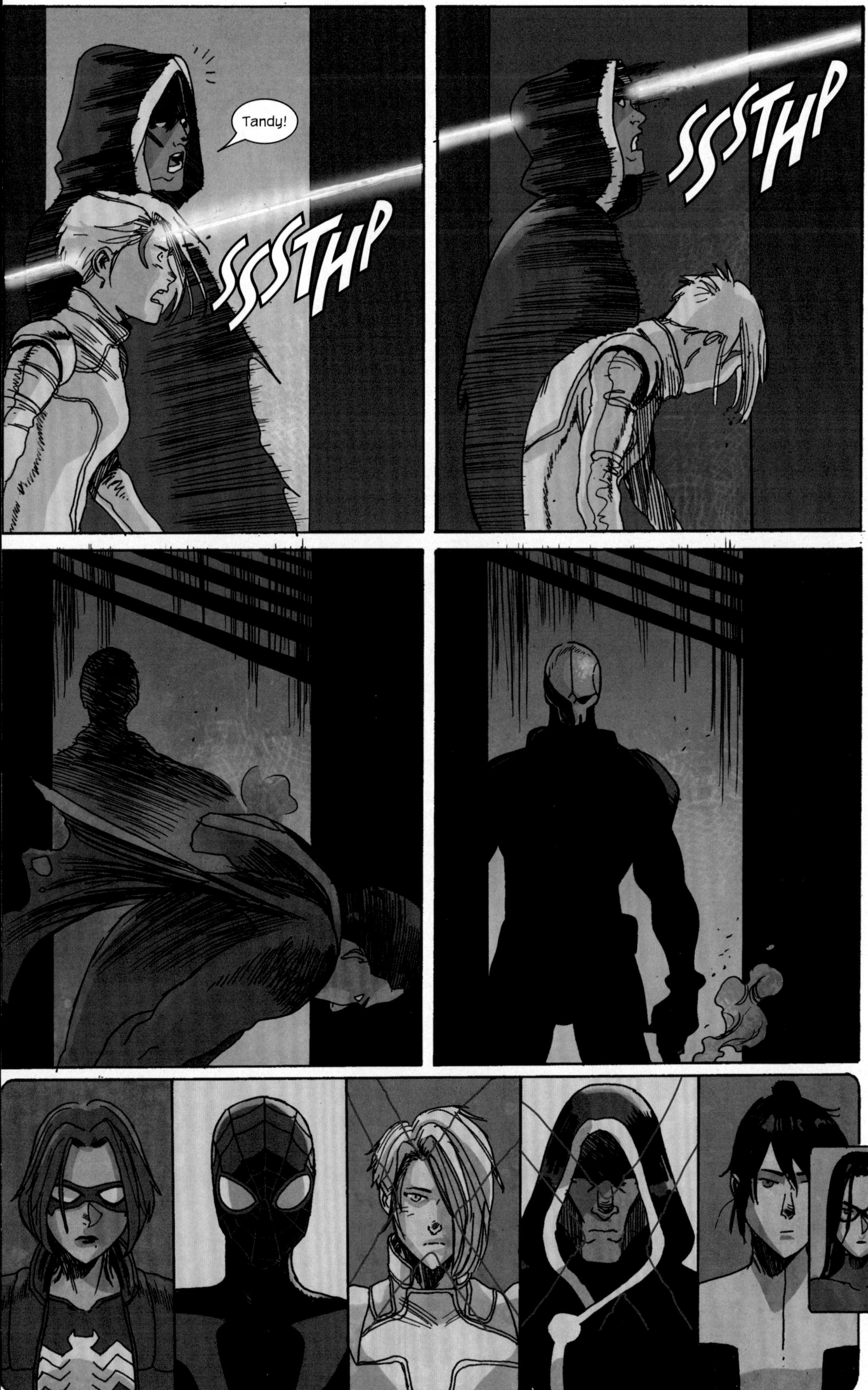
Tandy!
SSSTHP
SSSTHP

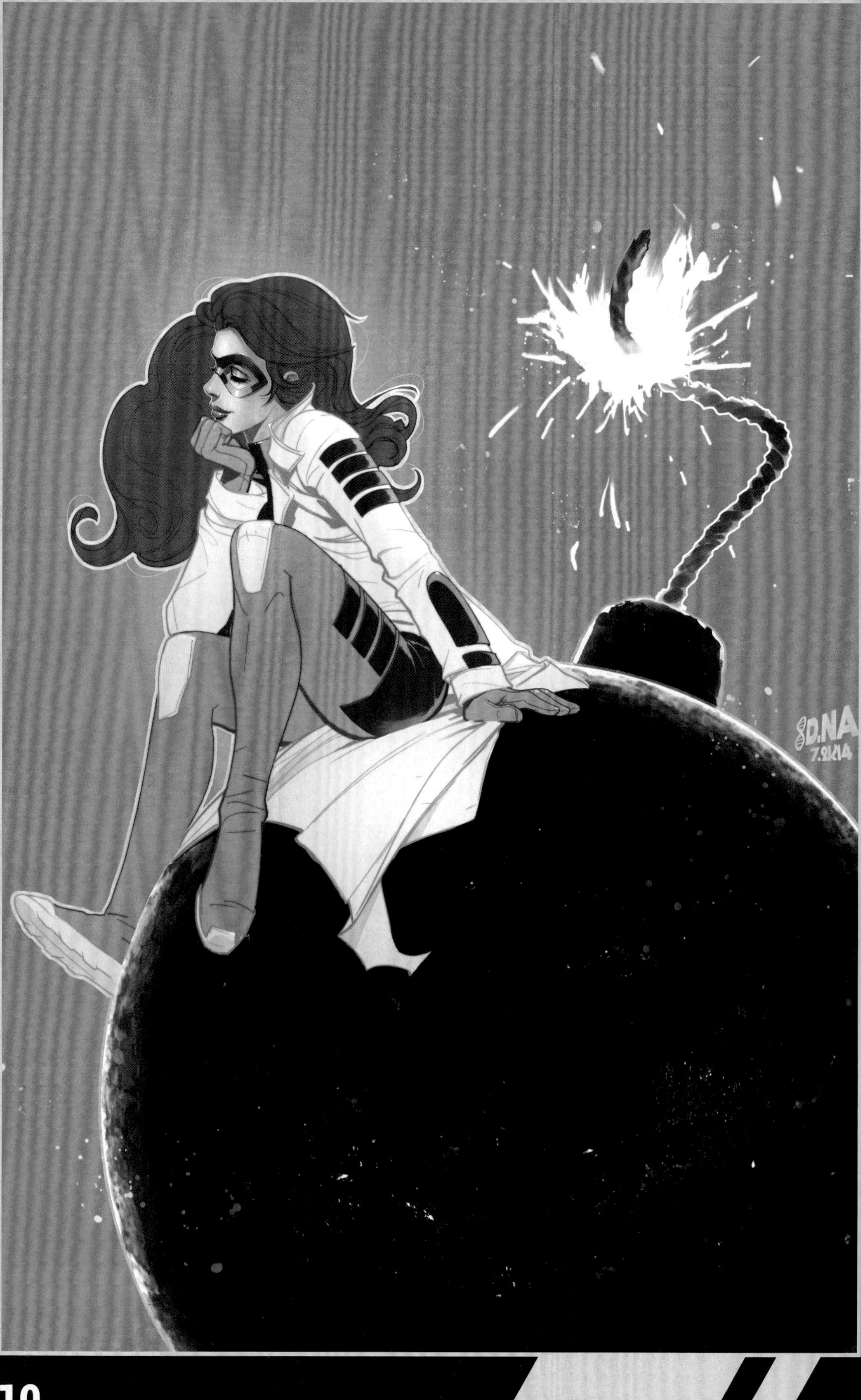
D.NA
7.2K14

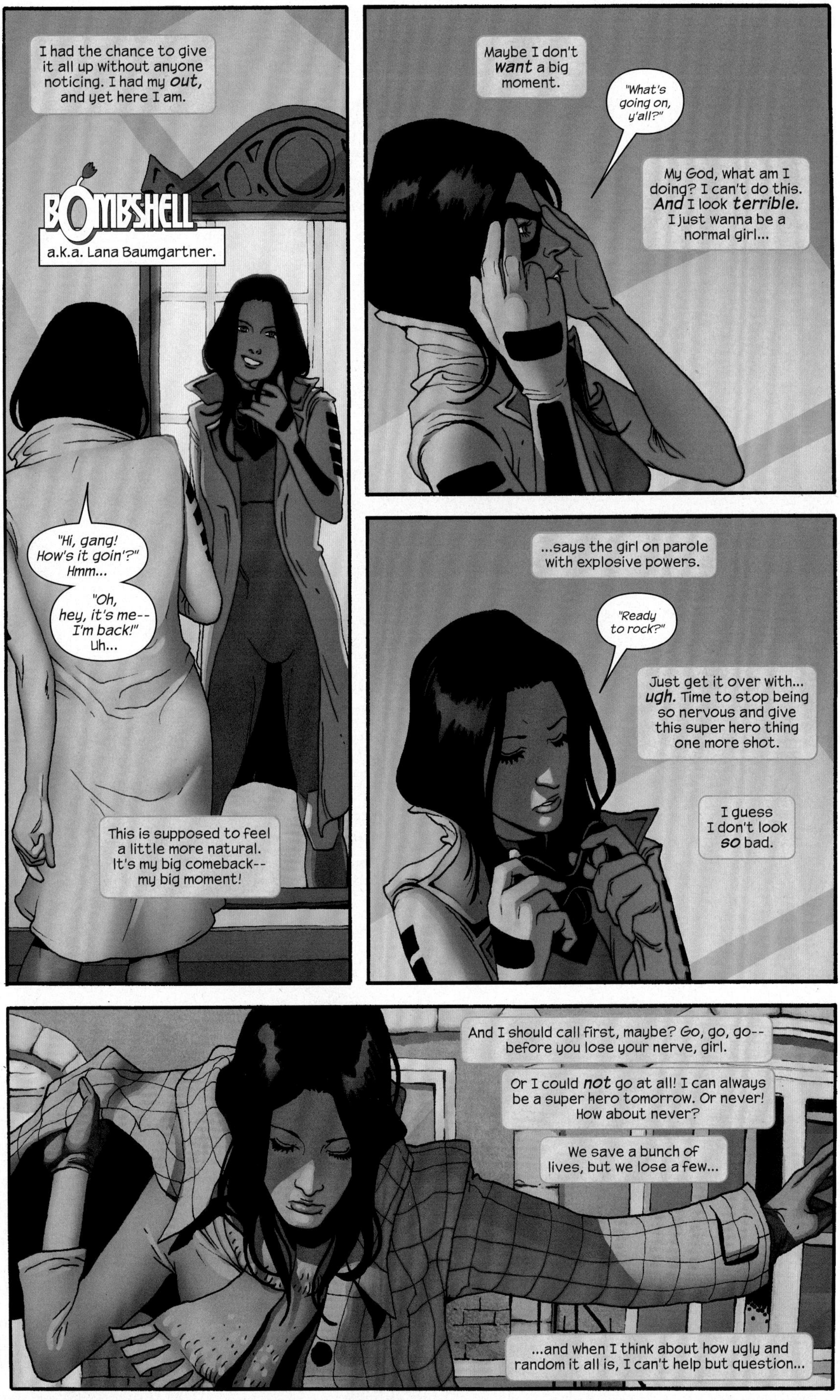

I had the chance to give it all up without anyone noticing. I had my *out*, and yet here I am.
BOMBSHELL
a.k.a. Lana Baumgartner.
"Hi, gang! How's it goin'?" Hmm...
"Oh, hey, it's me-- I'm back!" Uh...
This is supposed to feel a little more natural. It's my big comeback-- my big moment!
Maybe I don't *want* a big moment.
"What's going on, y'all?"
My God, what am I doing? I can't do this. *And* I look *terrible.* I just wanna be a normal girl...
...says the girl on parole with explosive powers.
"Ready to rock?"
Just get it over with... *ugh.* Time to stop being so nervous and give this super hero thing one more shot.
I guess I don't look *so* bad.
And I should call first, maybe? Go, go, go-- before you lose your nerve, girl.
Or I could *not* go at all! I can always be a super hero tomorrow. Or never! How about never?
We save a bunch of lives, but we lose a few...
...and when I think about how ugly and random it all is, I can't help but question...

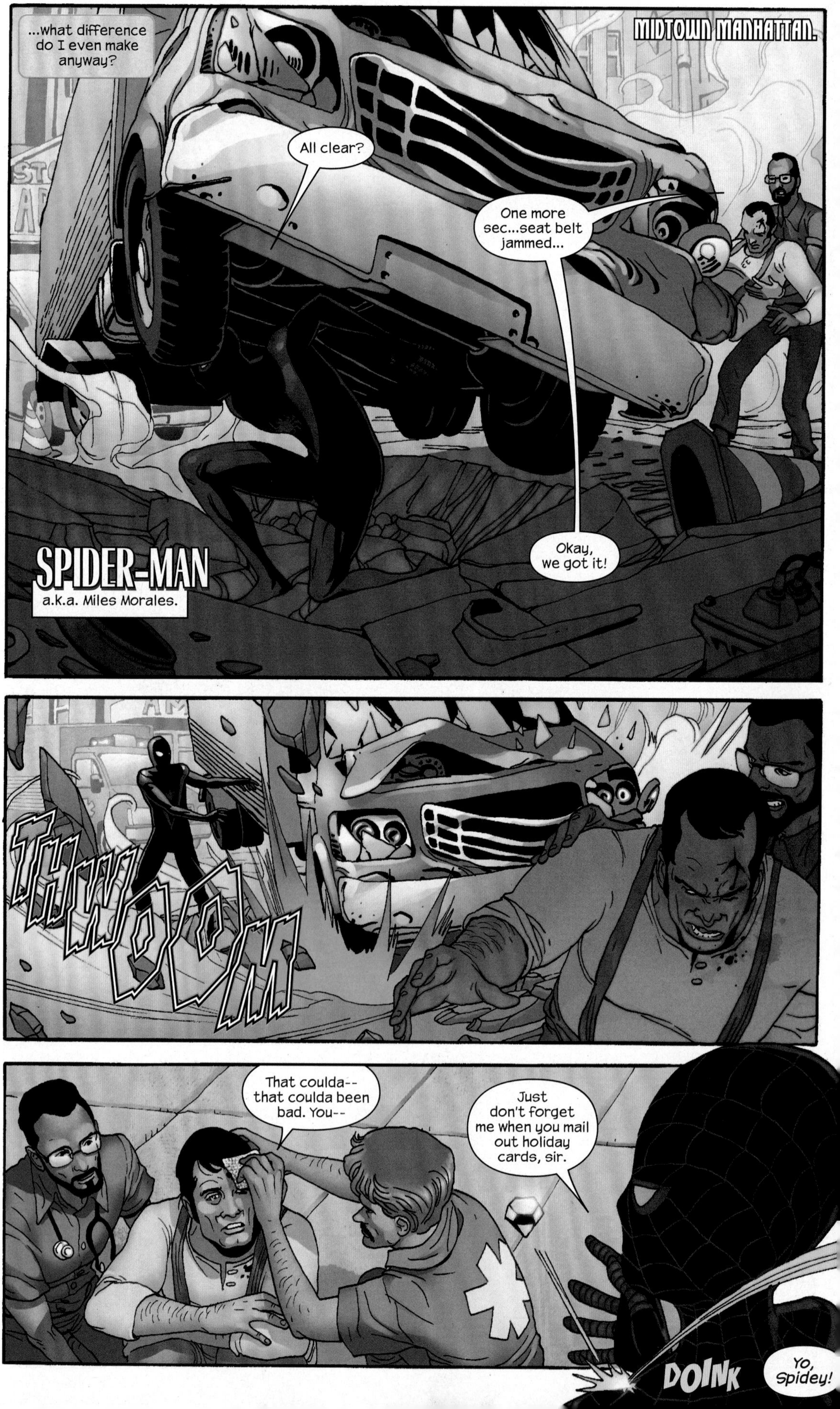

...what difference do I even make anyway?
MIDTOWN MANHATTAN.
All clear?
One more sec...seat belt jammed...
Okay, we got it!
SPIDER-MAN
a.k.a. Miles Morales.
THWOOM
That coulda-- that coulda been bad. You--
Just don't forget me when you mail out holiday cards, sir.
DOINK
Yo, Spidey!

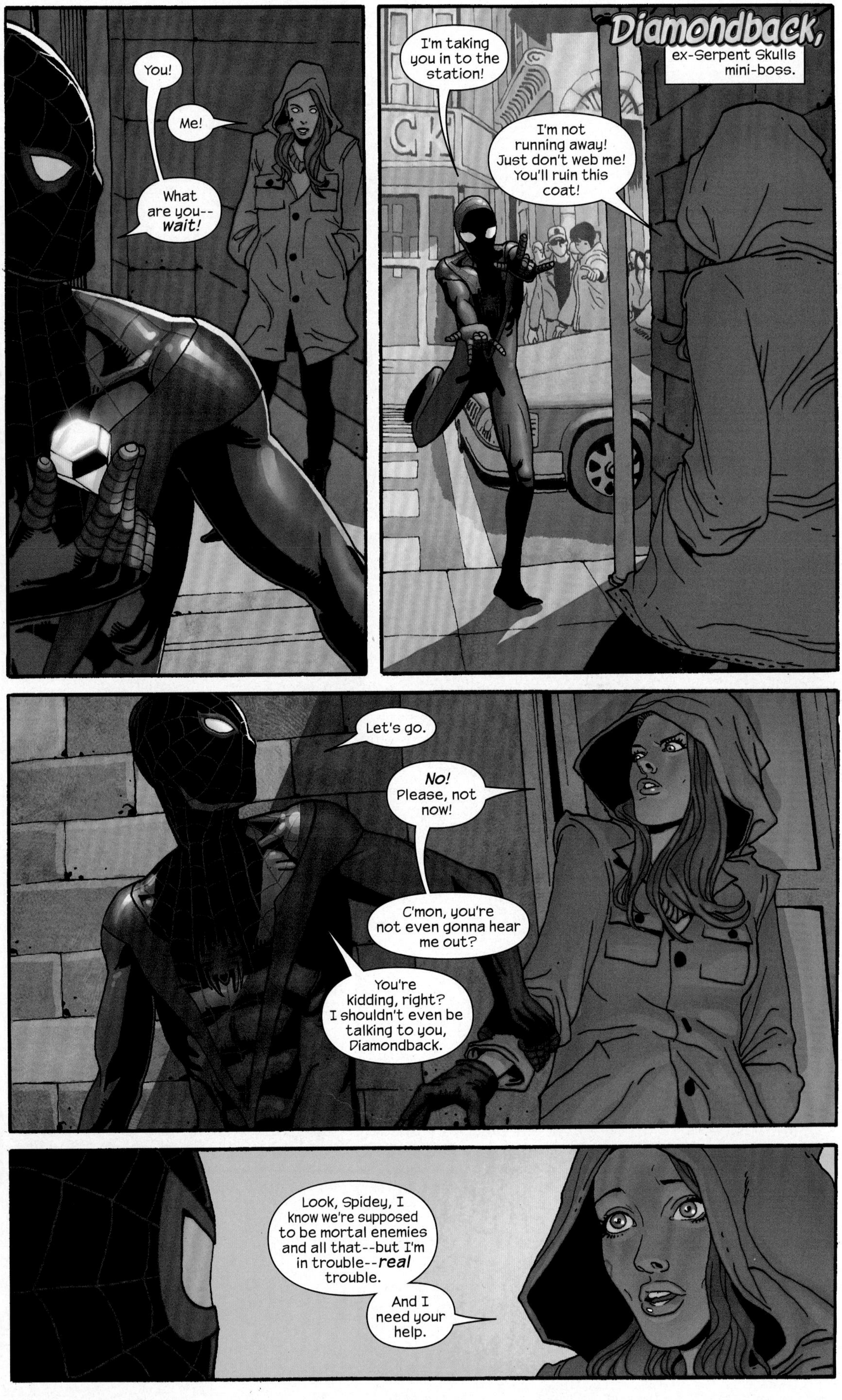
You!
Me!
What are you-- *wait!*
Diamondback,
ex-Serpent Skulls mini-boss.
I'm taking you in to the station!
I'm not running away! Just don't web me! You'll ruin this coat!
Let's go.
No! Please, not now!
C'mon, you're not even gonna hear me out?
You're kidding, right? I shouldn't even be talking to you, Diamondback.
Look, Spidey, I know we're supposed to be mortal enemies and all that--but I'm in trouble--*real* trouble.
And I need your help.

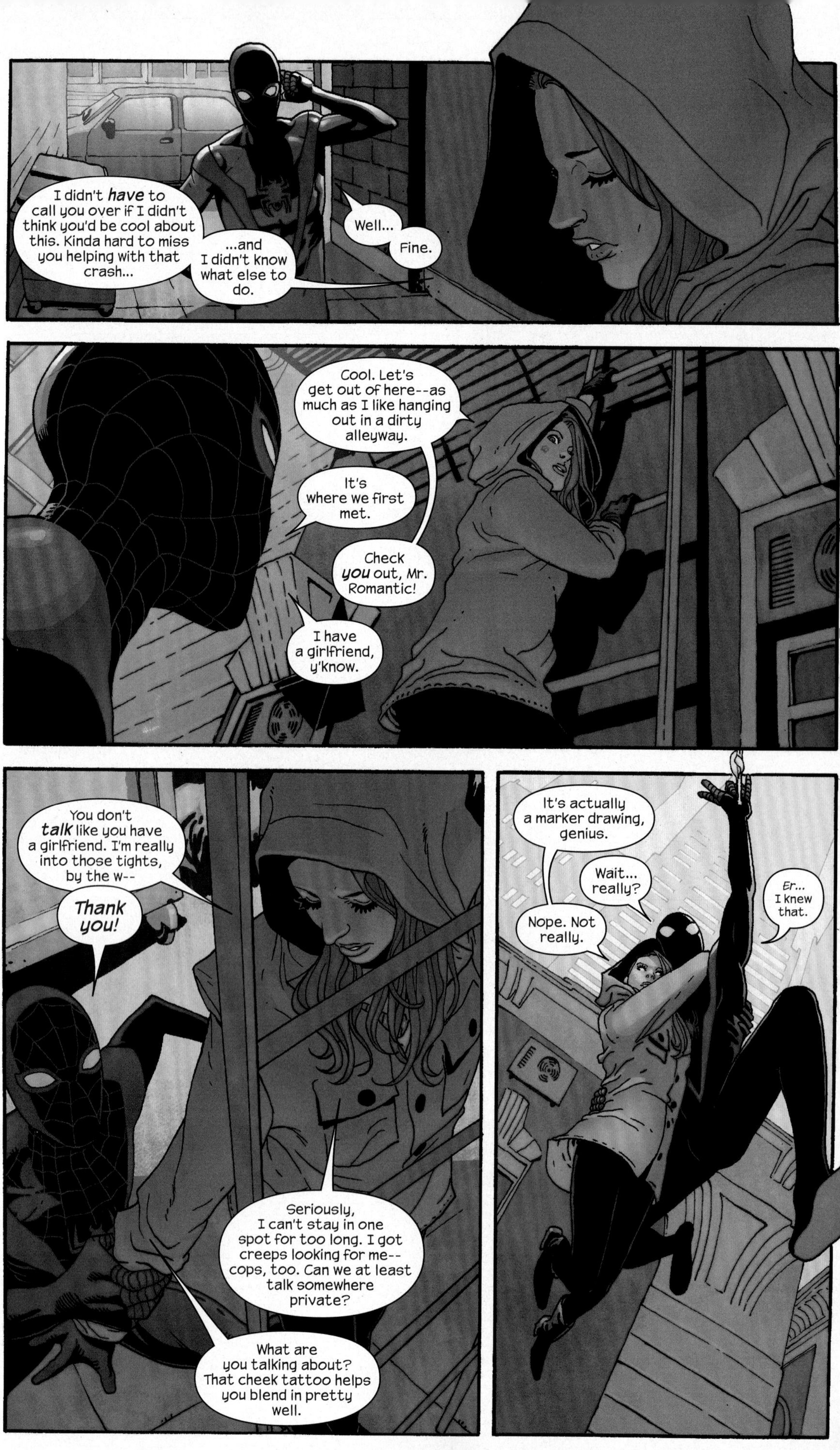
I didn't *have* to call you over if I didn't think you'd be cool about this. Kinda hard to miss you helping with that crash...
...and I didn't know what else to do.
Well...
Fine.
Cool. Let's get out of here--as much as I like hanging out in a dirty alleyway.
It's where we first met.
Check *you* out, Mr. Romantic!
I have a girlfriend, y'know.
You don't *talk* like you have a girlfriend. I'm really into those tights, by the w--
Thank you!
Seriously, I can't stay in one spot for too long. I got creeps looking for me--cops, too. Can we at least talk somewhere private?
What are you talking about? That cheek tattoo helps you blend in pretty well.
It's actually a marker drawing, genius.
Wait... really?
Nope. Not really.
Er... I knew that.

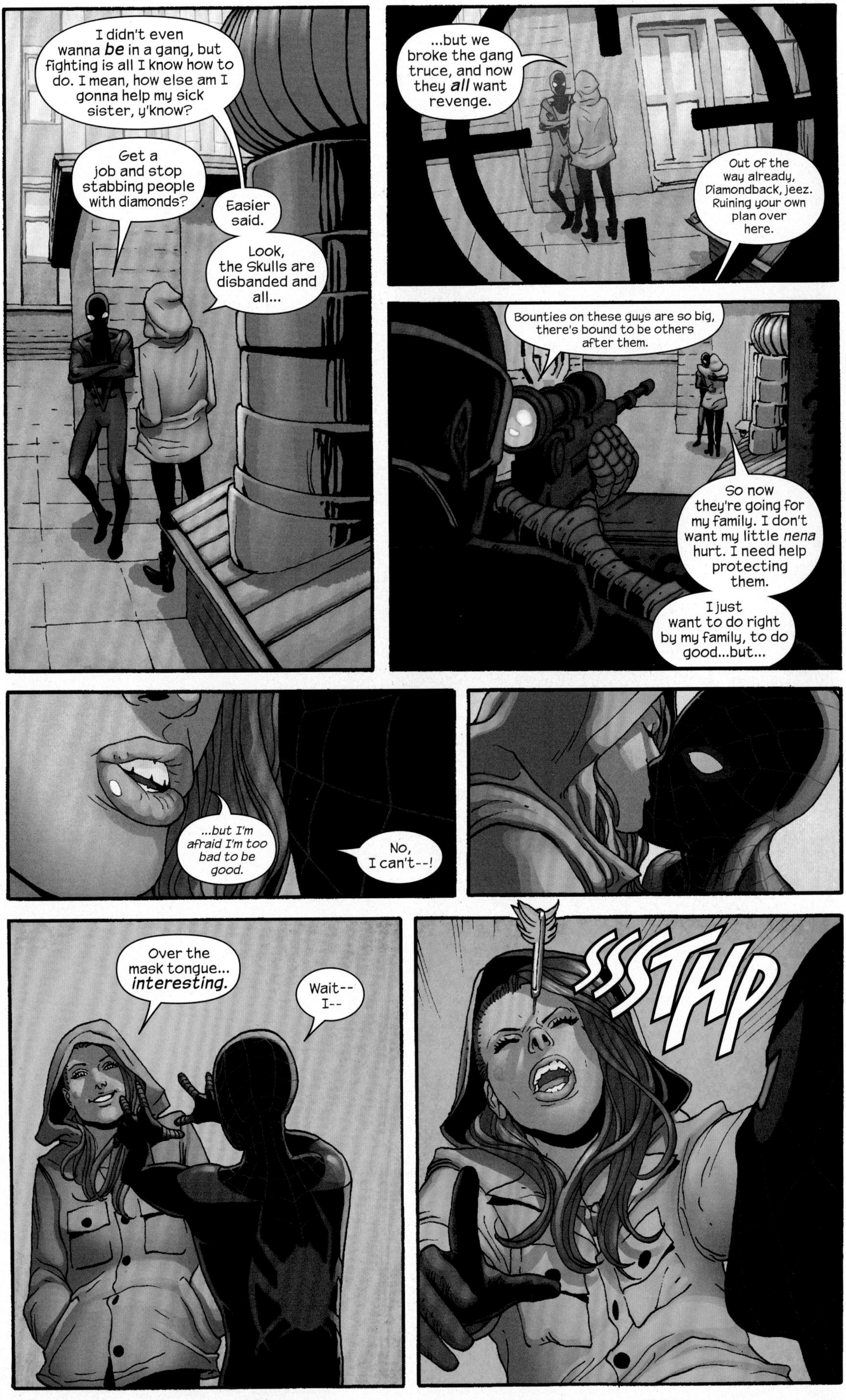
I didn't even wanna *be* in a gang, but fighting is all I know how to do. I mean, how else am I gonna help my sick sister, y'know?
Get a job and stop stabbing people with diamonds?
Easier said.
Look, the Skulls are disbanded and all...
...but we broke the gang truce, and now they *all* want revenge.
Out of the way already, Diamondback, jeez. Ruining your own plan over here.
Bounties on these guys are so big, there's bound to be others after them.
So now they're going for my family. I don't want my little *nena* hurt. I need help protecting them.
I just want to do right by my family, to do good...but...
...but I'm afraid I'm too bad to be good.
No, I can't--!
Over the mask tongue... *interesting.*
Wait-- I--
SSSTHP

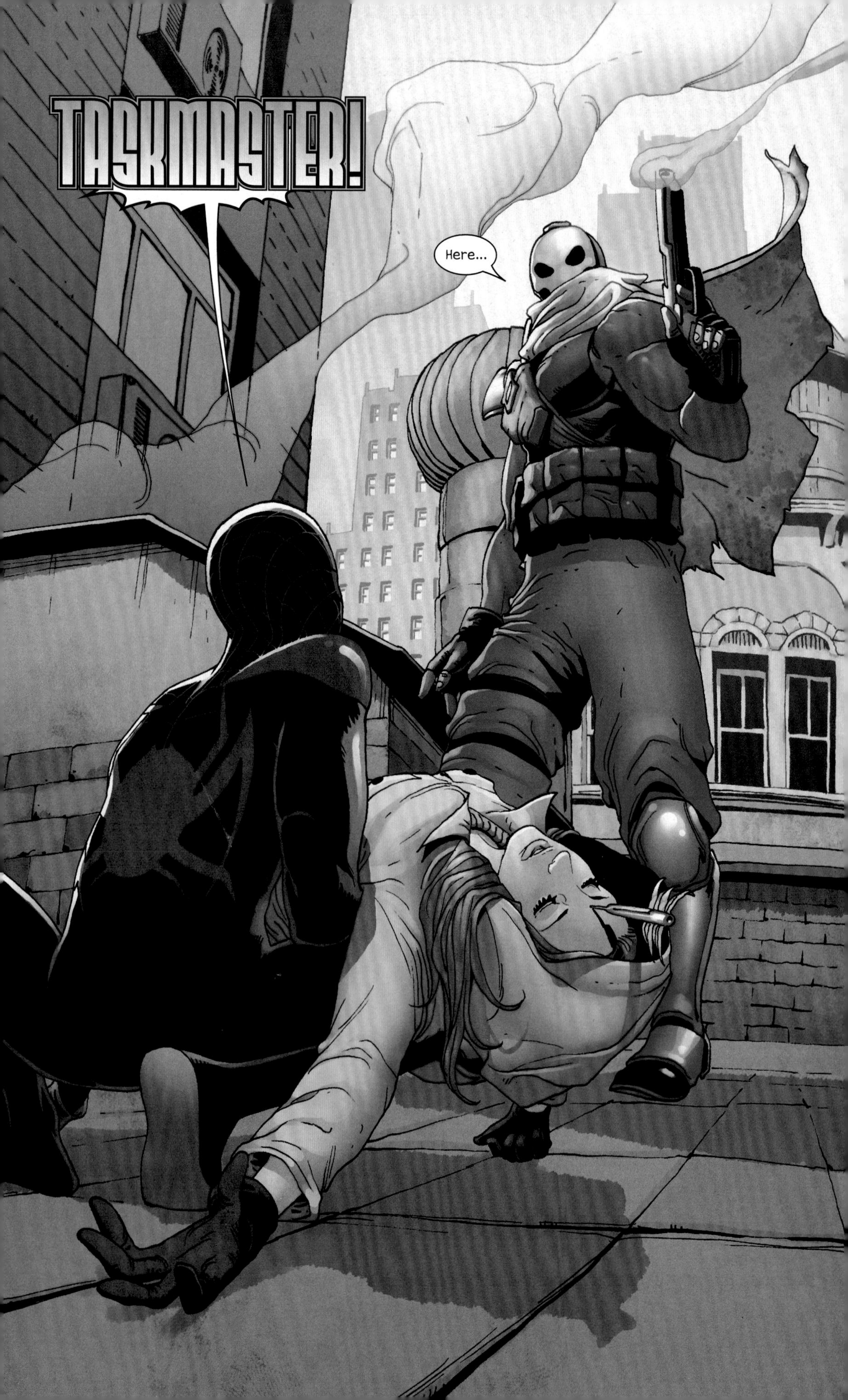
TASKMASTER!
Here...

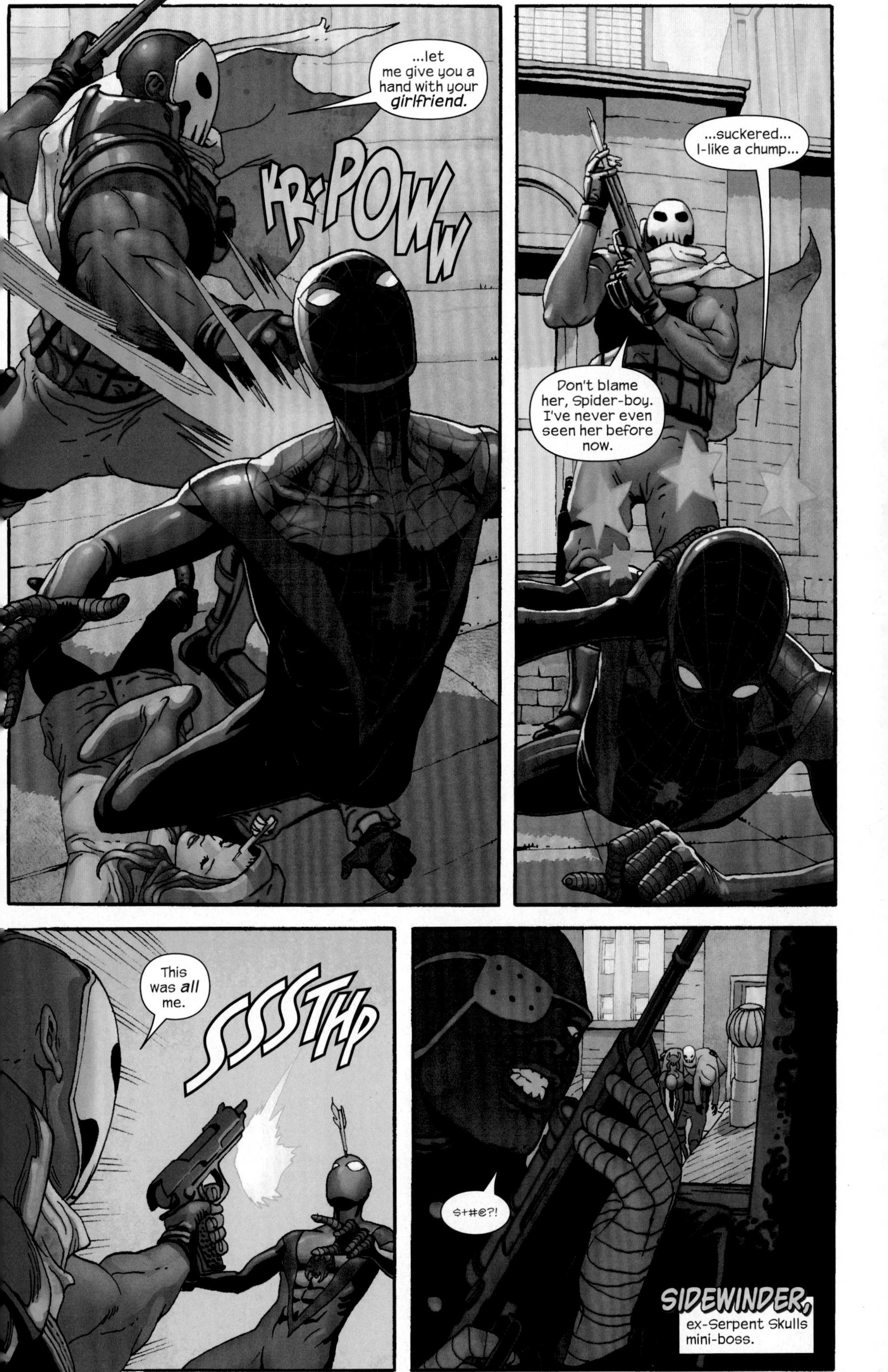
...let me give you a hand with your *girlfriend.*
KR-POWW
...suckered... I-like a chump...
Don't blame her, Spider-boy. I've never even seen her before now.
This was *all* me.
SSSTHP
$+#@?!
SIDEWINDER,
ex-Serpent Skulls mini-boss.

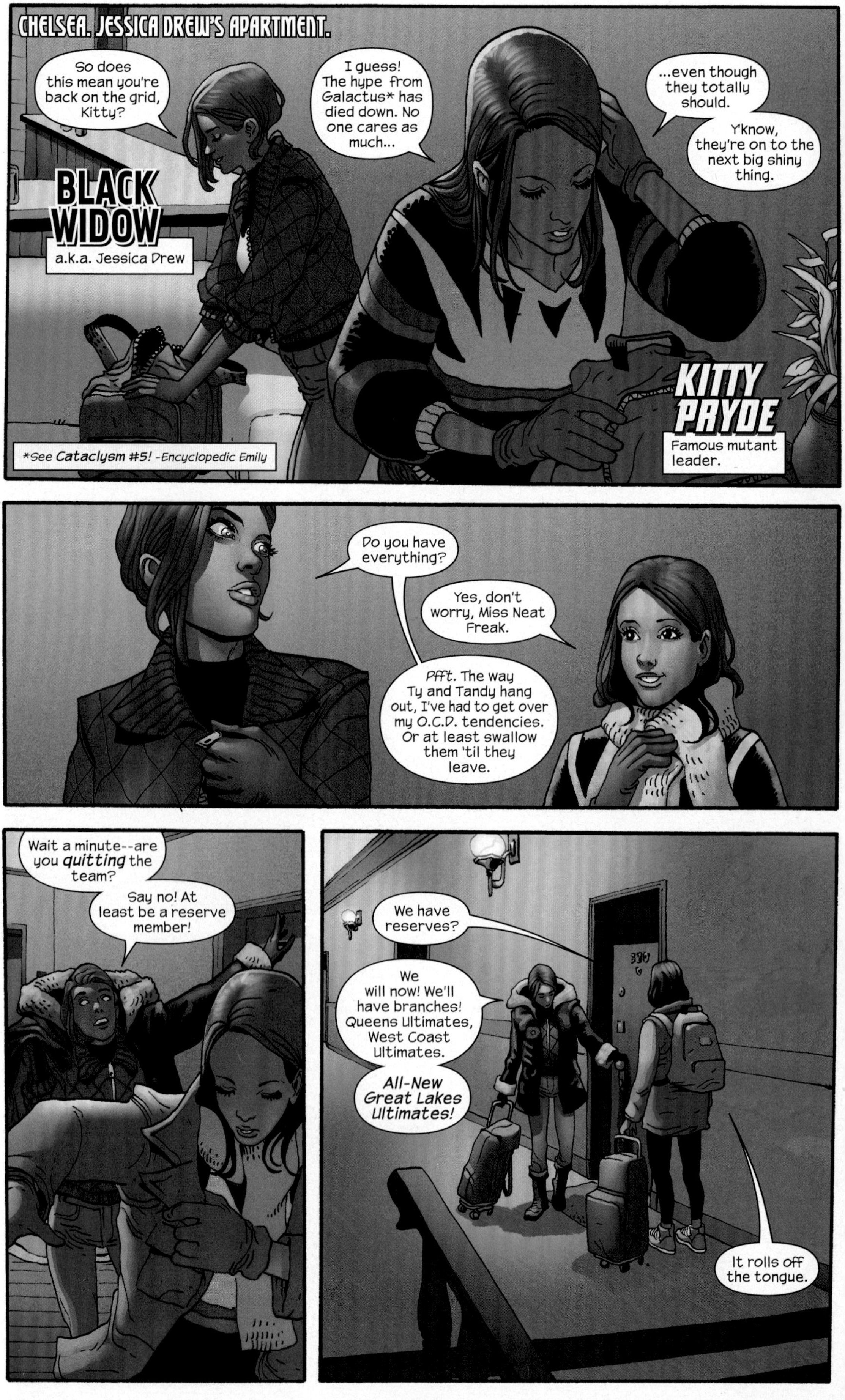
CHELSEA. JESSICA DREW'S APARTMENT.
So does this mean you're back on the grid, Kitty?
BLACK WIDOW
a.k.a. Jessica Drew
I guess! The hype from Galactus* has died down. No one cares as much...
...even though they totally should.
Y'know, they're on to the next big shiny thing.
KITTY PRYDE
Famous mutant leader.
*See Cataclysm #5! -Encyclopedic Emily
Do you have everything?
Yes, don't worry, Miss Neat Freak.
Pfft. The way Ty and Tandy hang out, I've had to get over my O.C.D. tendencies. Or at least swallow them 'til they leave.
Wait a minute--are you quitting the team?
Say no! At least be a reserve member!
We have reserves?
We will now! We'll have branches! Queens Ultimates, West Coast Ultimates.
All-New Great Lakes Ultimates!
It rolls off the tongue.

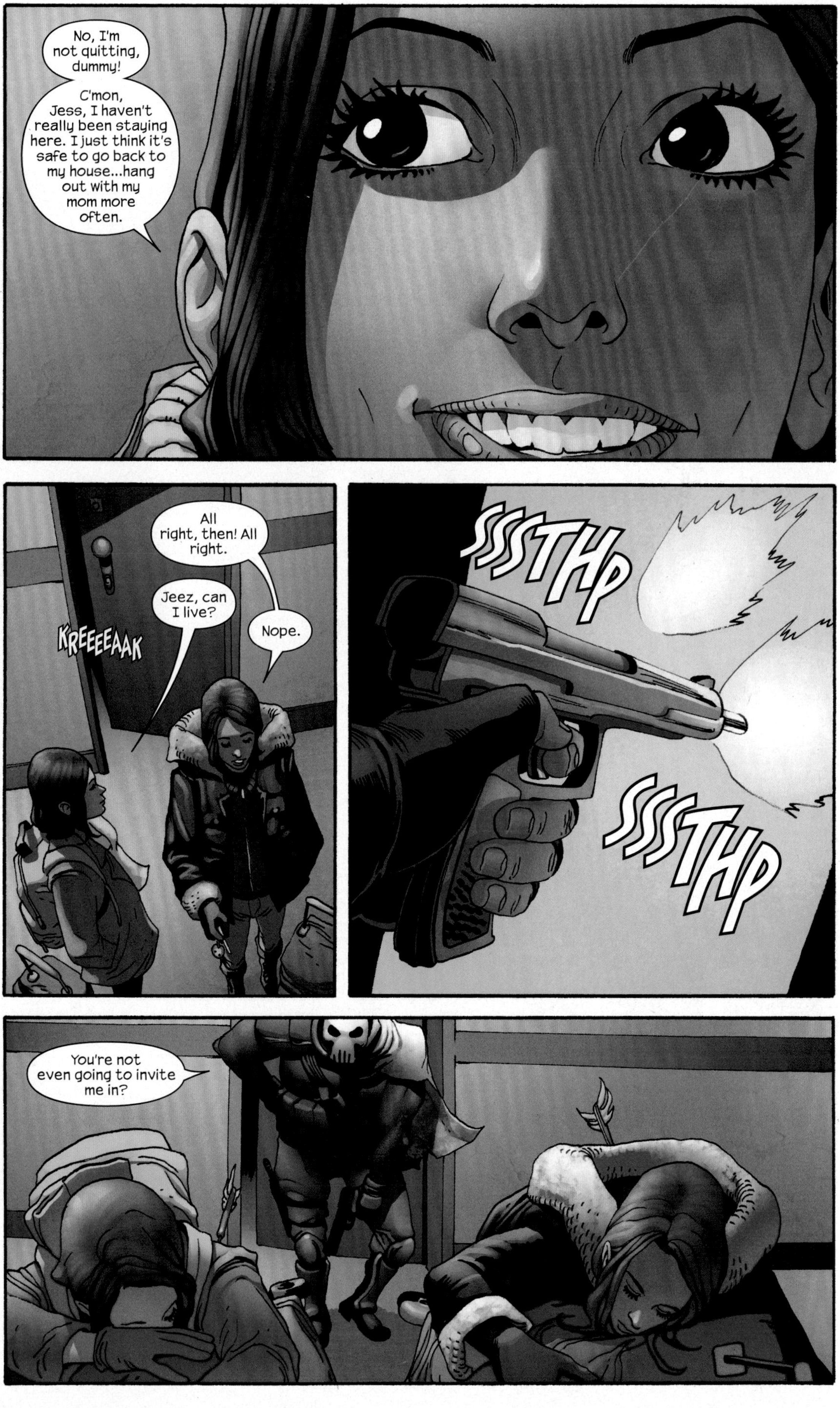
No, I'm not quitting, dummy!
C'mon, Jess, I haven't really been staying here. I just think it's safe to go back to my house...hang out with my mom more often.
KREEEEAAK
All right, then! All right.
Jeez, can I live?
Nope.
SSSTHP
SSSTHP
You're not even going to invite me in?

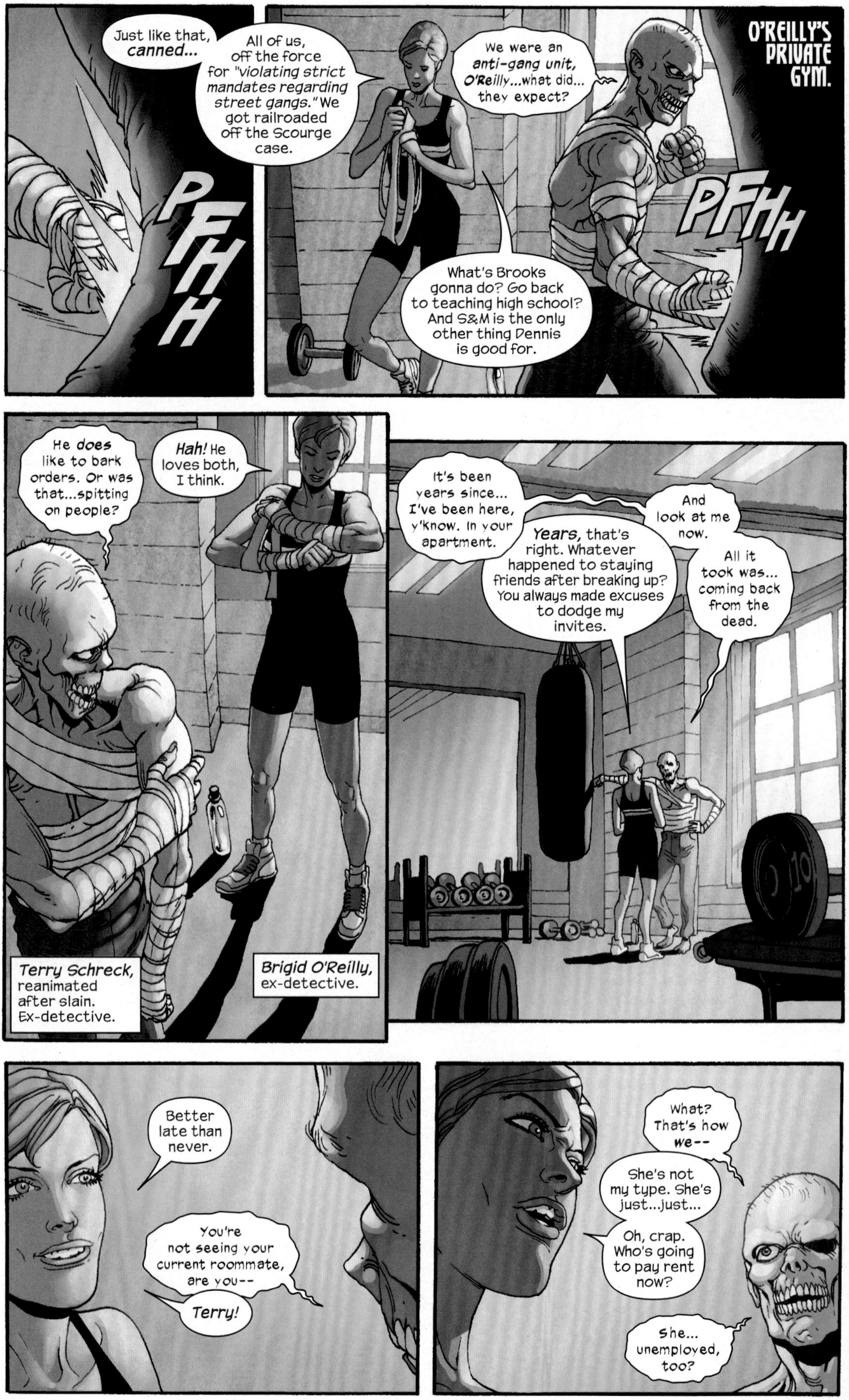
Just like that, canned...
All of us, off the force for "violating strict mandates regarding street gangs." We got railroaded off the Scourge case.
We were an anti-gang unit, O'Reilly...what did... they expect?
O'REILLY'S PRIVATE GYM.
PFHH
PFHH
What's Brooks gonna do? Go back to teaching high school? And S&M is the only other thing Dennis is good for.
He does like to bark orders. Or was that...spitting on people?
Hah! He loves both, I think.
Terry Schreck, reanimated after slain. Ex-detective.
Brigid O'Reilly, ex-detective.
It's been years since... I've been here, y'know. In your apartment.
Years, that's right. Whatever happened to staying friends after breaking up? You always made excuses to dodge my invites.
And look at me now.
All it took was... coming back from the dead.
Better late than never.
You're not seeing your current roommate, are you--
Terry!
What? That's how we--
She's not my type. She's just...just...
Oh, crap. Who's going to pay rent now?
She... unemployed, too?

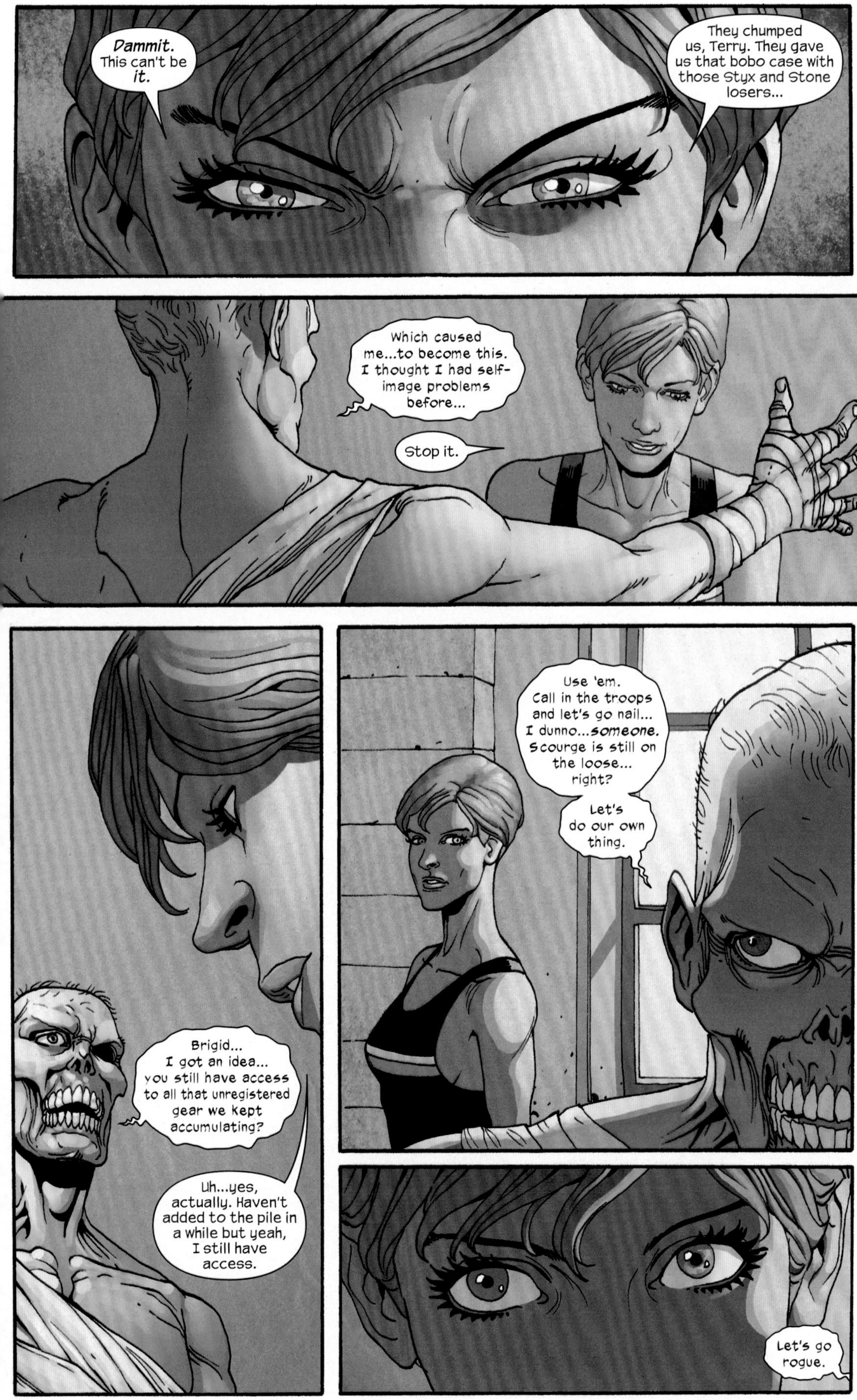
Dammit. This can't be *it.*
They chumped us, Terry. They gave us that bobo case with those Styx and Stone losers...
Which caused me...to become this. I thought I had self-image problems before...
Stop it.
Brigid... I got an idea... you still have access to all that unregistered gear we kept accumulating?
Uh...yes, actually. Haven't added to the pile in a while but yeah, I still have access.
Use 'em. Call in the troops and let's go nail... I dunno...*someone.* Scourge is still on the loose... right?
Let's do our own thing.
Let's go rogue.

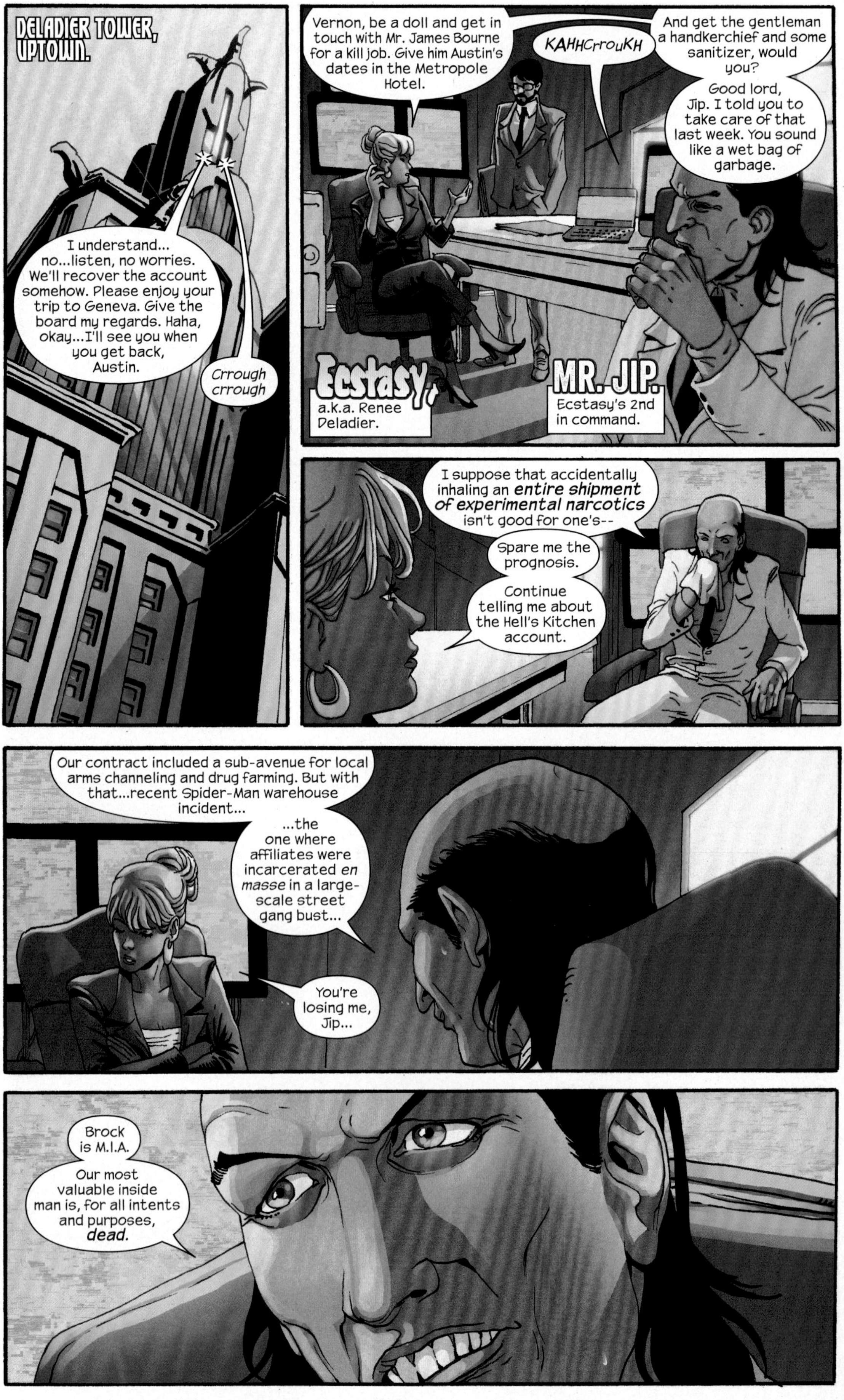
DELADIER TOWER, UPTOWN.
I understand... no...listen, no worries. We'll recover the account somehow. Please enjoy your trip to Geneva. Give the board my regards. Haha, okay...I'll see you when you get back, Austin.
Crrough crrough
Vernon, be a doll and get in touch with Mr. James Bourne for a kill job. Give him Austin's dates in the Metropole Hotel.
KAHHCrrouKH
And get the gentleman a handkerchief and some sanitizer, would you?
Good lord, Jip. I told you to take care of that last week. You sound like a wet bag of garbage.
Ecstasy,
a.k.a. Renee Deladier.
MR. JIP.
Ecstasy's 2nd in command.
I suppose that accidentally inhaling an *entire shipment of experimental narcotics* isn't good for one's--
Spare me the prognosis.
Continue telling me about the Hell's Kitchen account.
Our contract included a sub-avenue for local arms channeling and drug farming. But with that...recent Spider-Man warehouse incident...
...the one where affiliates were incarcerated *en masse* in a large-scale street gang bust...
You're losing me, Jip...
Brock is M.I.A.
Our most valuable inside man is, for all intents and purposes, ***dead.***

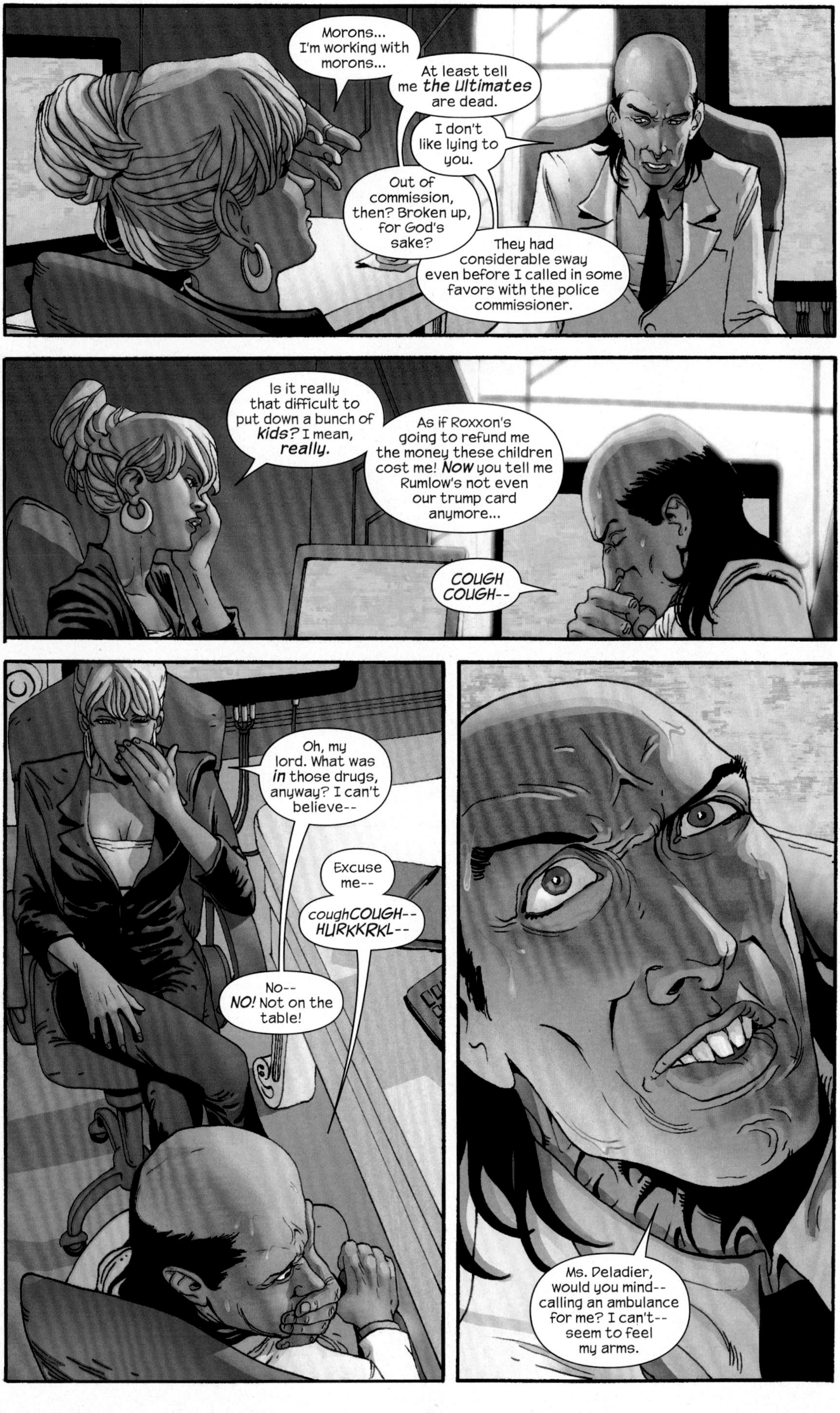
Morons... I'm working with morons...
At least tell me *the Ultimates* are dead.
I don't like lying to you.
Out of commission, then? Broken up, for God's sake?
They had considerable sway even before I called in some favors with the police commissioner.
Is it really that difficult to put down a bunch of *kids?* I mean, ***really.***
As if Roxxon's going to refund me the money these children cost me! *NOW* you tell me Rumlow's not even our trump card anymore...
COUGH COUGH--
Oh, my lord. What was *in* those drugs, anyway? I can't believe--
Excuse me--
coughCOUGH-- HURKKRKL--
No-- *NO!* Not on the table!
Ms. Deladier, would you mind-- calling an ambulance for me? I can't-- seem to feel my arms.

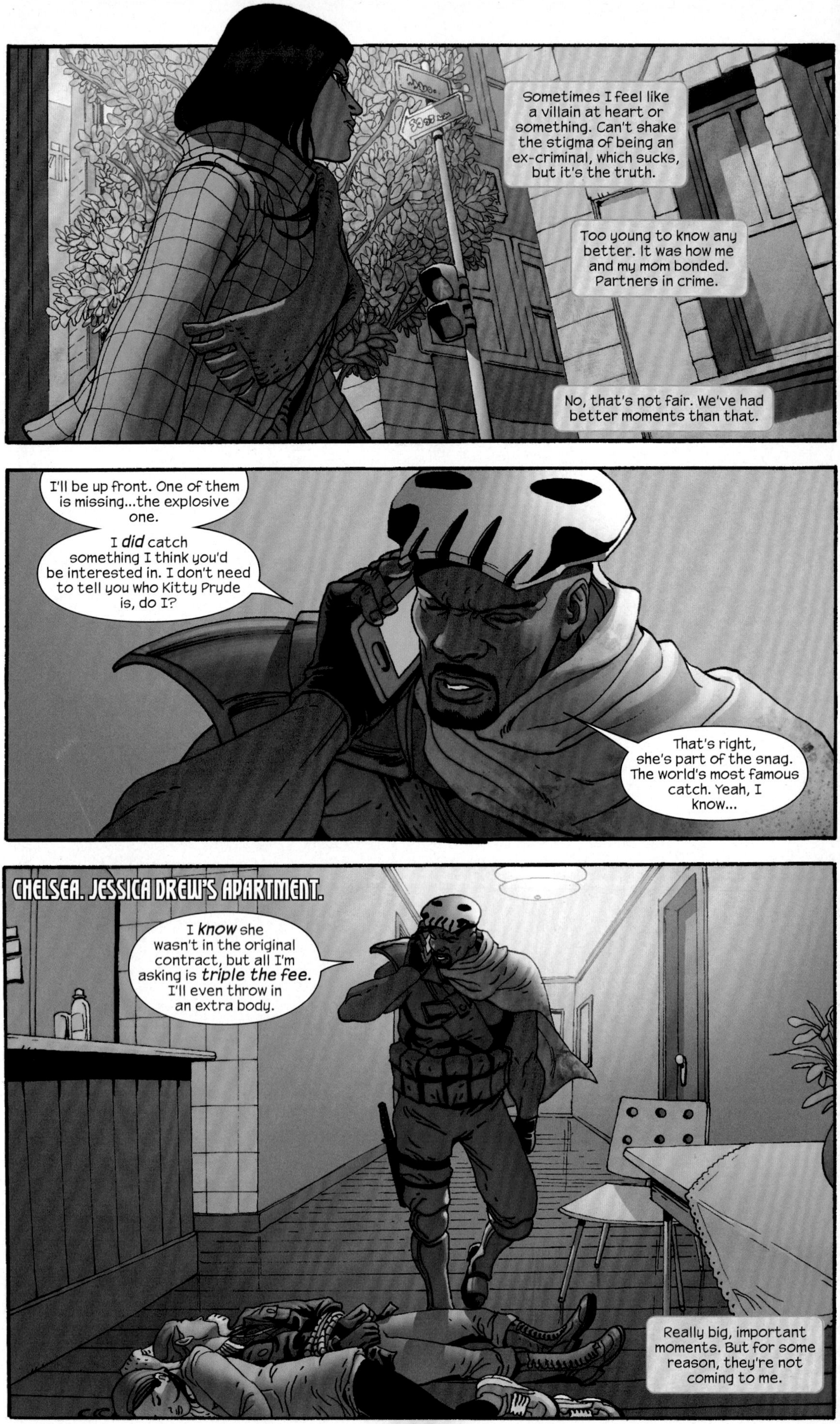

Sometimes I feel like a villain at heart or something. Can't shake the stigma of being an ex-criminal, which sucks, but it's the truth.
Too young to know any better. It was how me and my mom bonded. Partners in crime.
No, that's not fair. We've had better moments than that.
I'll be up front. One of them is missing...the explosive one.
I *did* catch something I think you'd be interested in. I don't need to tell you who Kitty Pryde is, do I?
That's right, she's part of the snag. The world's most famous catch. Yeah, I know...
CHELSEA. JESSICA DREW'S APARTMENT.
I *know* she wasn't in the original contract, but all I'm asking is *triple the fee.* I'll even throw in an extra body.
Really big, important moments. But for some reason, they're not coming to me.

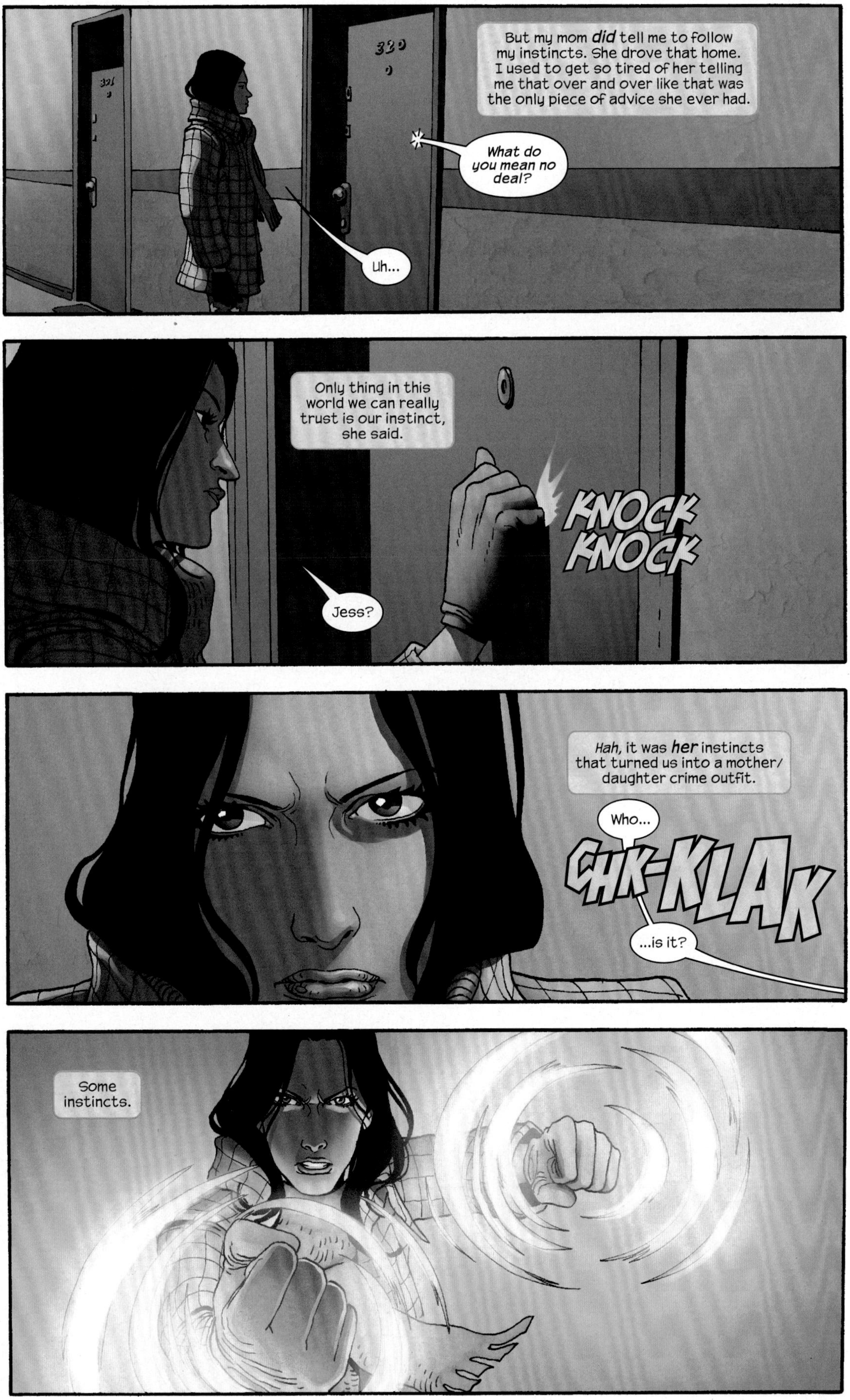

But my mom did tell me to follow my instincts. She drove that home. I used to get so tired of her telling me that over and over like that was the only piece of advice she ever had.
What do you mean no deal?
Uh...
Only thing in this world we can really trust is our instinct, she said.
KNOCK KNOCK
Jess?
Hah, it was her instincts that turned us into a mother/daughter crime outfit.
Who...
CHK-KLAK
...is it?
Some instincts.

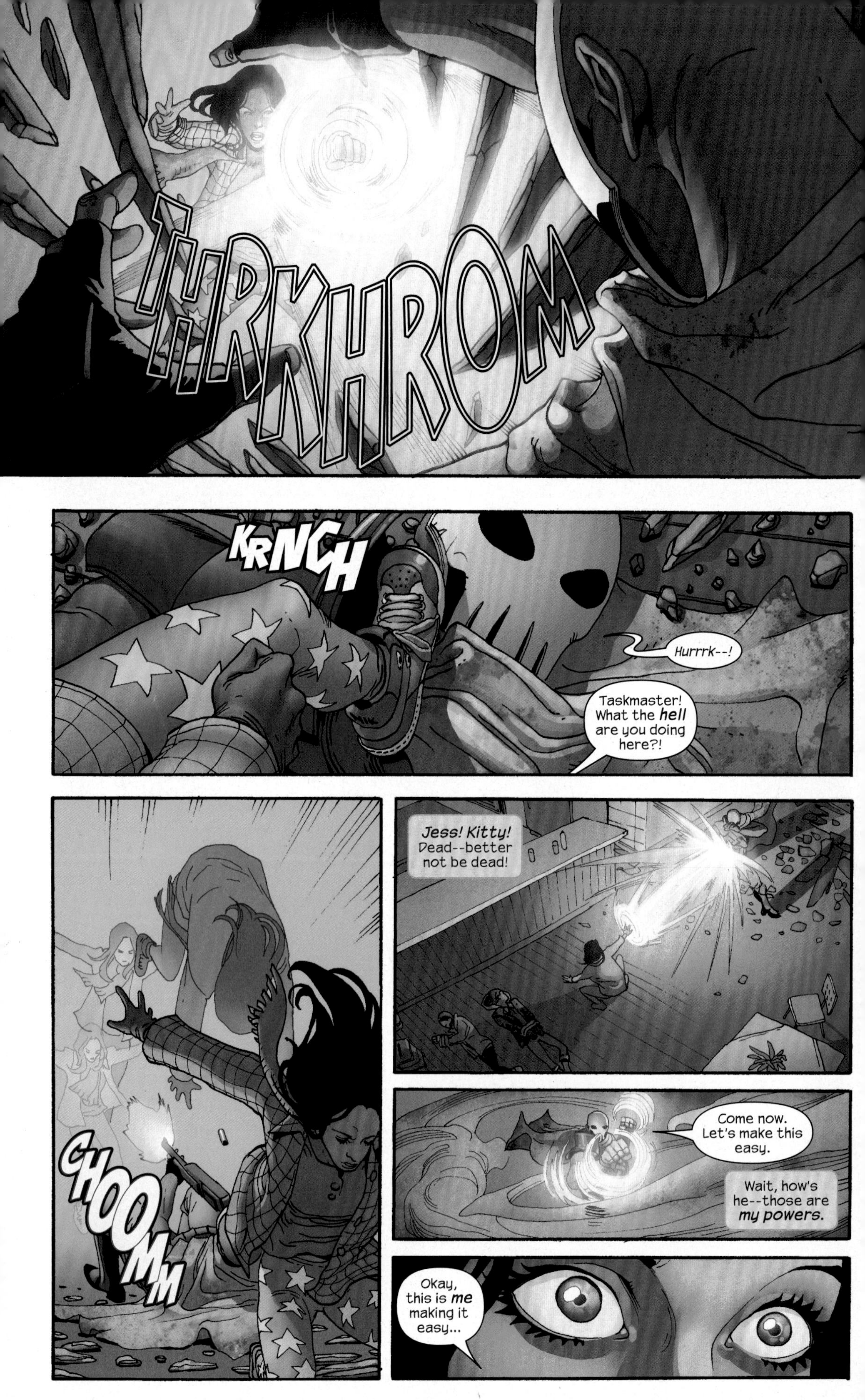
THRKHROM
KRNCH
Hurrrk--!
Taskmaster! What the hell are you doing here?!
CHOOMM
Jess! Kitty! Dead--better not be dead!
Come now. Let's make this easy.
Wait, how's he--those are my powers.
Okay, this is me making it easy...

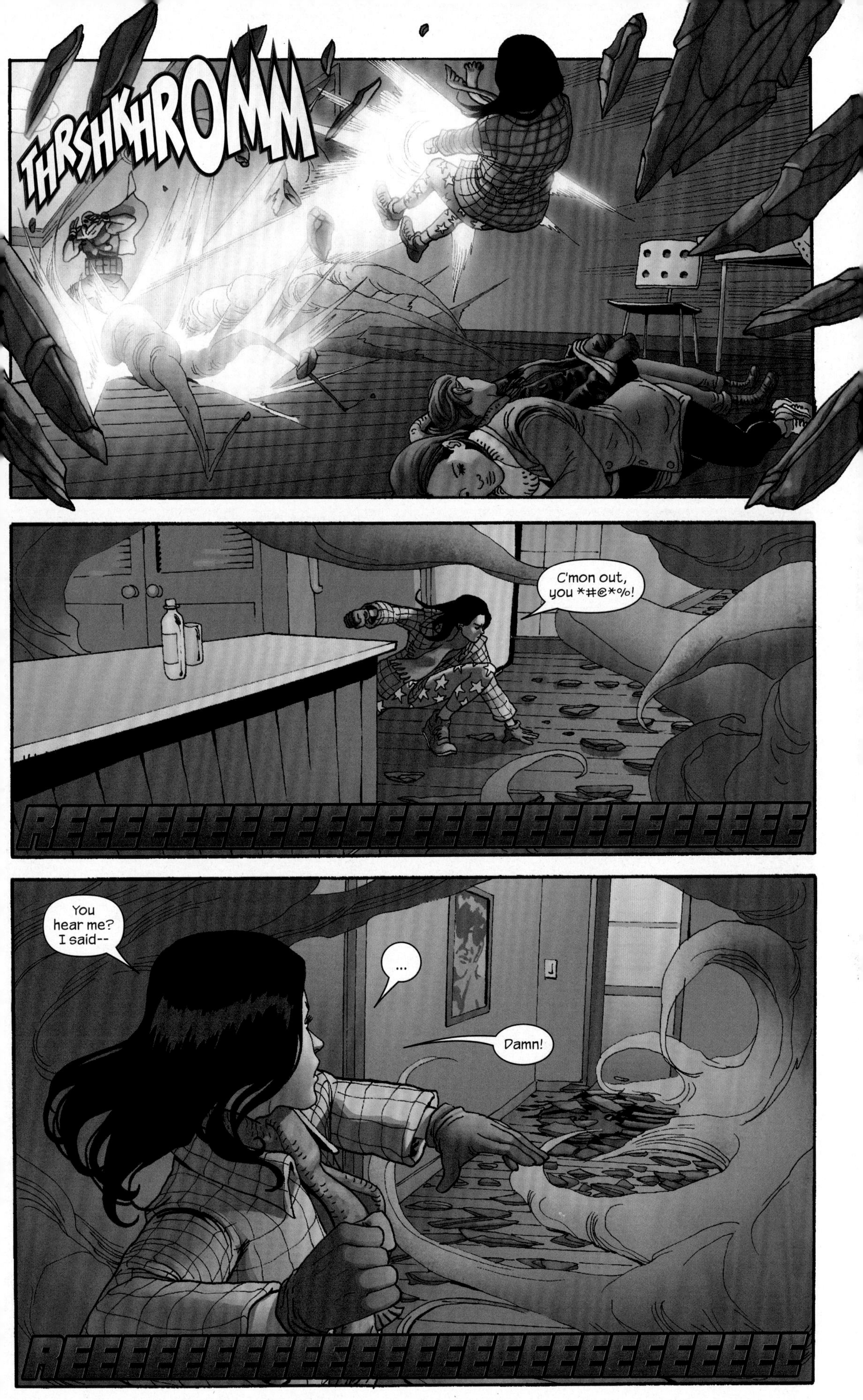
THRSHKHROMM
C'mon out, you *#@*%!
REEEEEEEEEEEEEEEEEEEEE
You hear me? I said--
...
Damn!
REEEEEEEEEEEEEEEEEEEEEEEE

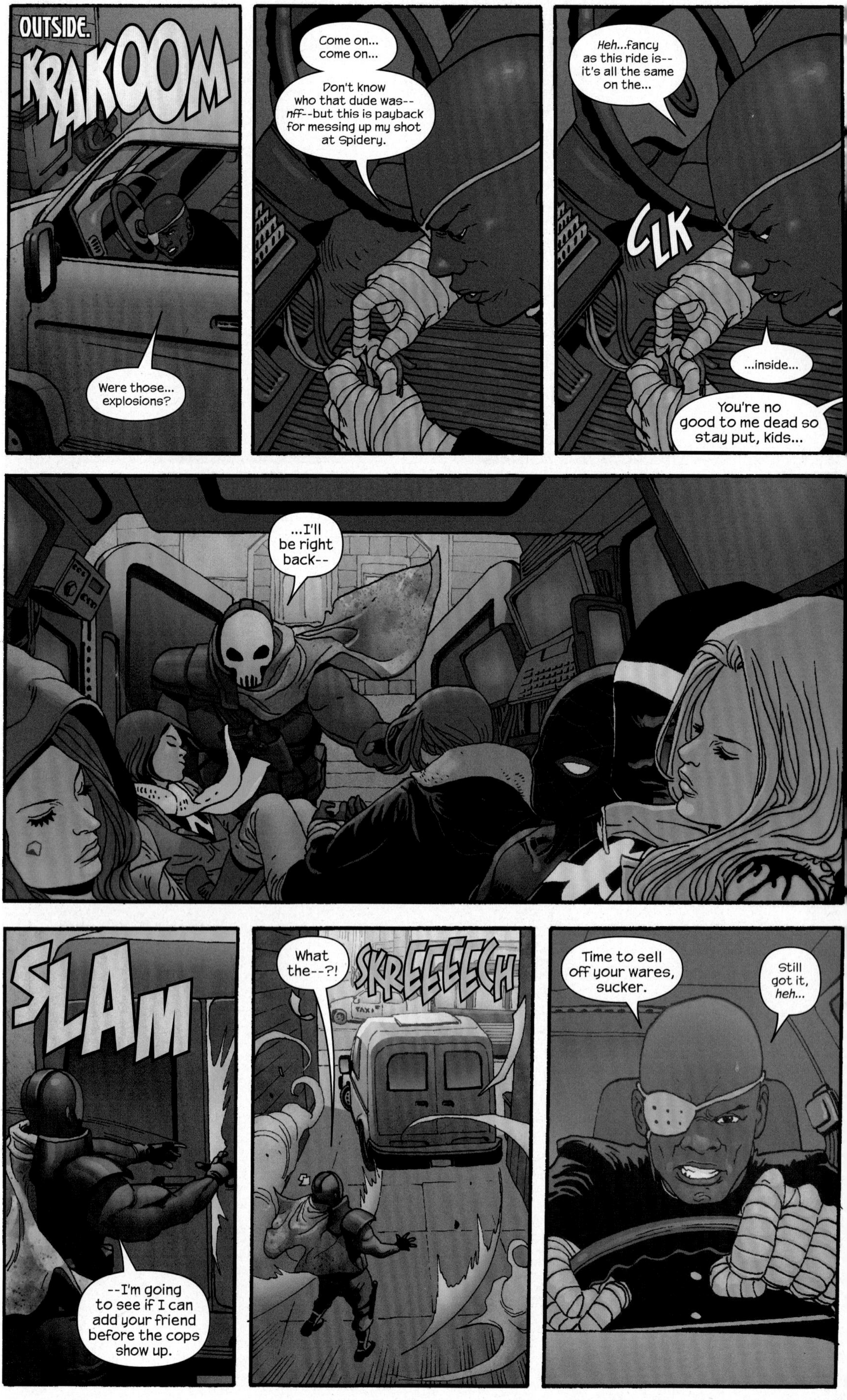
OUTSIDE.
KRAKOOM
Were those... explosions?
Come on... come on...
Don't know who that dude was-- nff--but this is payback for messing up my shot at Spidery.
Heh...fancy as this ride is-- it's all the same on the...
CLK
...inside...
You're no good to me dead so stay put, kids...
...I'll be right back--
SLAM
--I'm going to see if I can add your friend before the cops show up.
What the--?!
SKREEEEECH
TAXI
Time to sell off your wares, sucker.
Still got it, heh...

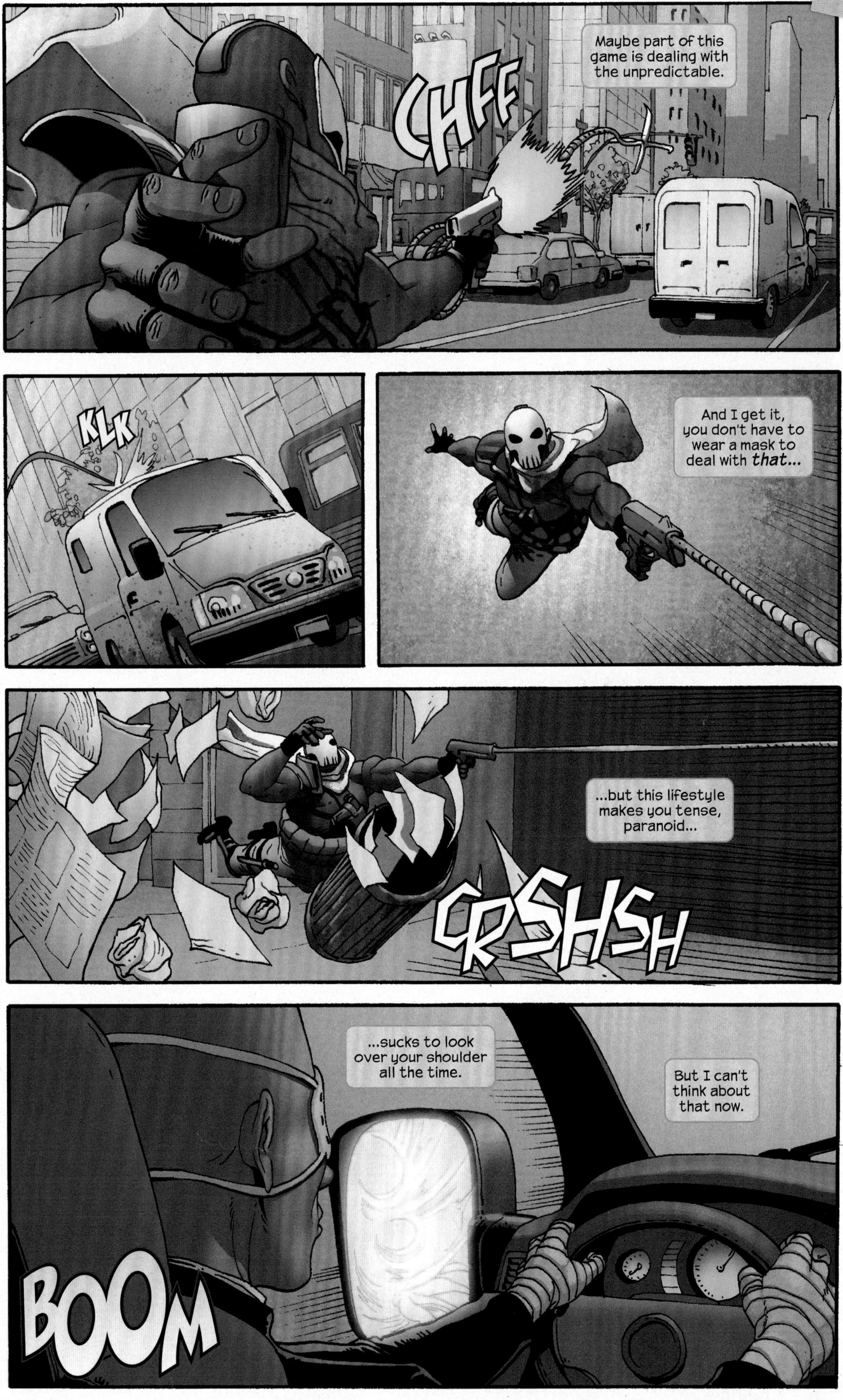

Maybe part of this game is dealing with the unpredictable.
CHFF
KLK
And I get it, you don't have to wear a mask to deal with *that*...
...but this lifestyle makes you tense, paranoid...
CRSHSH
...sucks to look over your shoulder all the time.
But I can't think about that now.
BOOM

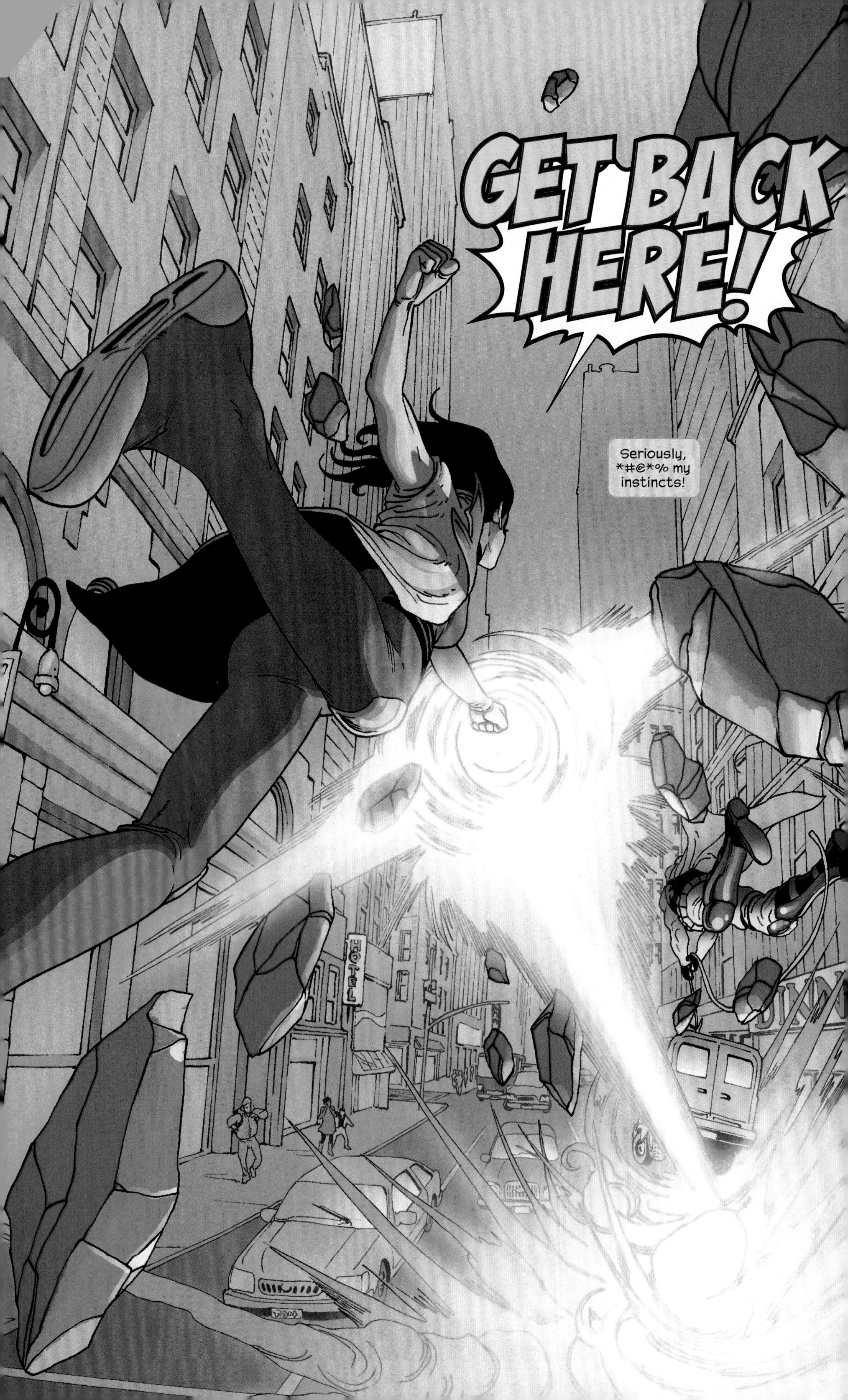
GET BACK HERE!
Seriously, *#@*% my instincts!

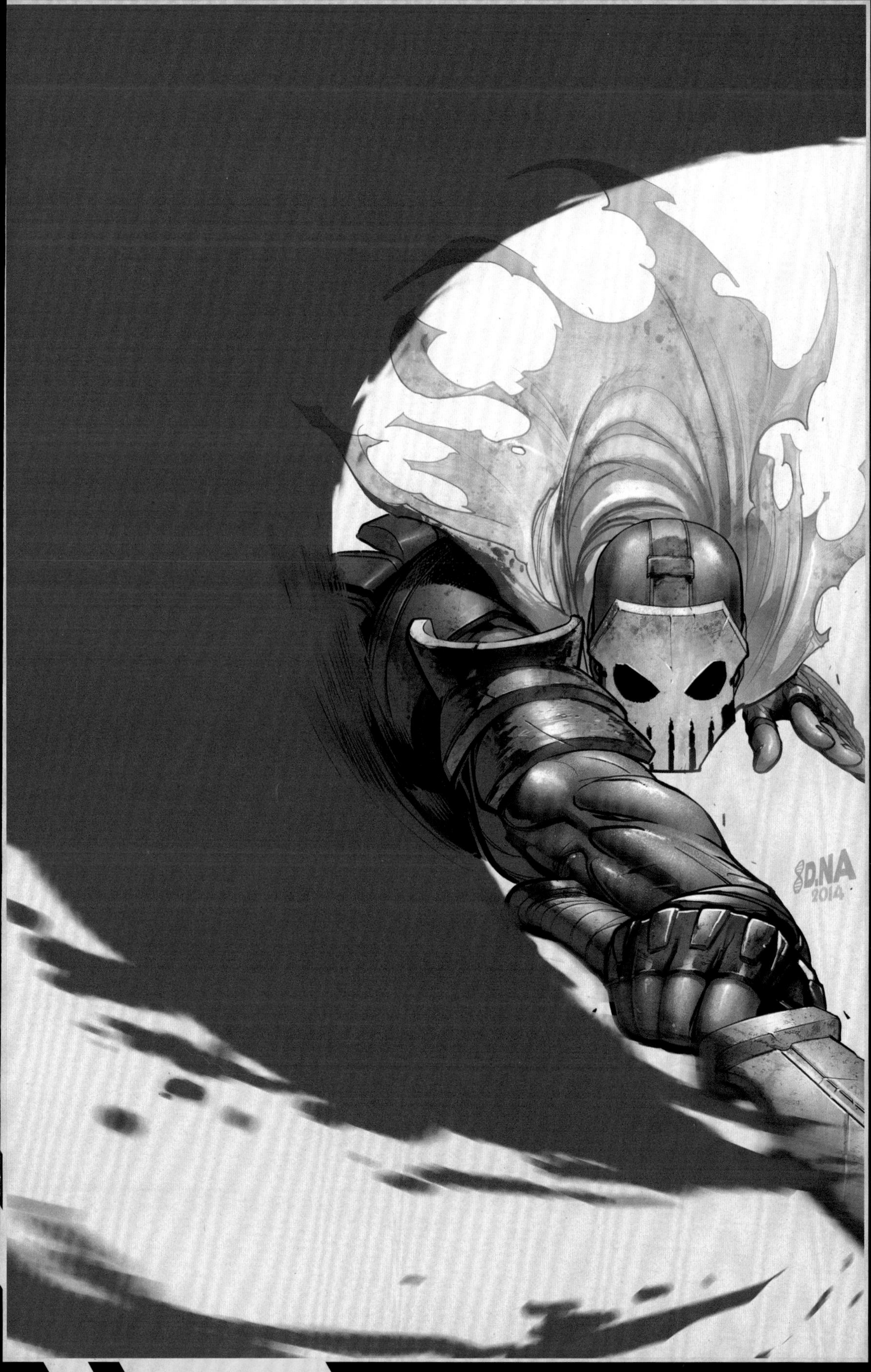
D.NA
2014

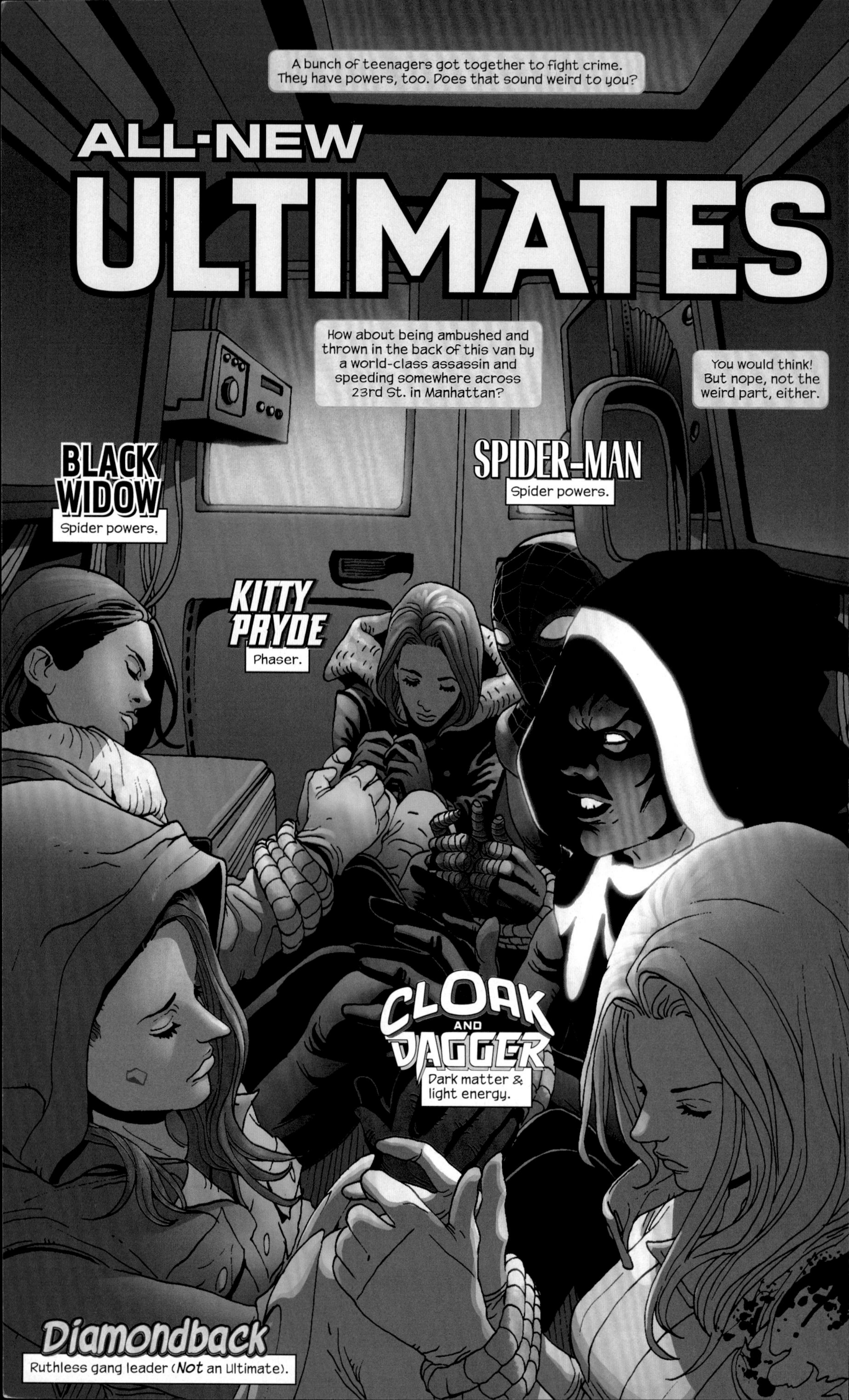
A bunch of teenagers got together to fight crime. They have powers, too. Does that sound weird to you?
ALL-NEW ULTIMATES
How about being ambushed and thrown in the back of this van by a world-class assassin and speeding somewhere across 23rd St. in Manhattan?
You would think! But nope, not the weird part, either.
BLACK WIDOW
Spider powers.
SPIDER-MAN
Spider powers.
KITTY PRYDE
Phaser.
CLOAK AND DAGGER
Dark matter & light energy.
Diamondback
Ruthless gang leader (Not an Ultimate).

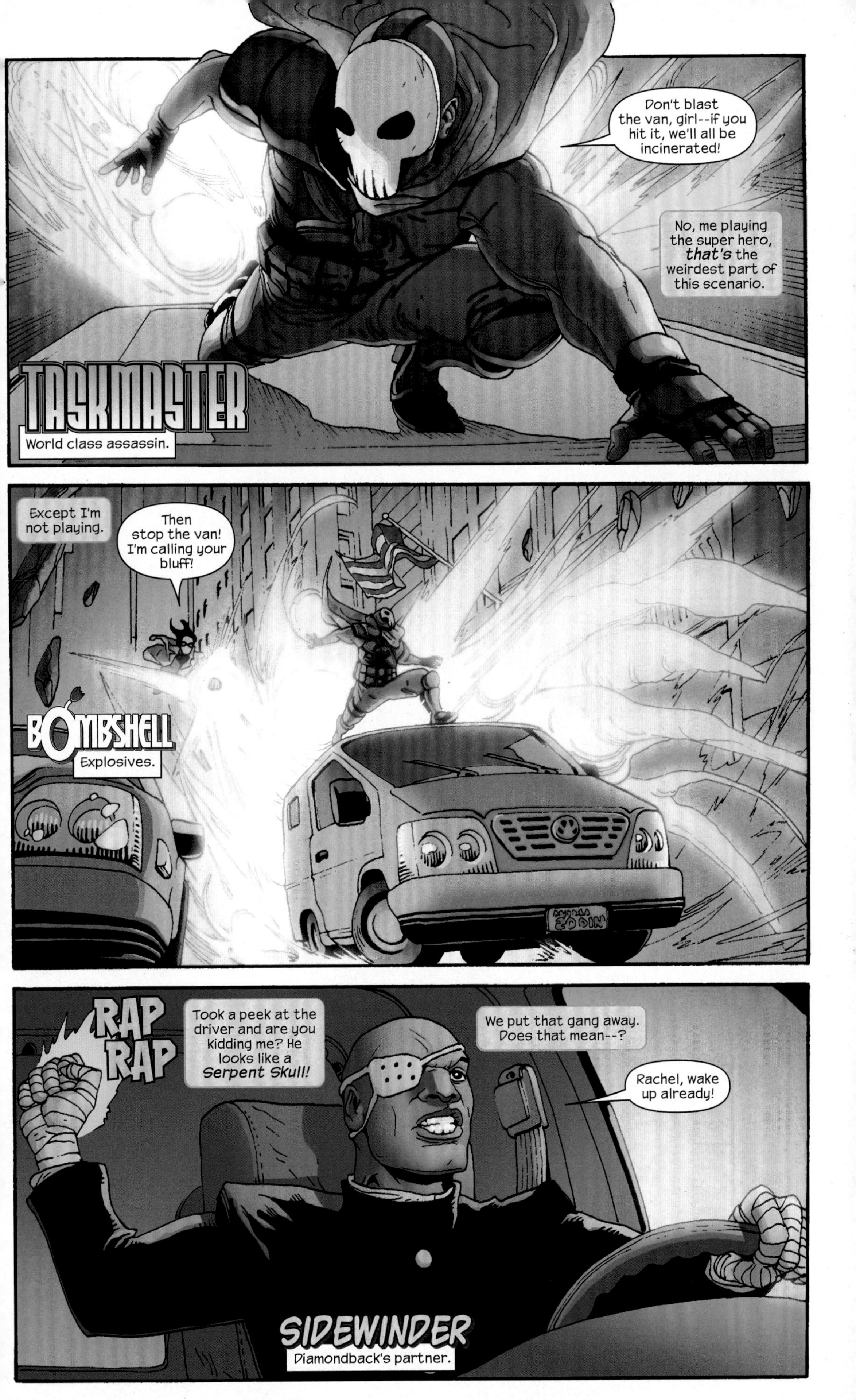
Don't blast the van, girl--if you hit it, we'll all be incinerated!
No, me playing the super hero, *that's* the weirdest part of this scenario.
TASKMASTER
World class assassin.
Except I'm not playing.
Then stop the van! I'm calling your bluff!
BOMBSHELL
Explosives.
RAP RAP
Took a peek at the driver and are you kidding me? He looks like a *Serpent Skull!*
We put that gang away. Does that mean--?
Rachel, wake up already!
SIDEWINDER
Diamondback's partner.

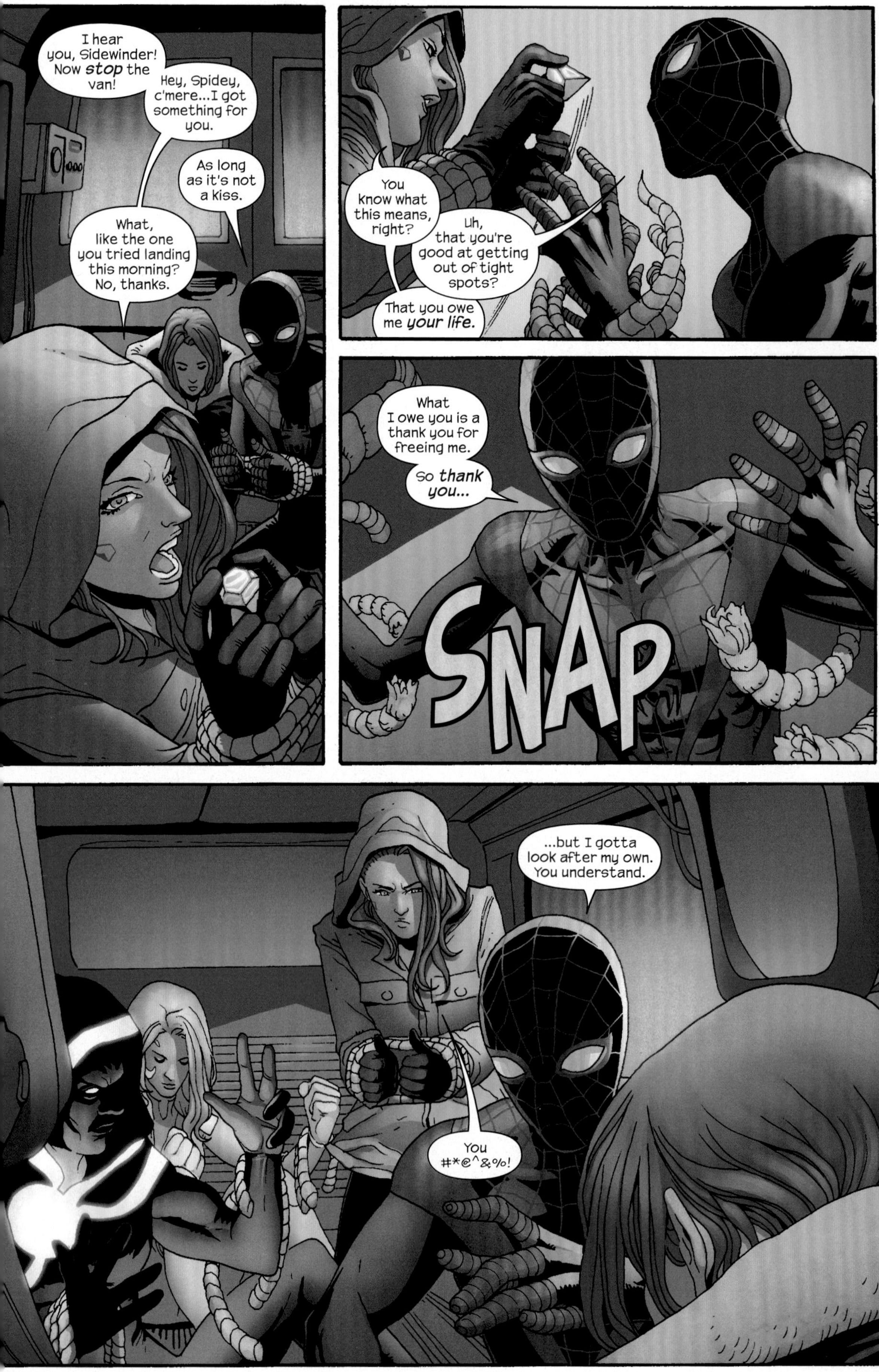
I hear you, Sidewinder! Now stop the van!
Hey, Spidey, c'mere...I got something for you.
As long as it's not a kiss.
What, like the one you tried landing this morning? No, thanks.
You know what this means, right?
Uh, that you're good at getting out of tight spots?
That you owe me your life.
What I owe you is a thank you for freeing me.
So thank you...
SNAP
...but I gotta look after my own. You understand.
You #*@^&%!

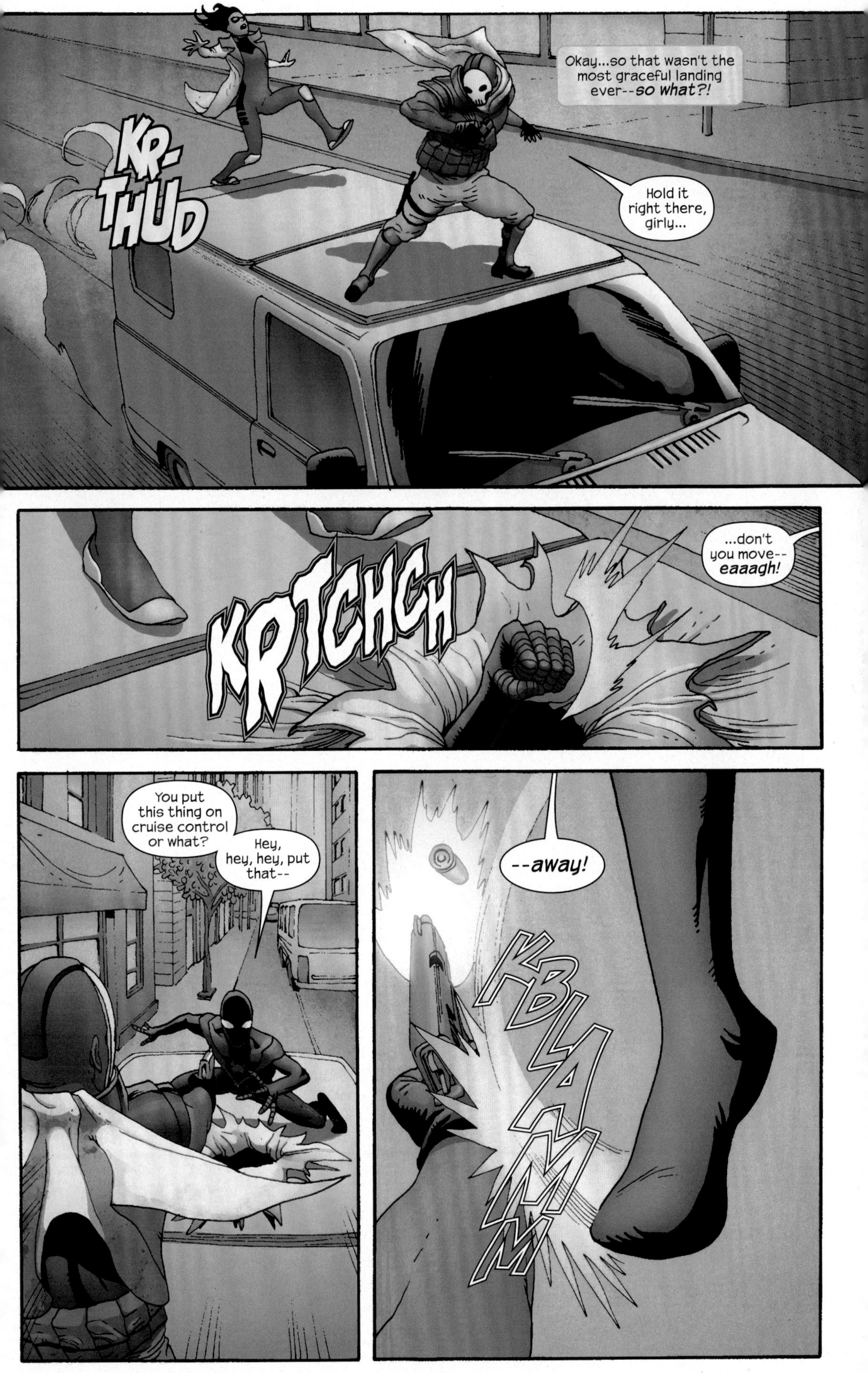
KR-THUD
Okay...so that wasn't the most graceful landing ever--so what?!
Hold it right there, girly...
KRTCHCH
...don't you move--eaaagh!
You put this thing on cruise control or what?
Hey, hey, hey, put that--
--away!
KBLAMM

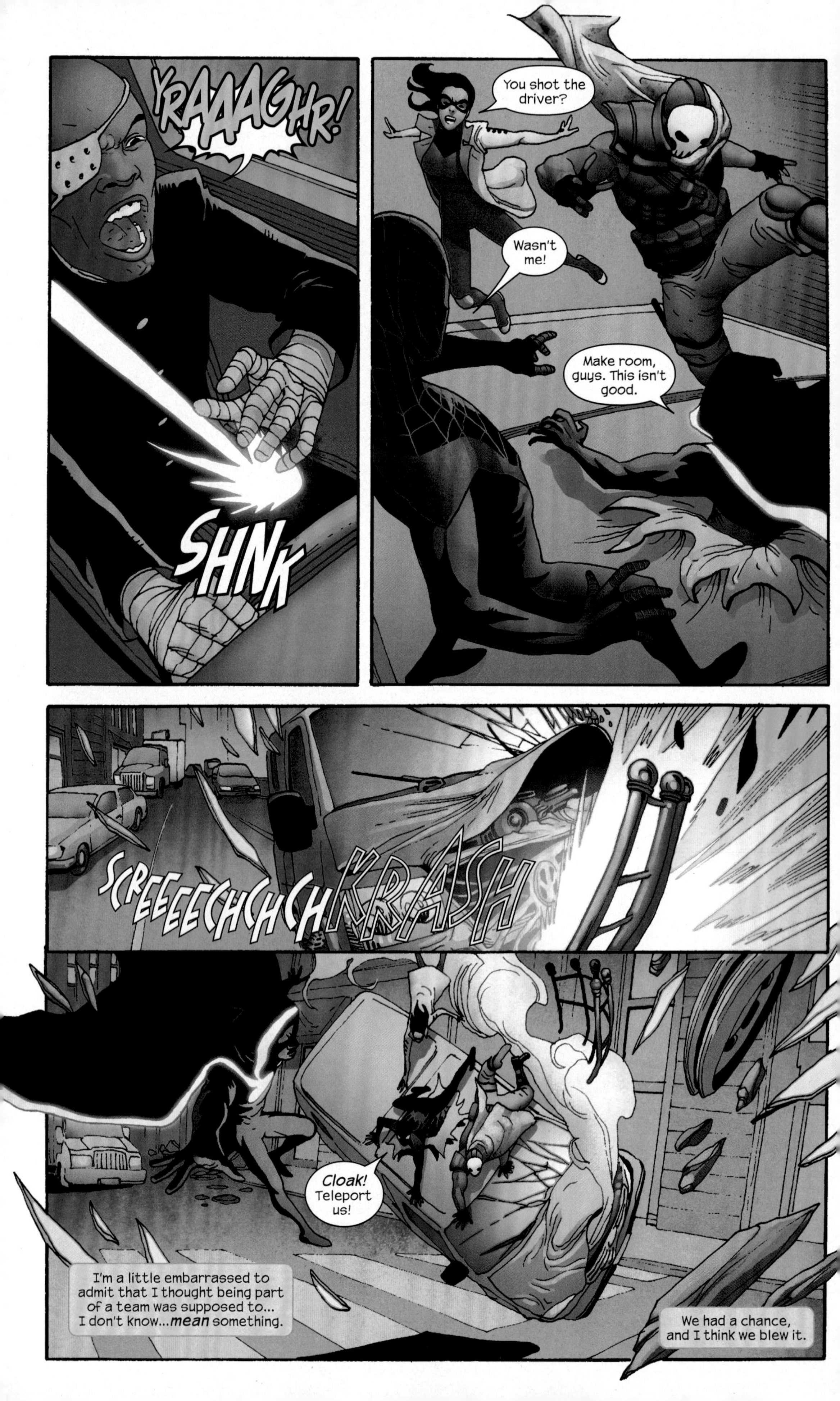
YRAAAGHR!
SHNK
You shot the driver?
Wasn't me!
Make room, guys. This isn't good.
SCREEEECHCHCH
KRASH
Cloak! Teleport us!
I'm a little embarrassed to admit that I thought being part of a team was supposed to... I don't know...*mean* something.
We had a chance, and I think we blew it.

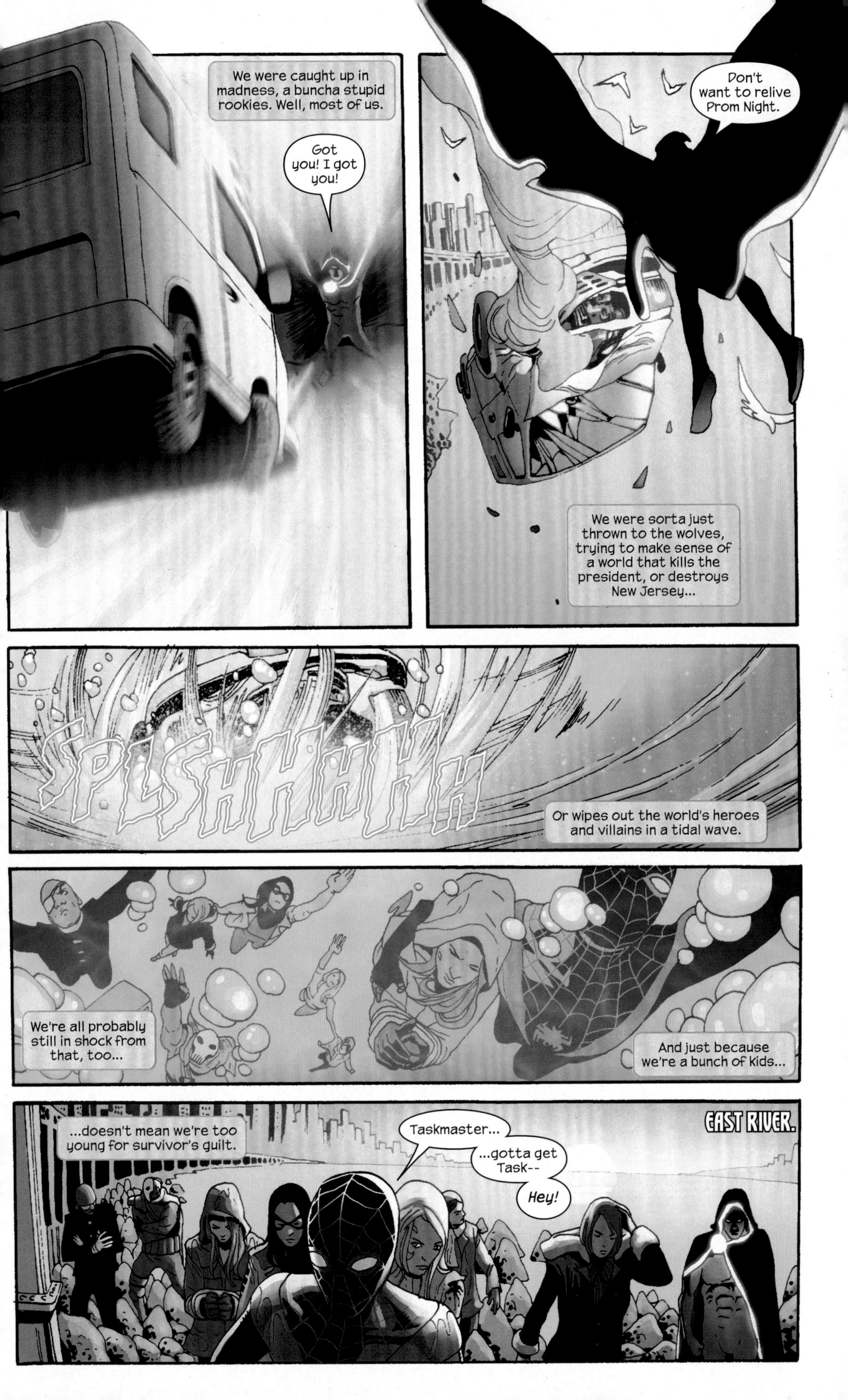
We were caught up in madness, a buncha stupid rookies. Well, most of us.
Got you! I got you!
Don't want to relive Prom Night.
We were sorta just thrown to the wolves, trying to make sense of a world that kills the president, or destroys New Jersey...
SPLSHHHHHH
Or wipes out the world's heroes and villains in a tidal wave.
We're all probably still in shock from that, too...
And just because we're a bunch of kids...
...doesn't mean we're too young for survivor's guilt.
EAST RIVER.
Taskmaster...
...gotta get Task--
Hey!

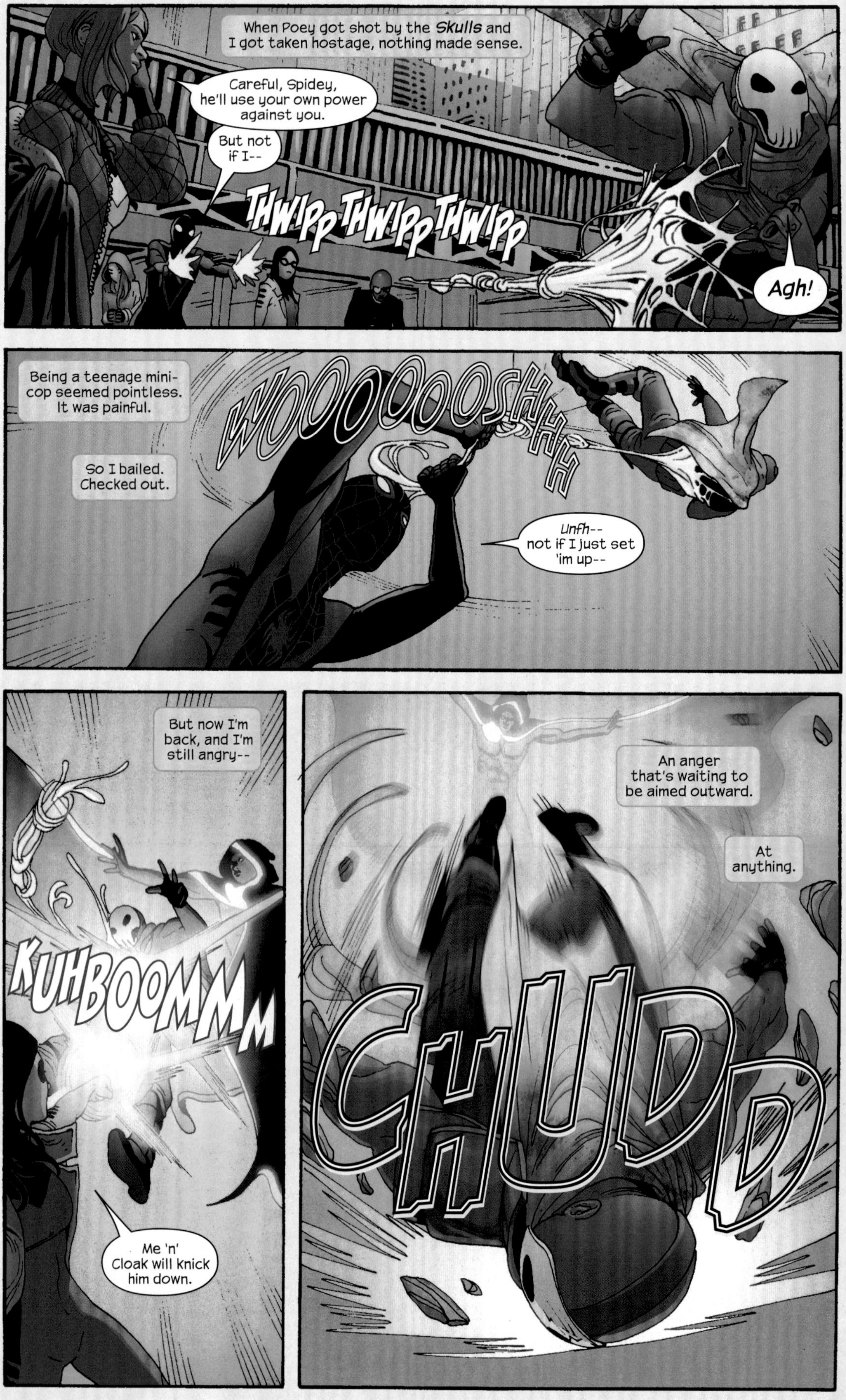
When Poey got shot by the Skulls and I got taken hostage, nothing made sense.
Careful, Spidey, he'll use your own power against you.
But not if I--
THWIPP THWIPP THWIPP
Agh!
Being a teenage mini-cop seemed pointless. It was painful.
WOOOOOOOSHHHH
So I bailed. Checked out.
Unfh-- not if I just set 'im up--
But now I'm back, and I'm still angry--
KUHBOOMMMM
Me 'n' Cloak will knick him down.
An anger that's waiting to be aimed outward.
At anything.
CHUDDD

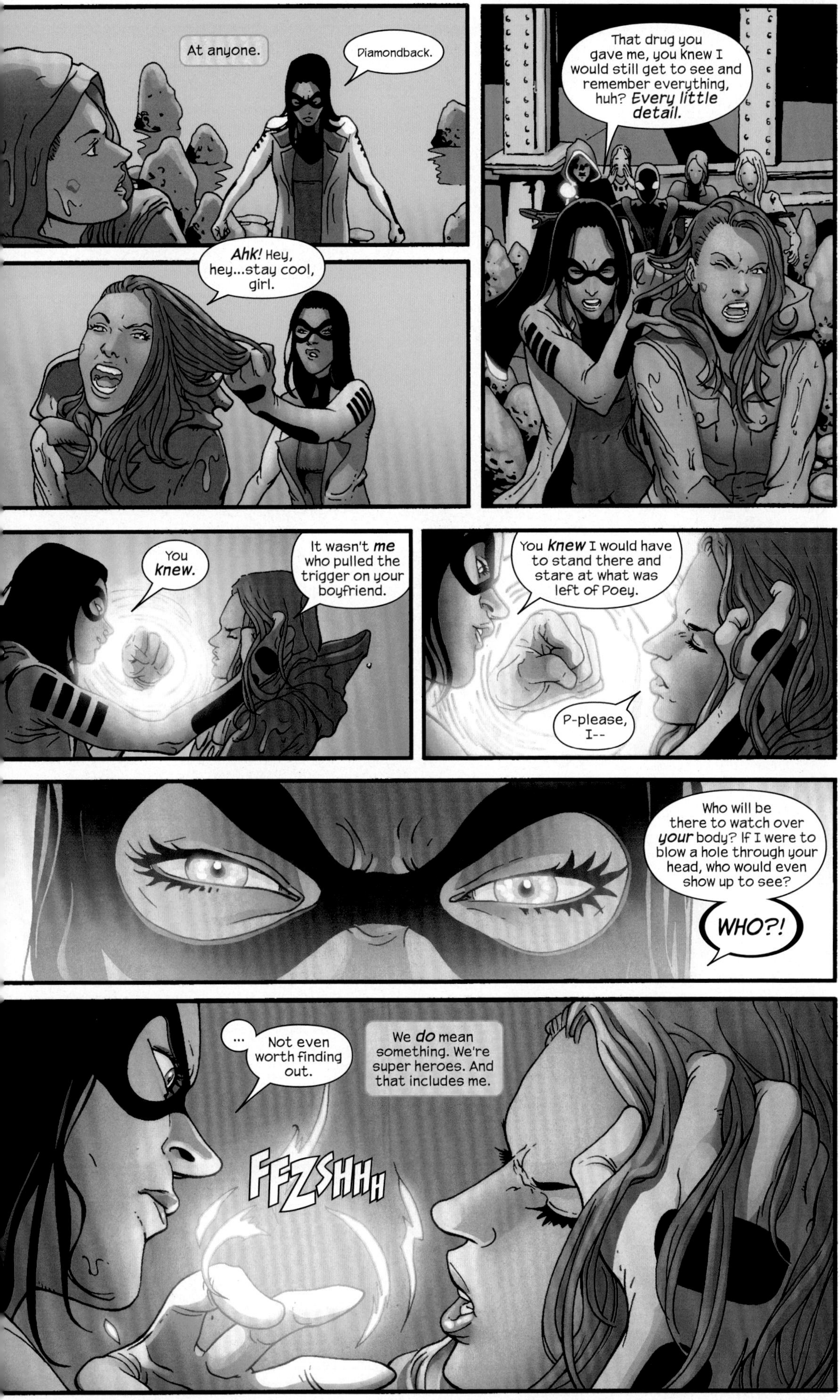
At anyone.
Diamondback.
That drug you gave me, you knew I would still get to see and remember everything, huh? Every little detail.
Ahk! Hey, hey...stay cool, girl.
You knew.
It wasn't me who pulled the trigger on your boyfriend.
You knew I would have to stand there and stare at what was left of Poey.
P-please, I--
Who will be there to watch over your body? If I were to blow a hole through your head, who would even show up to see?
WHO?!
... Not even worth finding out.
We do mean something. We're super heroes. And that includes me.
FFZSHHH

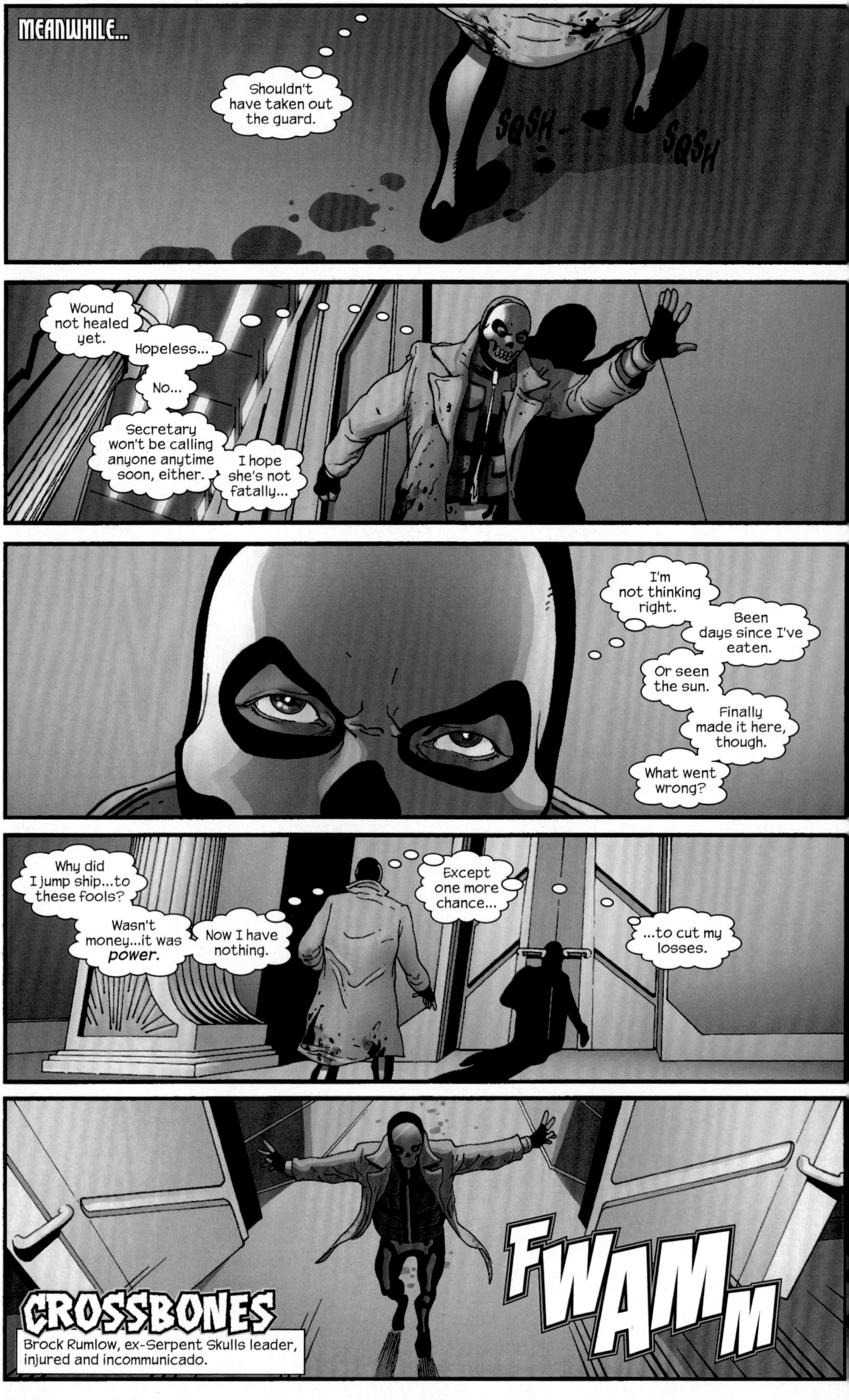
MEANWHILE...
Shouldn't have taken out the guard.
SQSH-
SQSH
Wound not healed yet.
Hopeless...
No...
Secretary won't be calling anyone anytime soon, either.
I hope she's not fatally...
I'm not thinking right.
Been days since I've eaten.
Or seen the sun.
Finally made it here, though.
What went wrong?
Why did I jump ship...to these fools?
Wasn't money...it was *power*.
Now I have nothing.
Except one more chance...
...to cut my losses.
FWAMM
CROSSBONES
Brock Rumlow, ex-Serpent Skulls leader, injured and incommunicado.

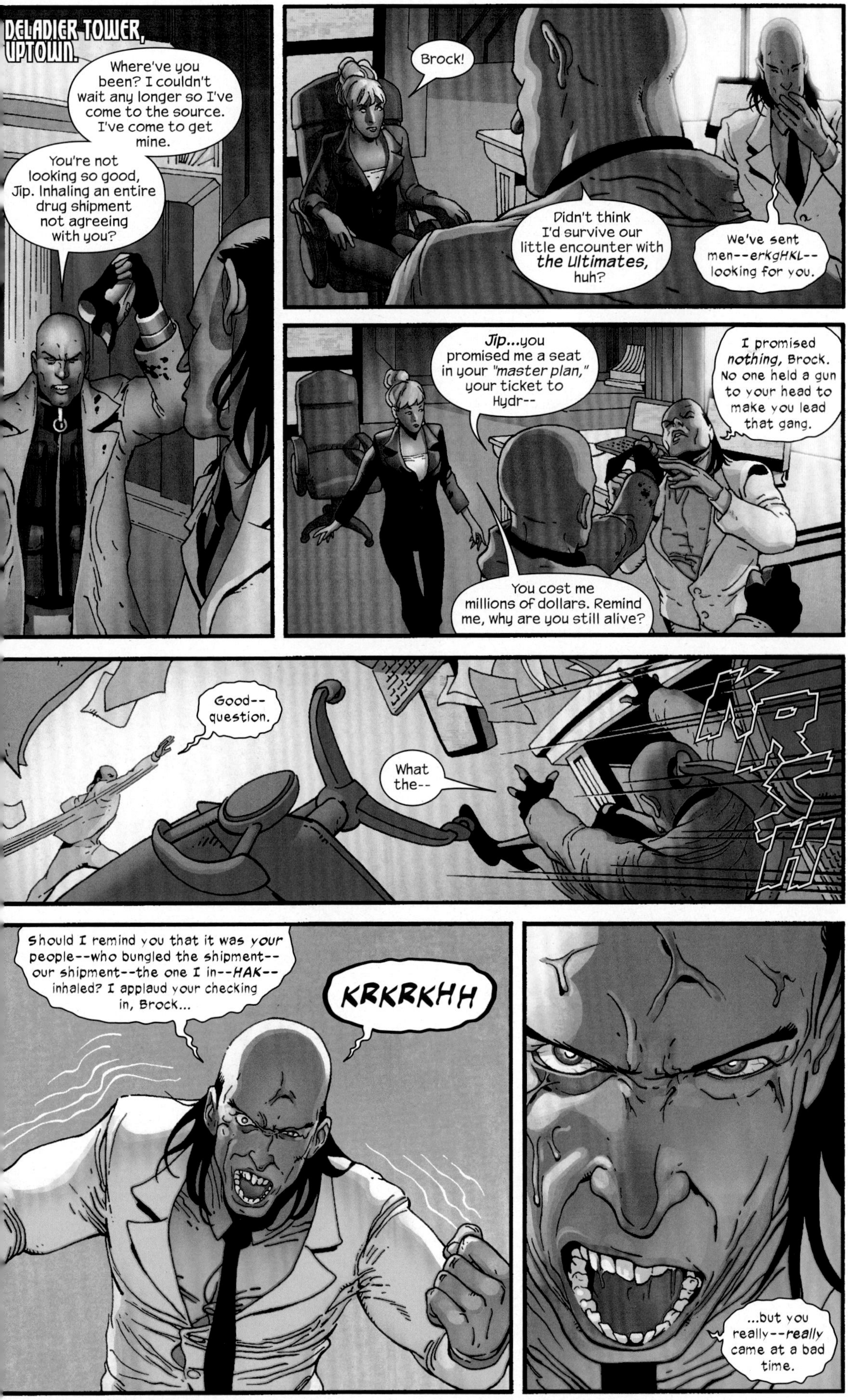
DELADIER TOWER, UPTOWN.
Where've you been? I couldn't wait any longer so I've come to the source. I've come to get mine.
You're not looking so good, Jip. Inhaling an entire drug shipment not agreeing with you?
Brock!
Didn't think I'd survive our little encounter with the Ultimates, huh?
We've sent men--erkgHKL--looking for you.
Jip...you promised me a seat in your "master plan," your ticket to Hydr--
I promised nothing, Brock. No one held a gun to your head to make you lead that gang.
You cost me millions of dollars. Remind me, why are you still alive?
Good--question.
What the--
KRSH
Should I remind you that it was your people--who bungled the shipment--our shipment--the one I in--HAK--inhaled? I applaud your checking in, Brock...
KRKRKHH
...but you really--really came at a bad time.

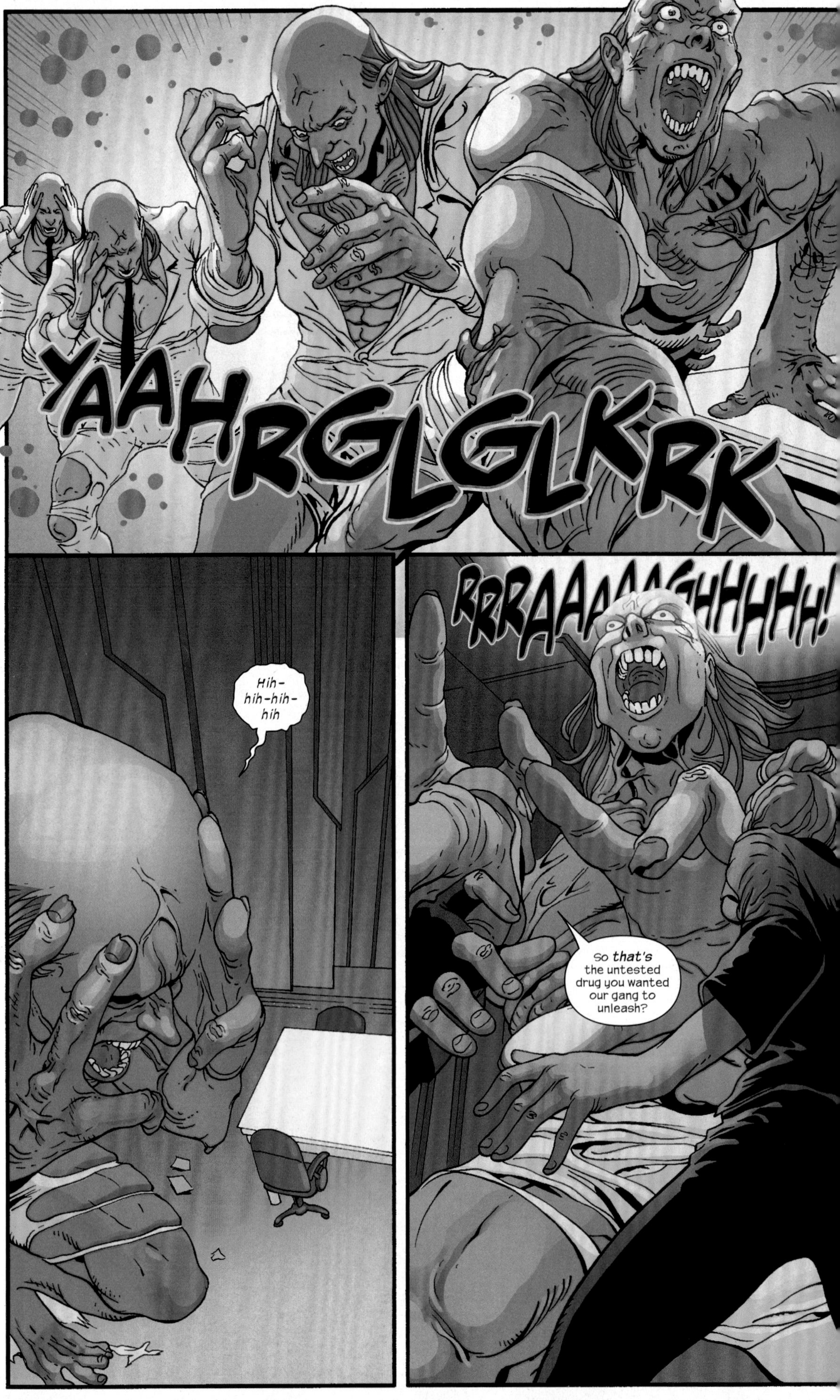
YAAHRGLGLKRK
Hih-hih-hih-hih
RRRAAAAAGHHHHH!
So that's the untested drug you wanted our gang to unleash?

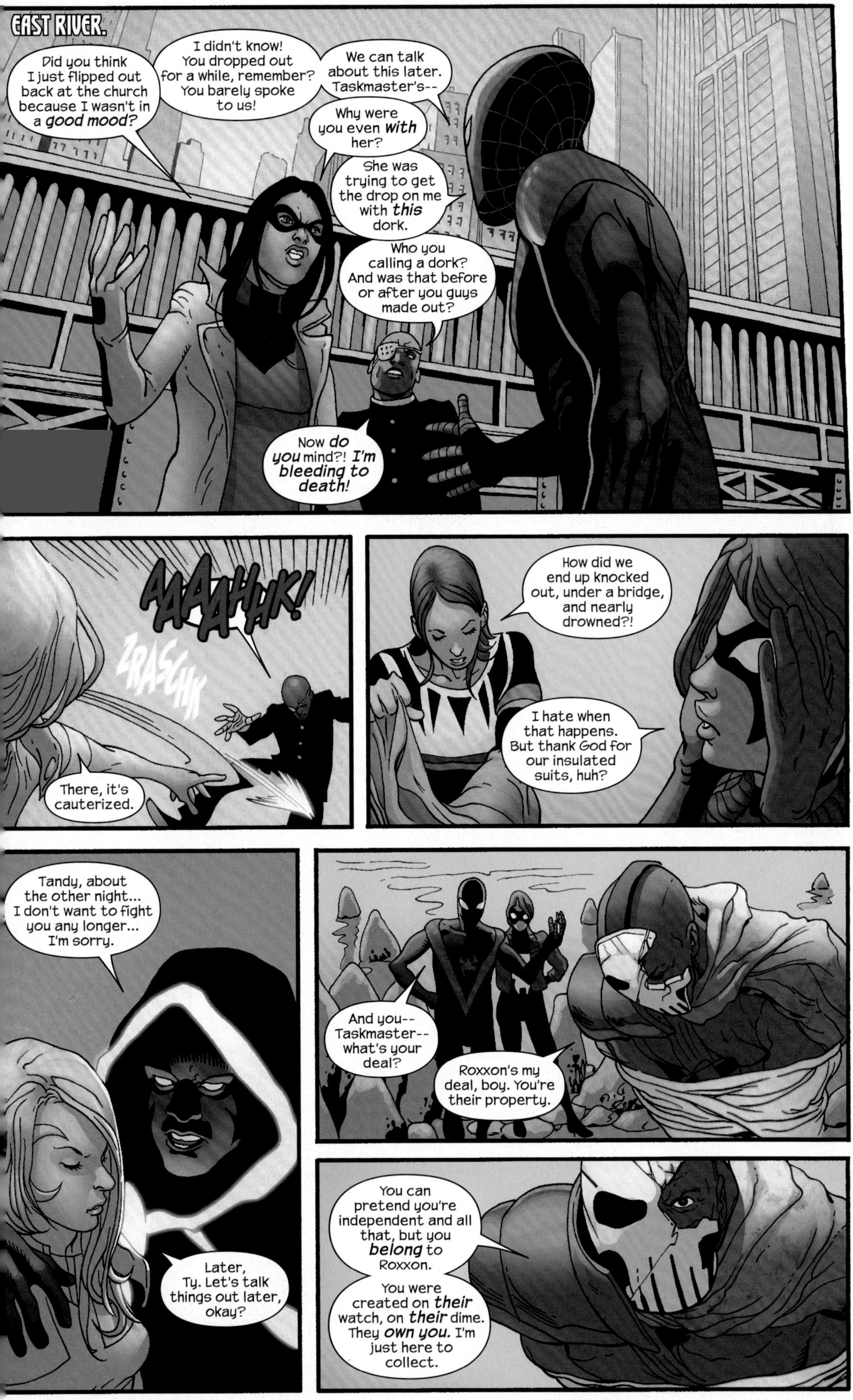
EAST RIVER.
Did you think I just flipped out back at the church because I wasn't in a good mood?
I didn't know! You dropped out for a while, remember? You barely spoke to us!
We can talk about this later. Taskmaster's--
Why were you even with her?
She was trying to get the drop on me with this dork.
Who you calling a dork? And was that before or after you guys made out?
Now do you mind?! I'm bleeding to death!
AAAAHHK!
ZRASCHK
There, it's cauterized.
How did we end up knocked out, under a bridge, and nearly drowned?!
I hate when that happens. But thank God for our insulated suits, huh?
Tandy, about the other night... I don't want to fight you any longer... I'm sorry.
Later, Ty. Let's talk things out later, okay?
And you-- Taskmaster-- what's your deal?
Roxxon's my deal, boy. You're their property.
You can pretend you're independent and all that, but you belong to Roxxon.
You were created on their watch, on their dime. They own you. I'm just here to collect.

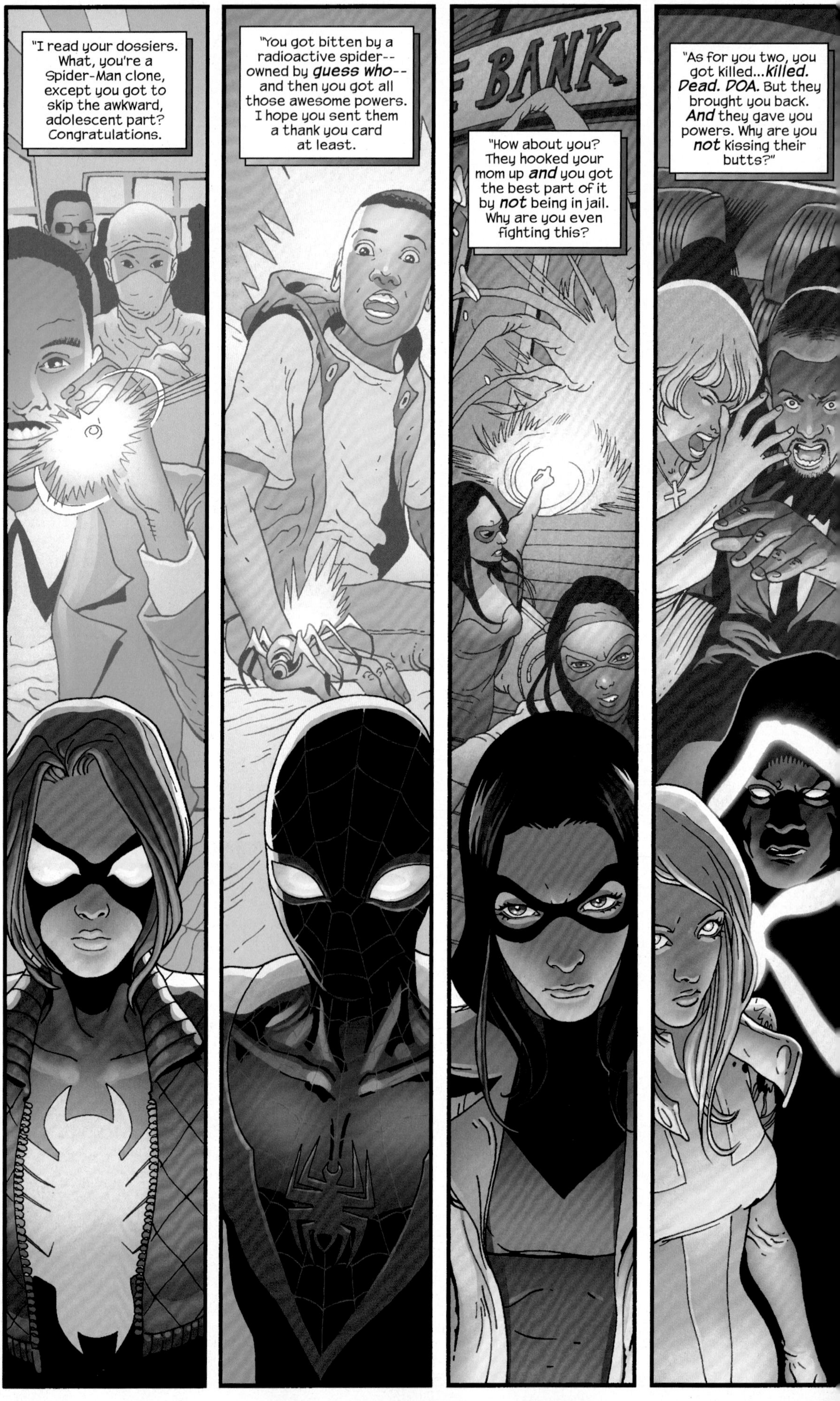
"I read your dossiers. What, you're a Spider-Man clone, except you got to skip the awkward, adolescent part? Congratulations.
"You got bitten by a radioactive spider--owned by ***guess who***--and then you got all those awesome powers. I hope you sent them a thank you card at least.
BANK
"How about you? They hooked your mom up ***and*** you got the best part of it by ***not*** being in jail. Why are you even fighting this?
"As for you two, you got killed...***killed. Dead. DOA.*** But they brought you back. ***And*** they gave you powers. Why are you ***not*** kissing their butts?"

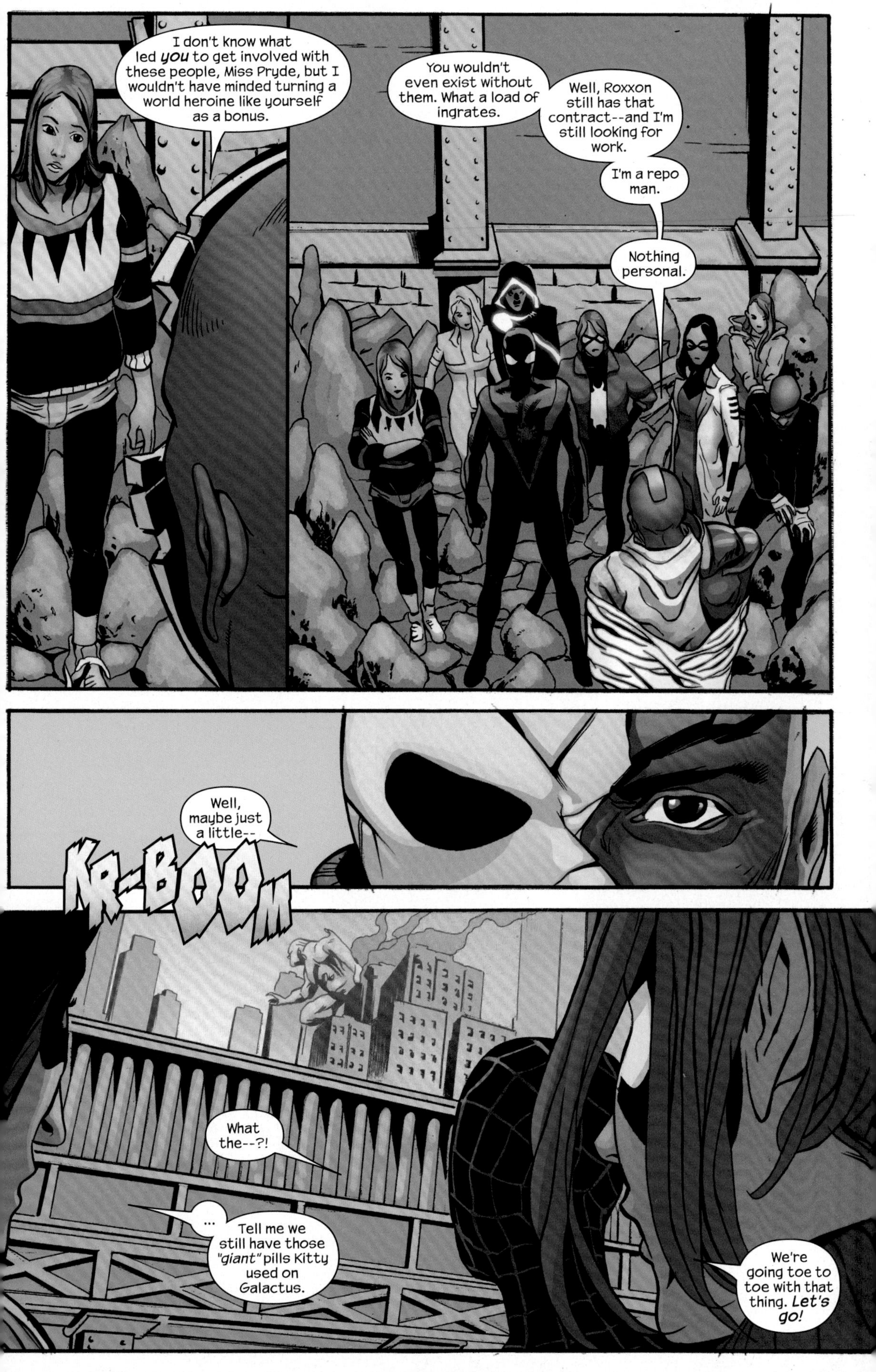
I don't know what led *you* to get involved with these people, Miss Pryde, but I wouldn't have minded turning a world heroine like yourself as a bonus.
You wouldn't even exist without them. What a load of ingrates.
Well, Roxxon still has that contract--and I'm still looking for work.
I'm a repo man.
Nothing personal.
Well, maybe just a little--
KR-BOOM
What the--?!
...
Tell me we still have those *"giant"* pills Kitty used on Galactus.
We're going toe to toe with that thing. *Let's go!*

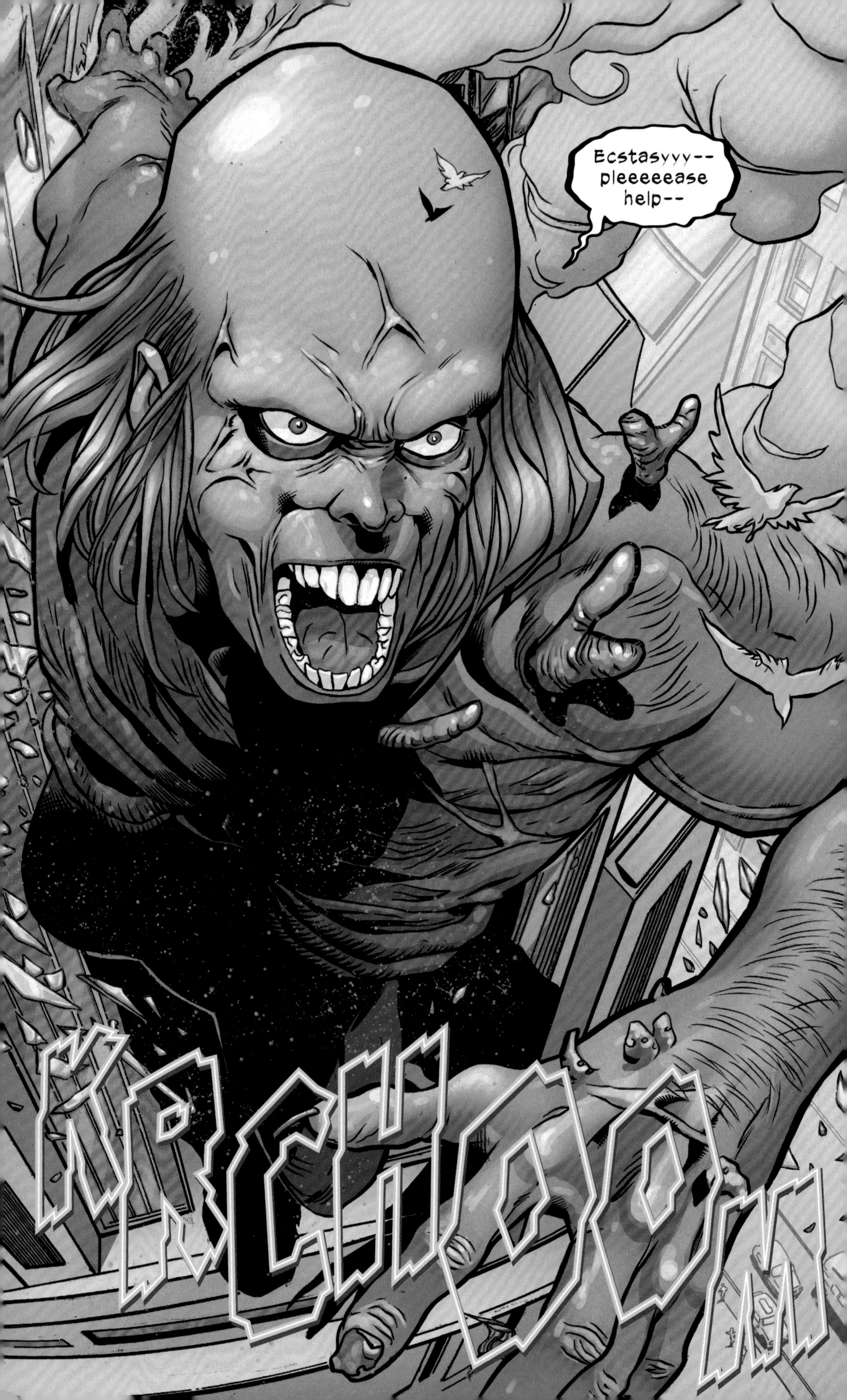
Ecstasyyy-- pleeeeease help--
KRCHOOM

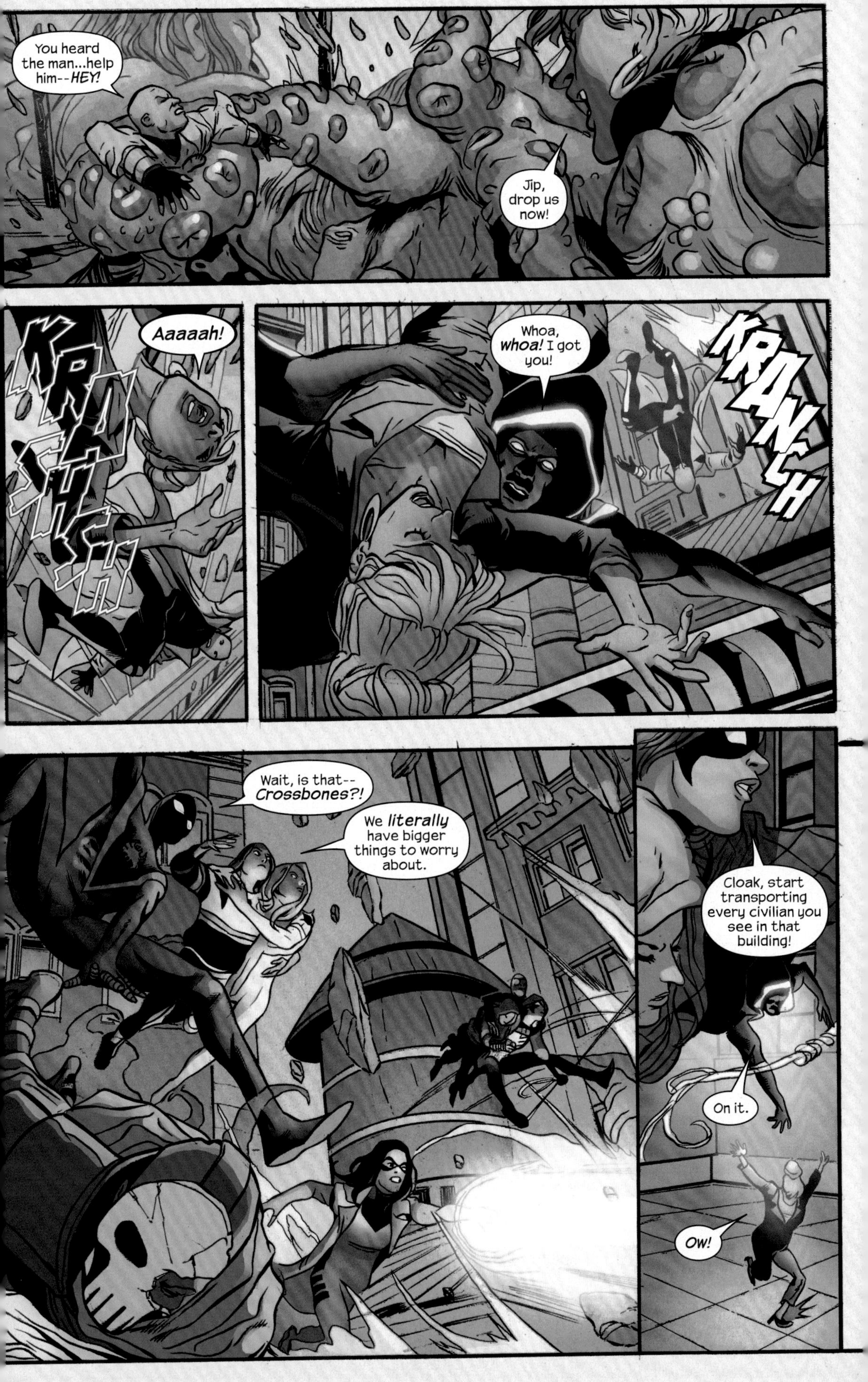
You heard the man...help him--HEY!
Jip, drop us now!
KRASHSHSH
Aaaaah!
Whoa, whoa! I got you!
KRANCH
Wait, is that-- Crossbones?!
We literally have bigger things to worry about.
Cloak, start transporting every civilian you see in that building!
On it.
Ow!

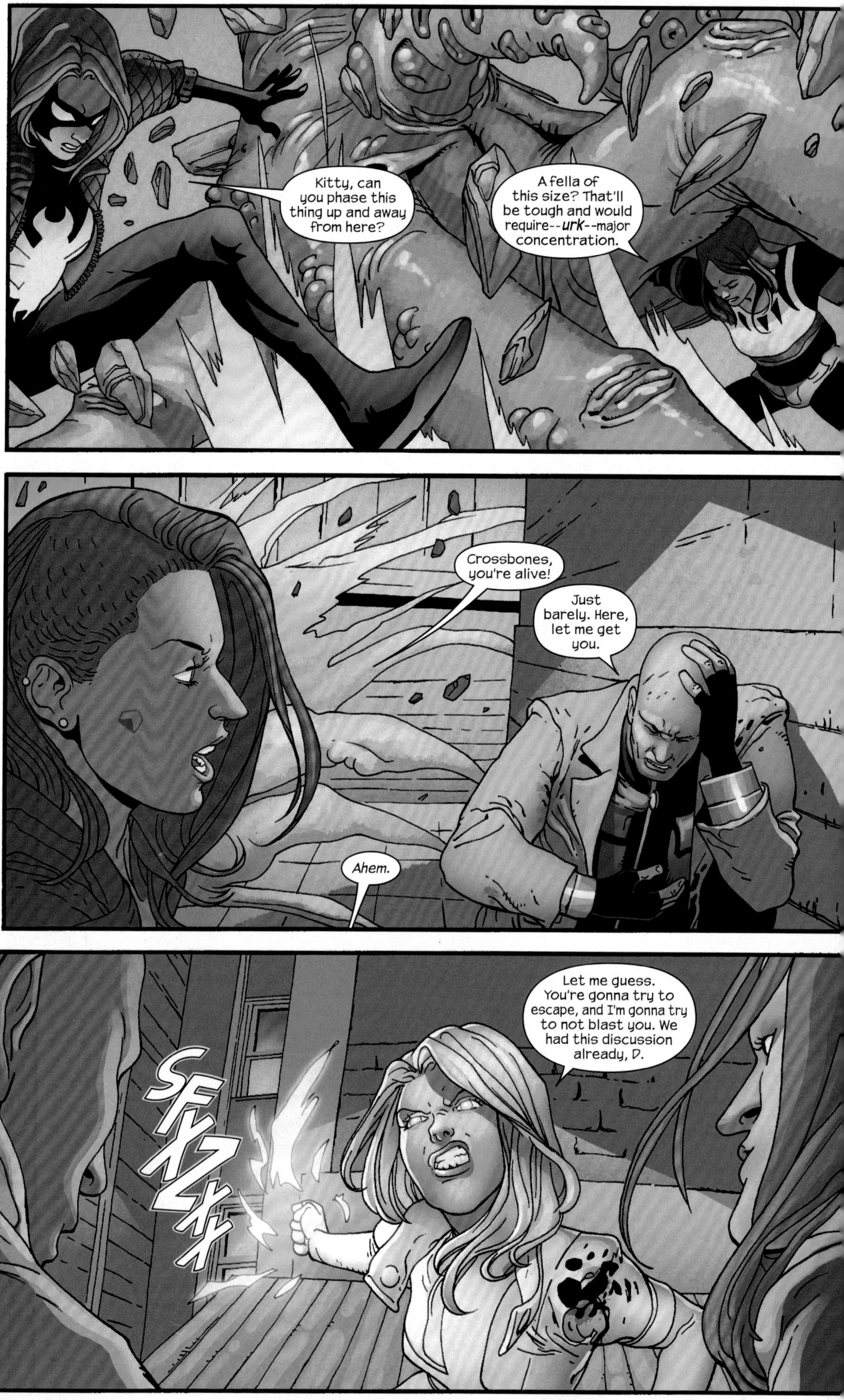
Kitty, can you phase this thing up and away from here?
A fella of this size? That'll be tough and would require--*urk*--major concentration.
Crossbones, you're alive!
Just barely. Here, let me get you.
Ahem.
Let me guess. You're gonna try to escape, and I'm gonna try to not blast you. We had this discussion already, D.

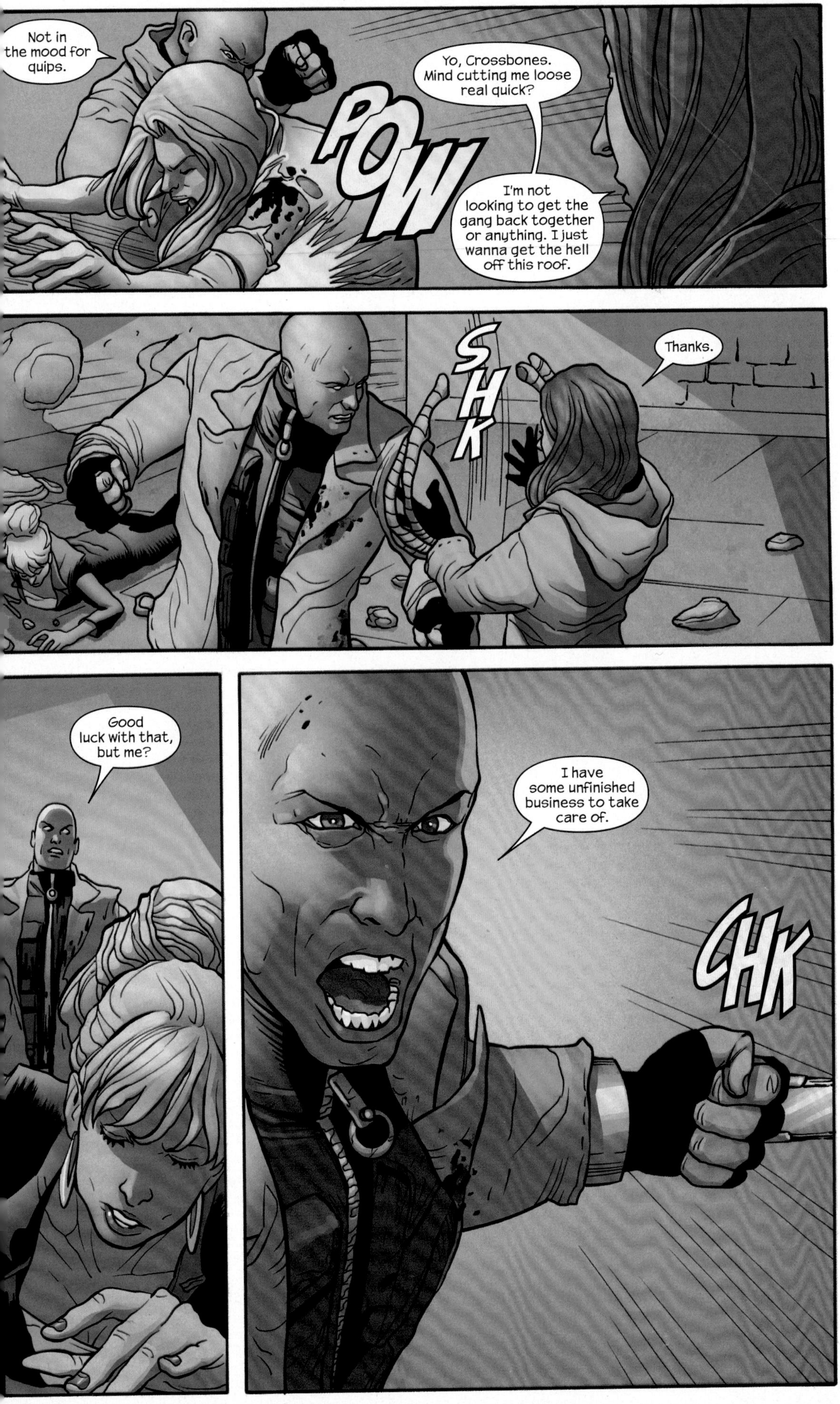

Not in the mood for quips.
POW
Yo, Crossbones. Mind cutting me loose real quick?
I'm not looking to get the gang back together or anything. I just wanna get the hell off this roof.
SHK
Thanks.
Good luck with that, but me?
I have some unfinished business to take care of.
CHK

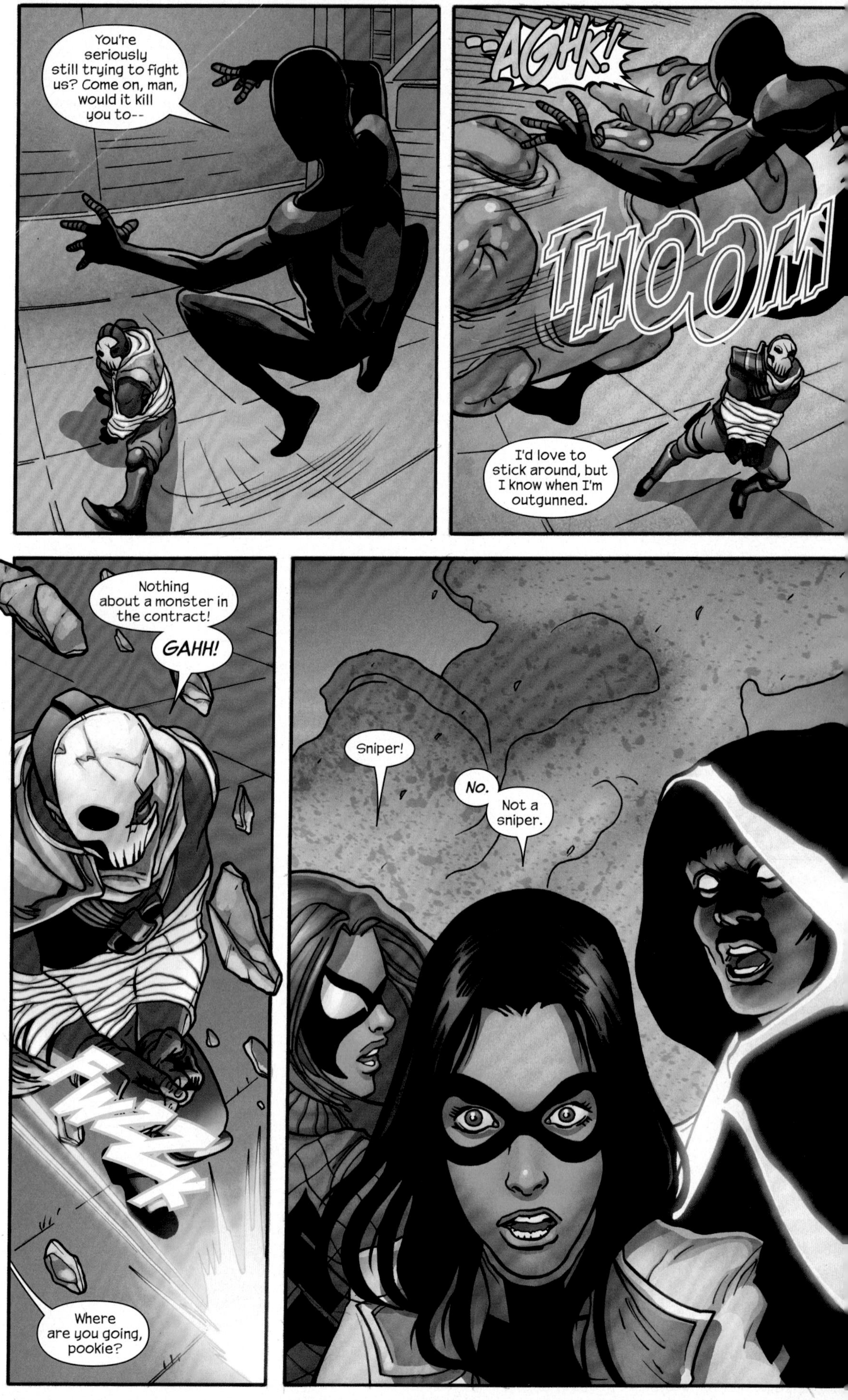
You're seriously still trying to fight us? Come on, man, would it kill you to--
--AGHK!
THOOM
I'd love to stick around, but I know when I'm outgunned.
Nothing about a monster in the contract!
GAHH!
FWZZK
Where are you going, pookie?
Sniper!
No.
Not a sniper.

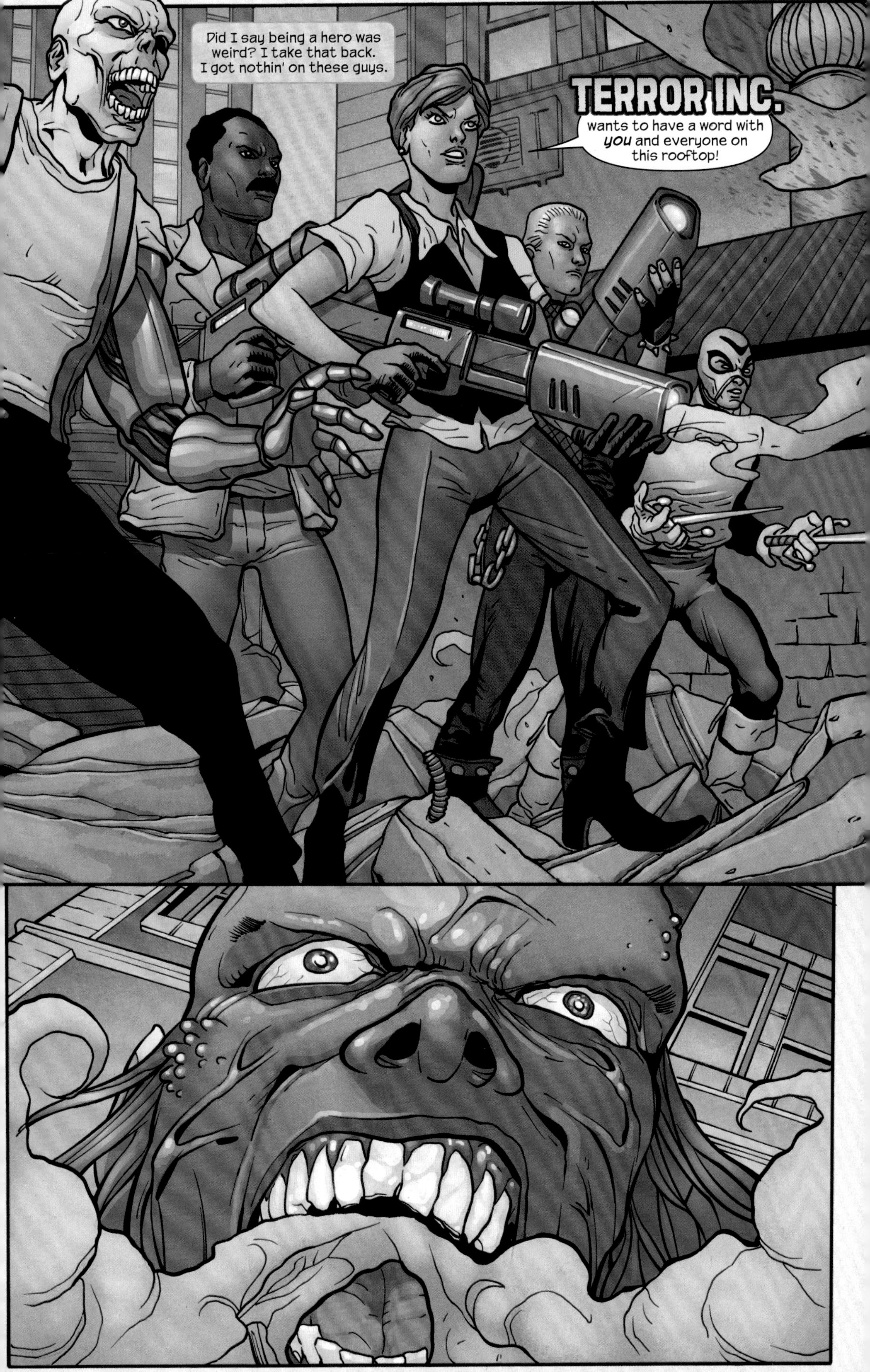
Did I say being a hero was weird? I take that back. I got nothin' on these guys.
TERROR INC.
wants to have a word with *you* and everyone on this rooftop!

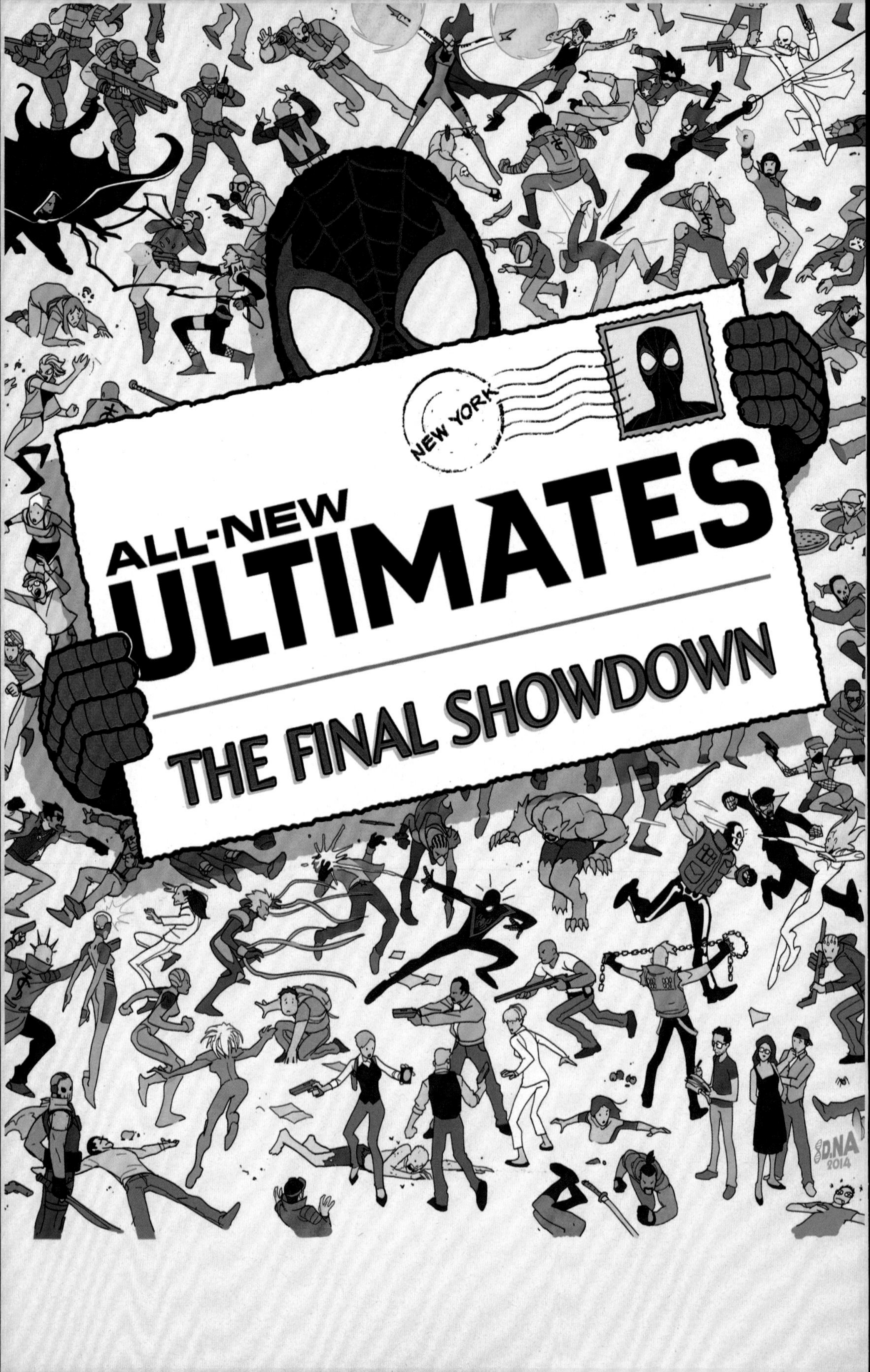
NEW YORK
ALL-NEW
ULTIMATES
THE FINAL SHOWDOWN
D.NA
2014

12

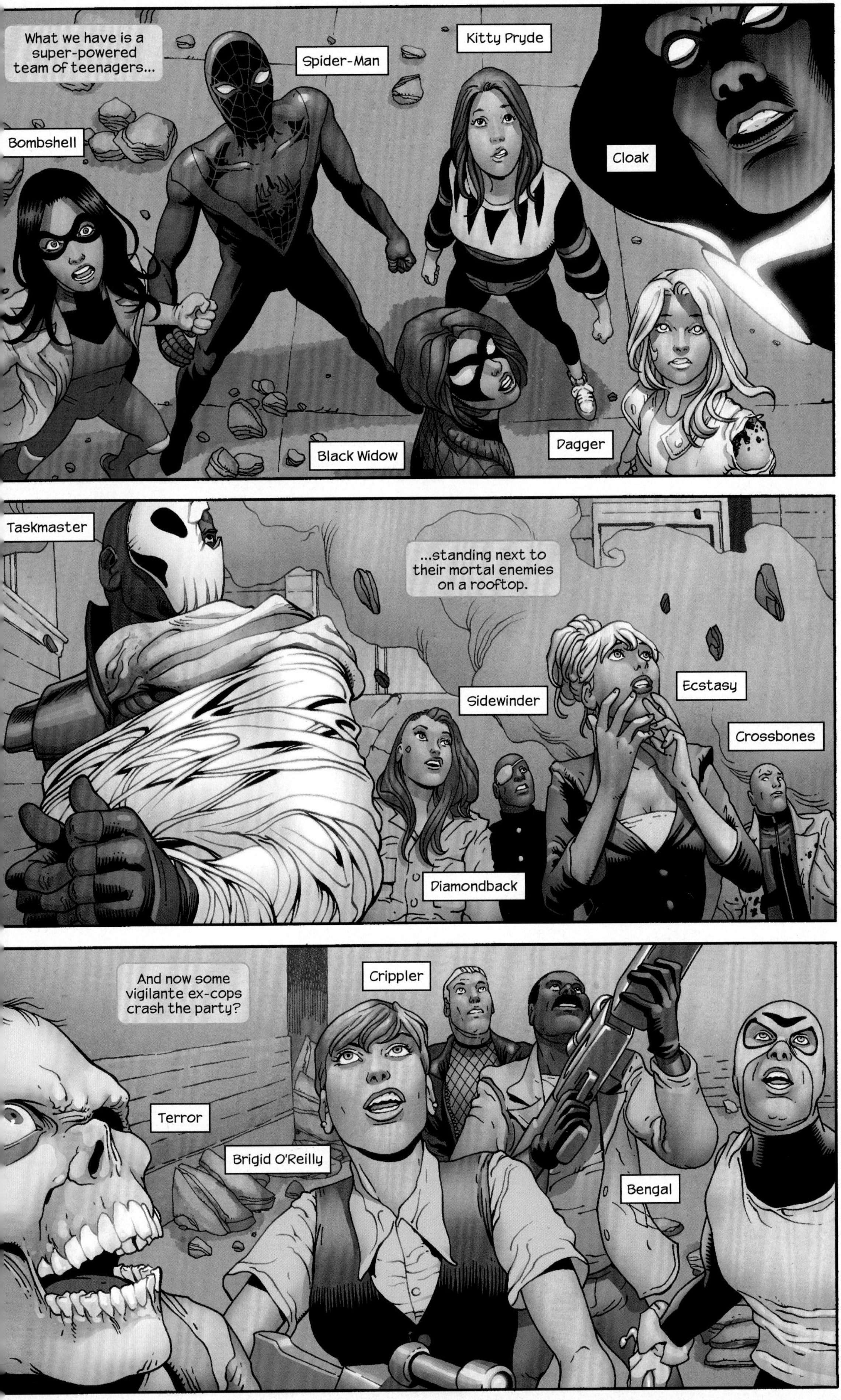

What we have is a super-powered team of teenagers...
Spider-Man
Kitty Pryde
Cloak
Bombshell
Black Widow
Dagger
Taskmaster
...standing next to their mortal enemies on a rooftop.
Sidewinder
Ecstasy
Crossbones
Diamondback
And now some vigilante ex-cops crash the party?
Crippler
Terror
Brigid O'Reilly
Bengal

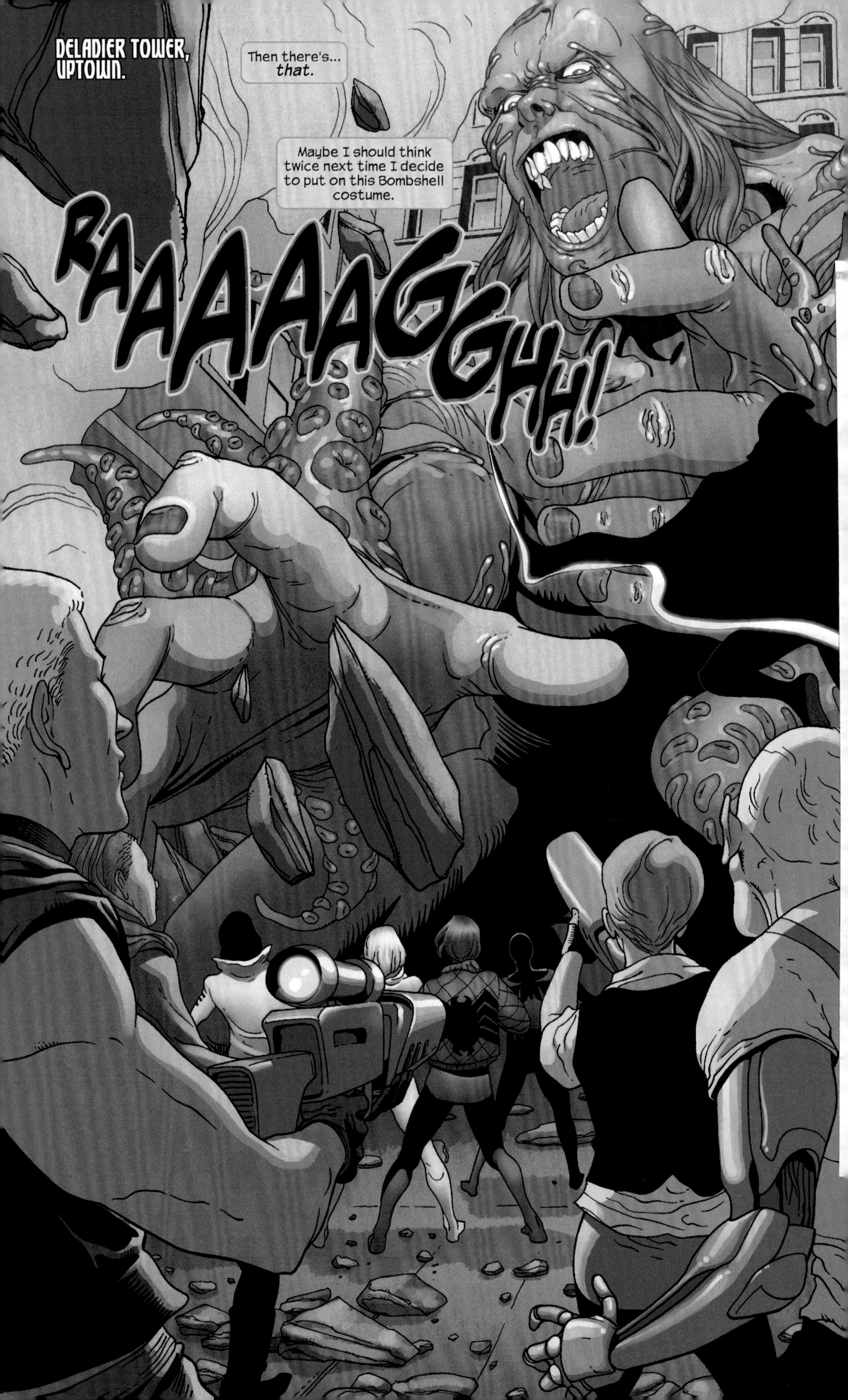
DELADIER TOWER, UPTOWN.
Then there's... *that.*
Maybe I should think twice next time I decide to put on this Bombshell costume.
RAAAAAAGGHH!

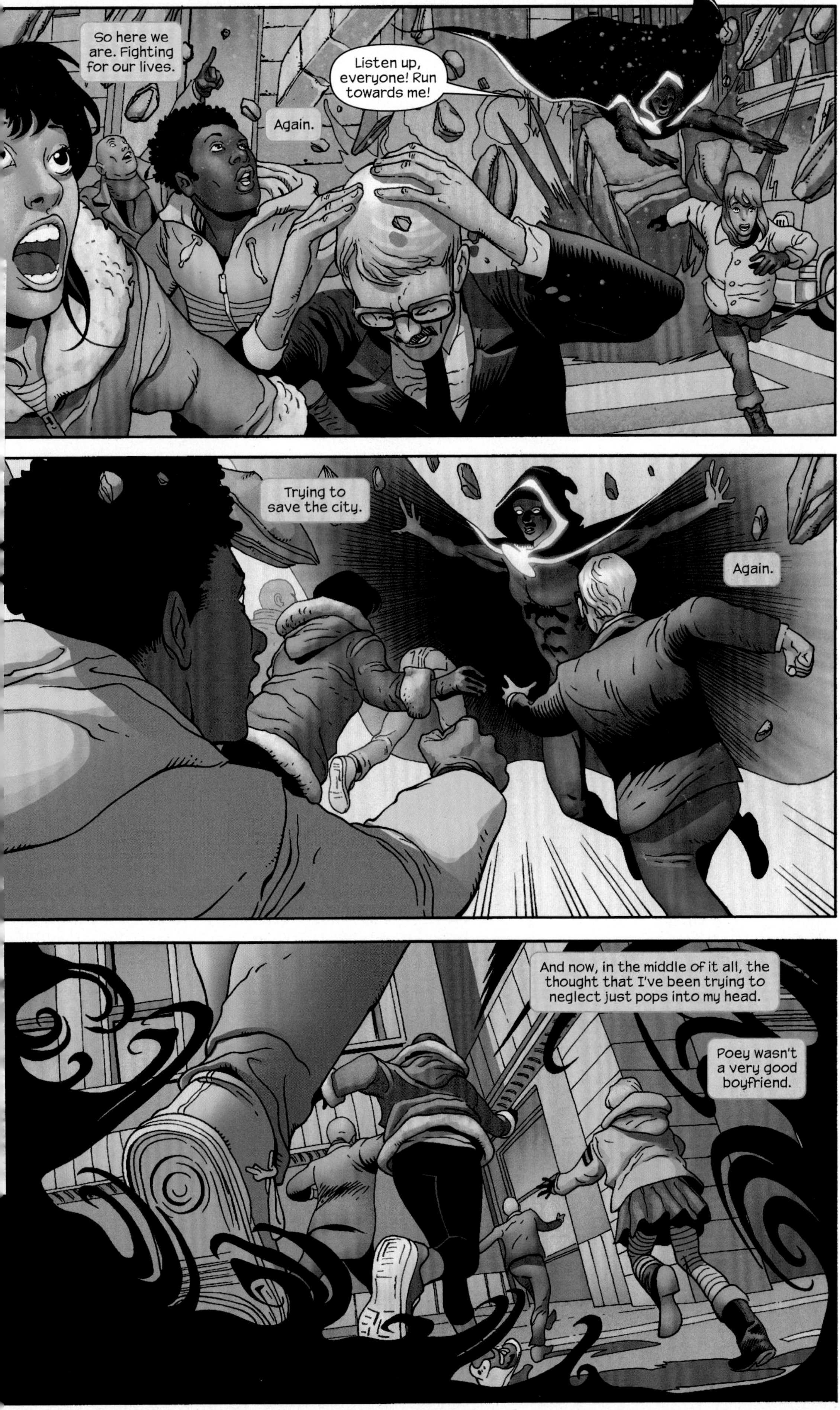
So here we are. Fighting for our lives.
Again.
Listen up, everyone! Run towards me!
Trying to save the city.
Again.
And now, in the middle of it all, the thought that I've been trying to neglect just pops into my head.
Poey wasn't a very good boyfriend.

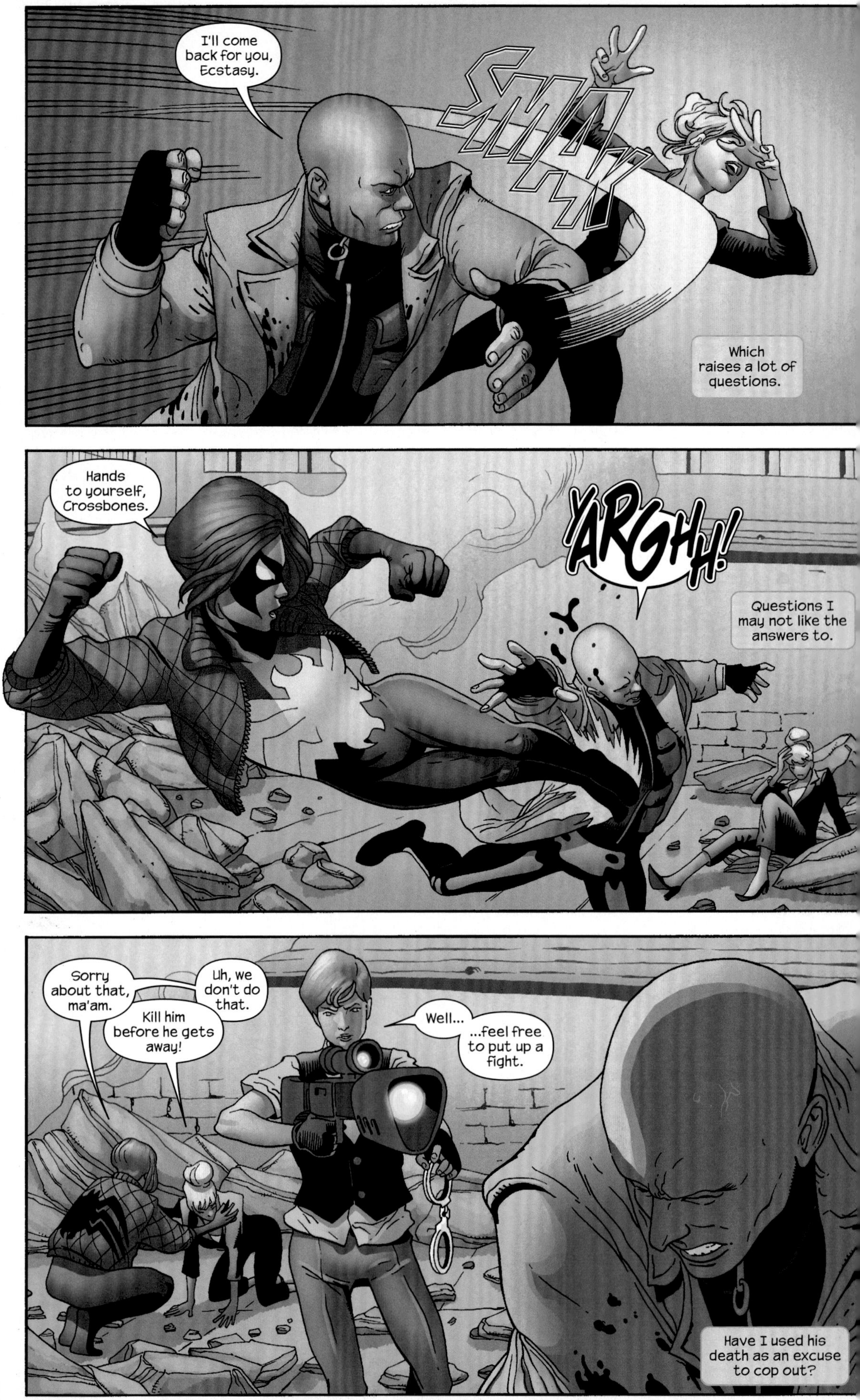
I'll come back for you, Ecstasy.
SMACK
Which raises a lot of questions.
Hands to yourself, Crossbones.
YARGHH!
Questions I may not like the answers to.
Sorry about that, ma'am.
Uh, we don't do that.
Kill him before he gets away!
Well...
...feel free to put up a fight.
Have I used his death as an excuse to cop out?

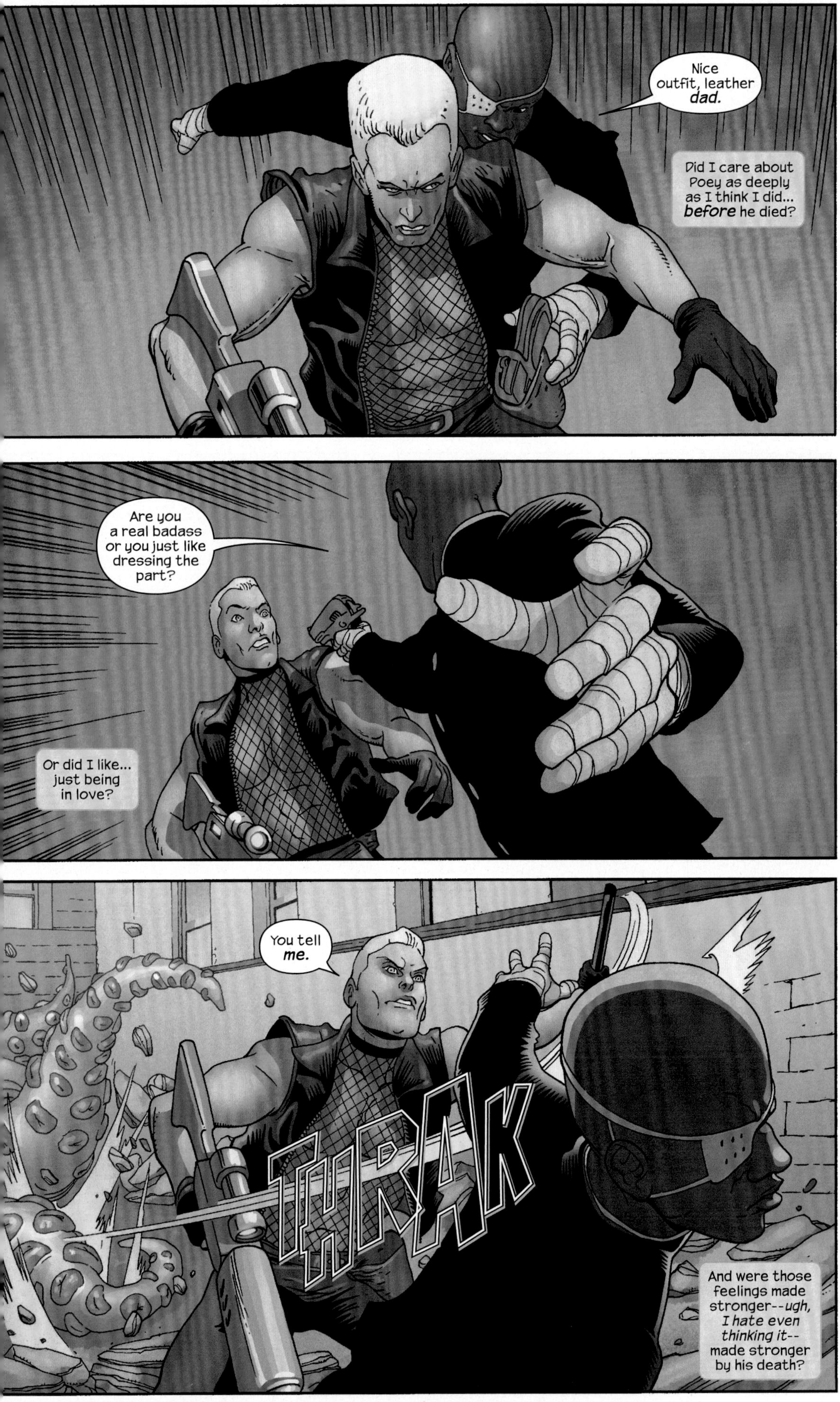
Nice outfit, leather *dad.*
Did I care about Poey as deeply as I think I did... *before* he died?
Are you a real badass or you just like dressing the part?
Or did I like... just being in love?
You tell *me.*
THRAK
And were those feelings made stronger--*ugh, I hate even thinking it*--made stronger by his death?

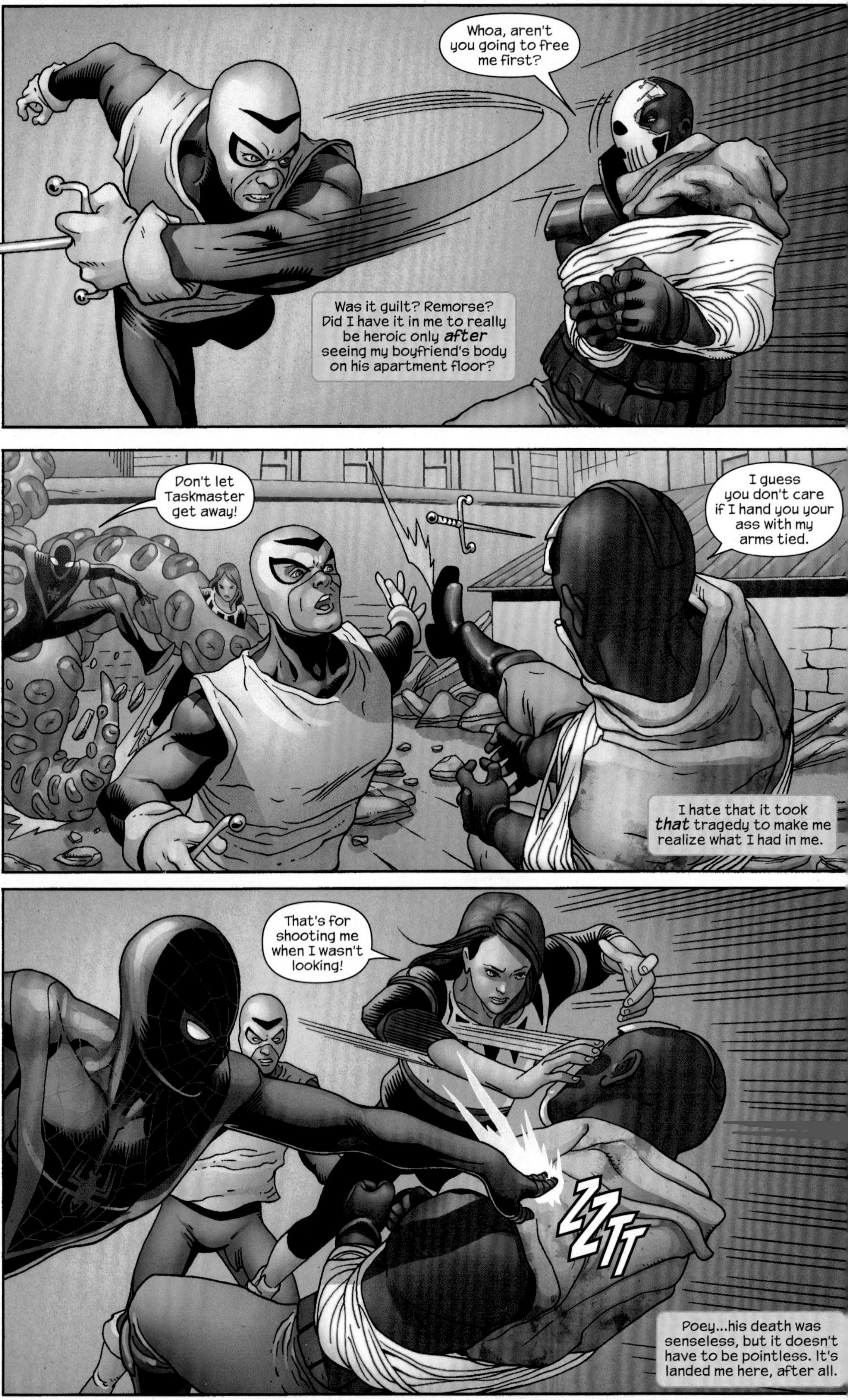
Whoa, aren't you going to free me first?
Was it guilt? Remorse? Did I have it in me to really be heroic only *after* seeing my boyfriend's body on his apartment floor?
Don't let Taskmaster get away!
I guess you don't care if I hand you your ass with my arms tied.
I hate that it took *that* tragedy to make me realize what I had in me.
That's for shooting me when I wasn't looking!
ZZTT
Poey...his death was senseless, but it doesn't have to be pointless. It's landed me here, after all.

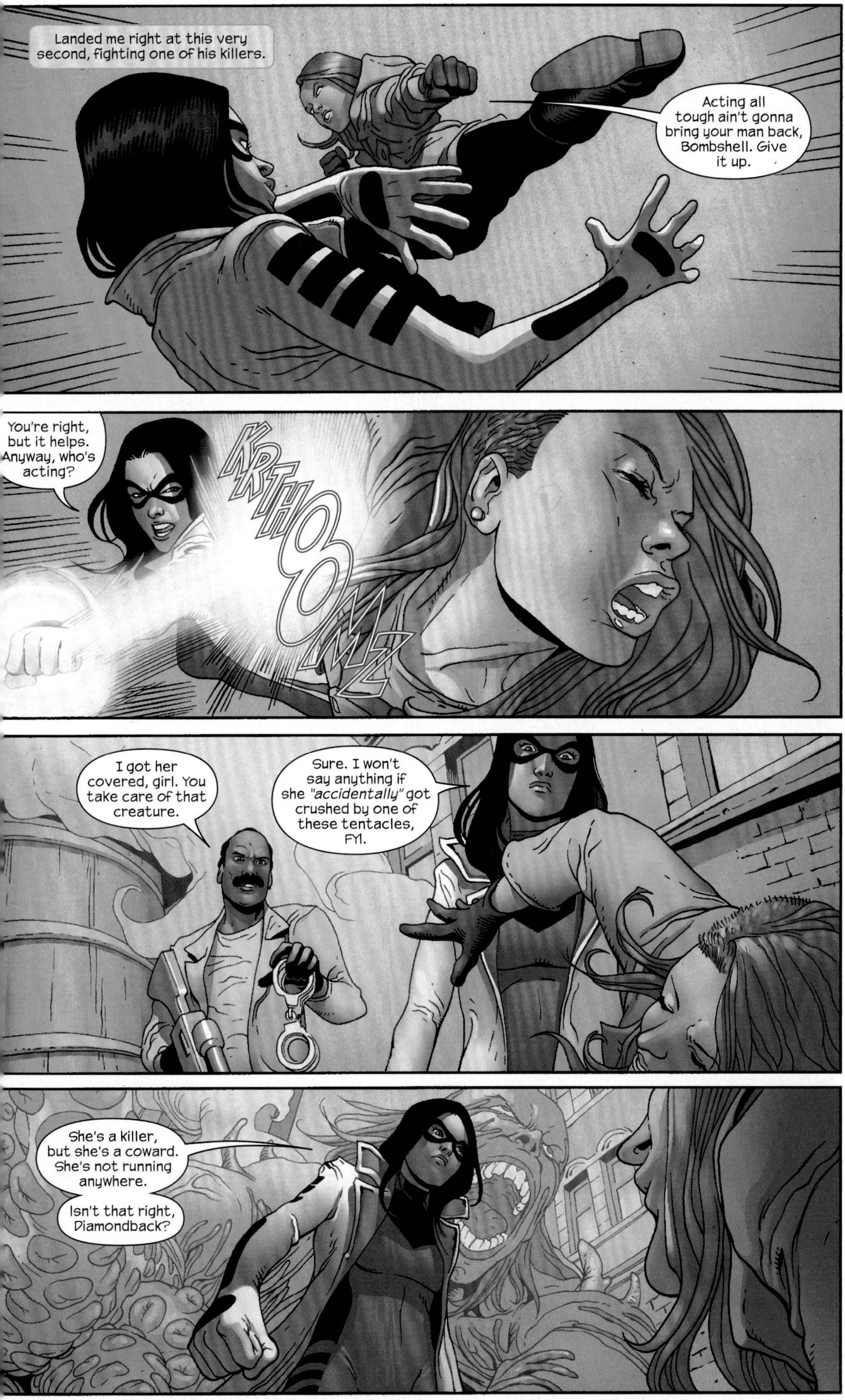
Landed me right at this very second, fighting one of his killers.
Acting all tough ain't gonna bring your man back, Bombshell. Give it up.
You're right, but it helps. Anyway, who's acting?
KRTHOOMZ
I got her covered, girl. You take care of that creature.
Sure. I won't say anything if she "accidentally" got crushed by one of these tentacles, FYI.
She's a killer, but she's a coward. She's not running anywhere.
Isn't that right, Diamondback?

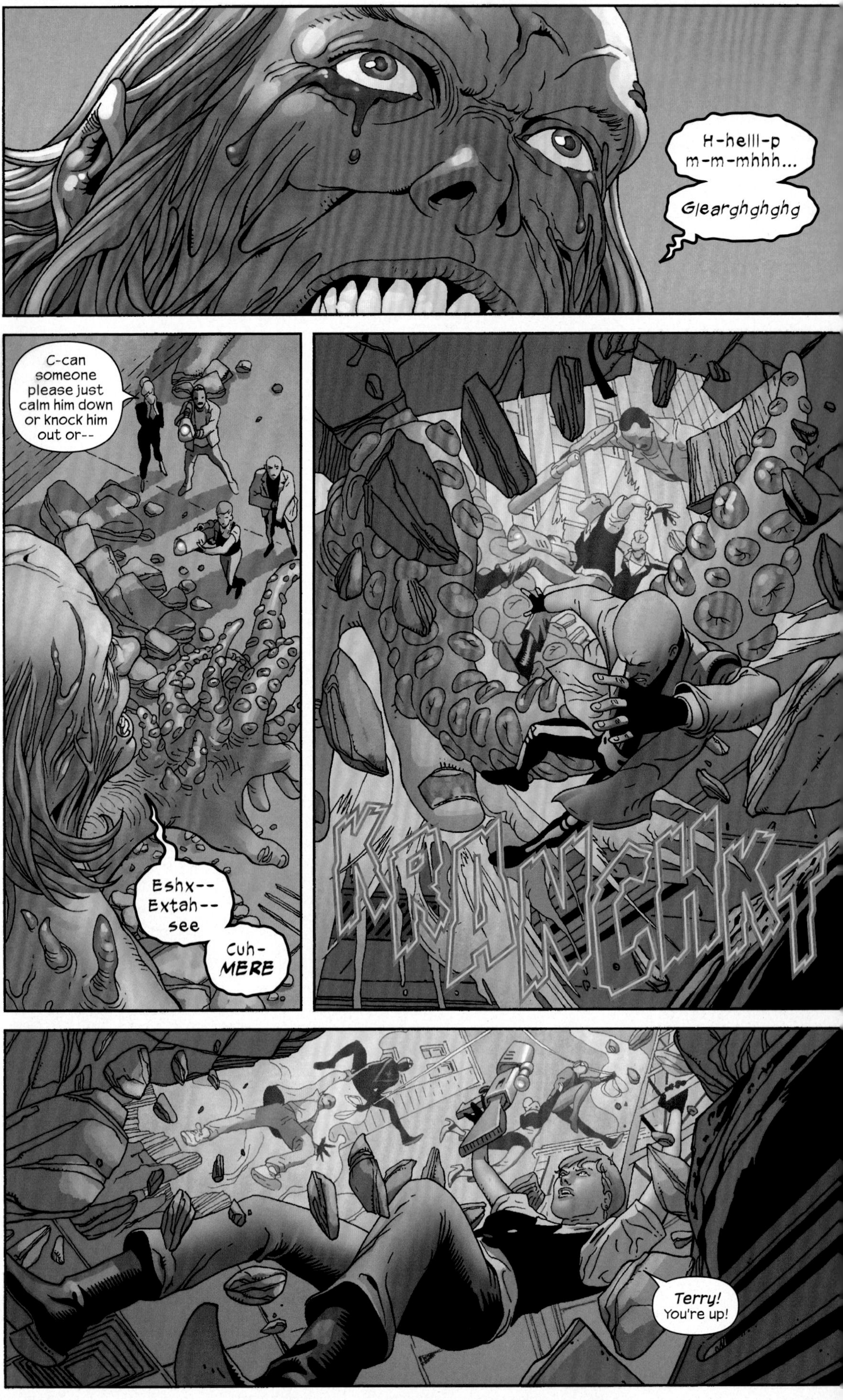
H-helll-p m-m-mhhh...
Glearghghghg
C-can someone please just calm him down or knock him out or--
Eshx-- Extah-- see
Cuh- MERE
KRANCHKT
Terry! You're up!

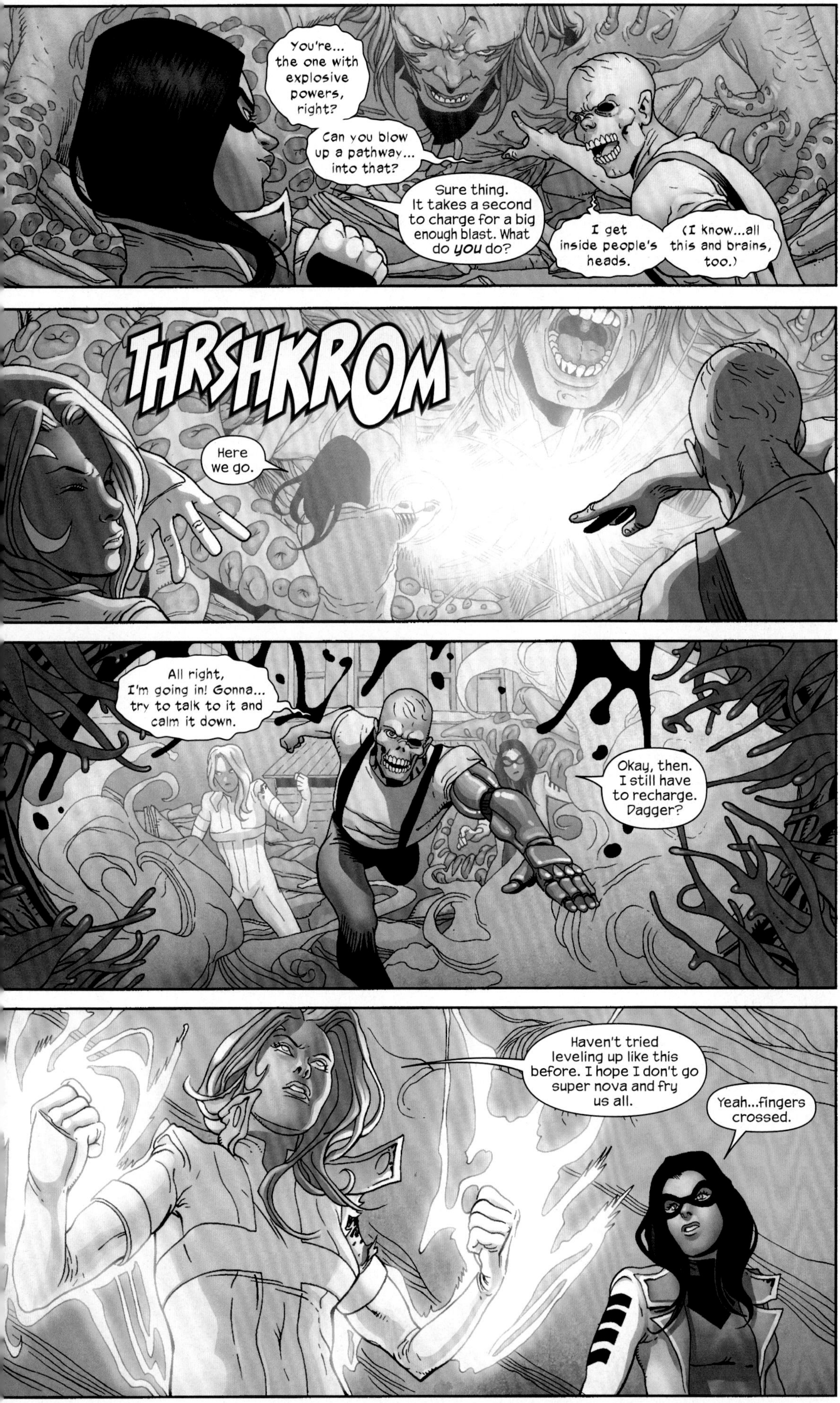
You're... the one with explosive powers, right?
Can you blow up a pathway... into that?
Sure thing. It takes a second to charge for a big enough blast. What do *you* do?
I get inside people's heads.
(I know...all this and brains, too.)
THRSHKROM
Here we go.
All right, I'm going in! Gonna... try to talk to it and calm it down.
Okay, then. I still have to recharge. Dagger?
Haven't tried leveling up like this before. I hope I don't go super nova and fry us all.
Yeah...fingers crossed.

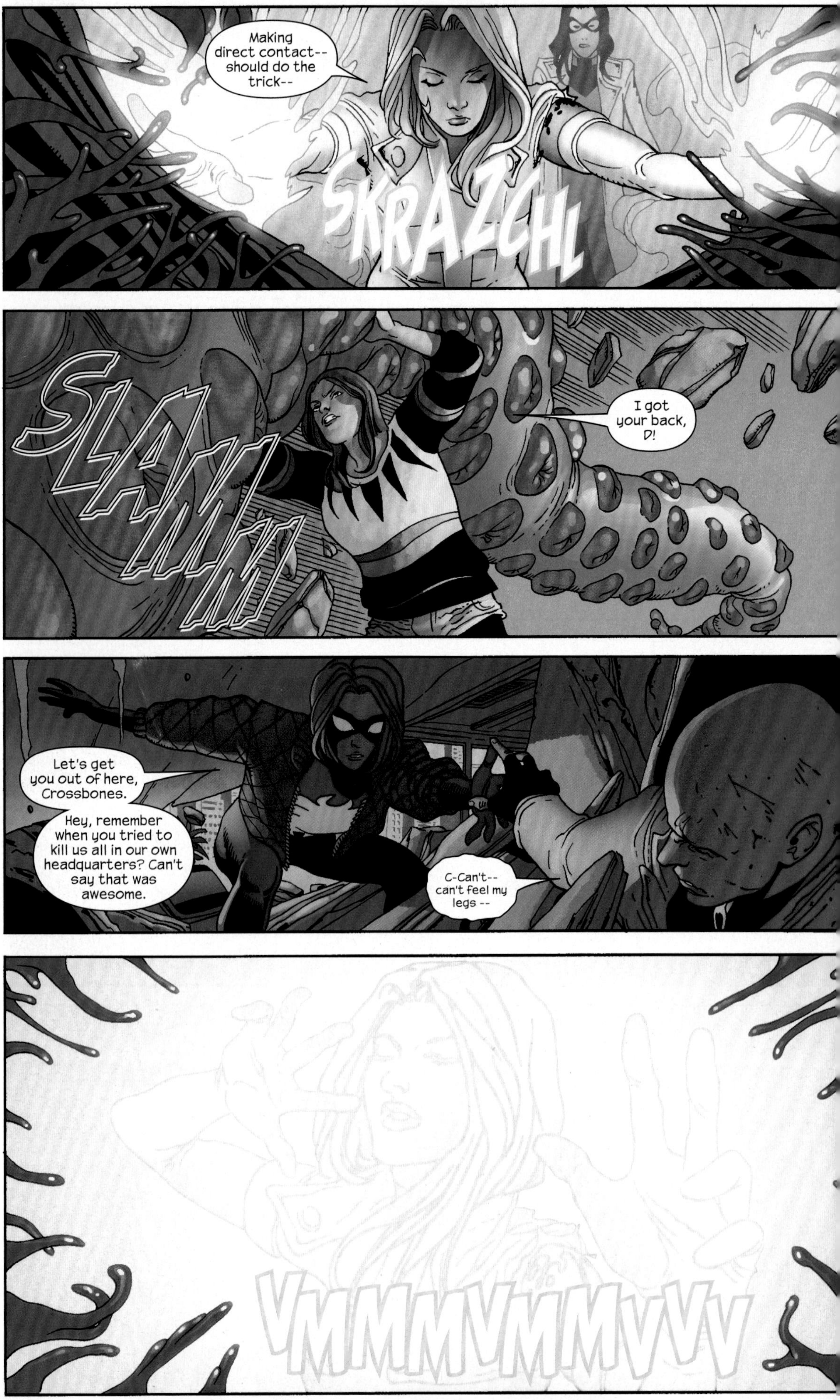
Making direct contact-- should do the trick--
SKRAZCHL
SLAMM
I got your back, D!
Let's get you out of here, Crossbones.
Hey, remember when you tried to kill us all in our own headquarters? Can't say that was awesome.
C-Can't-- can't feel my legs --
VMMMVMMMVVV

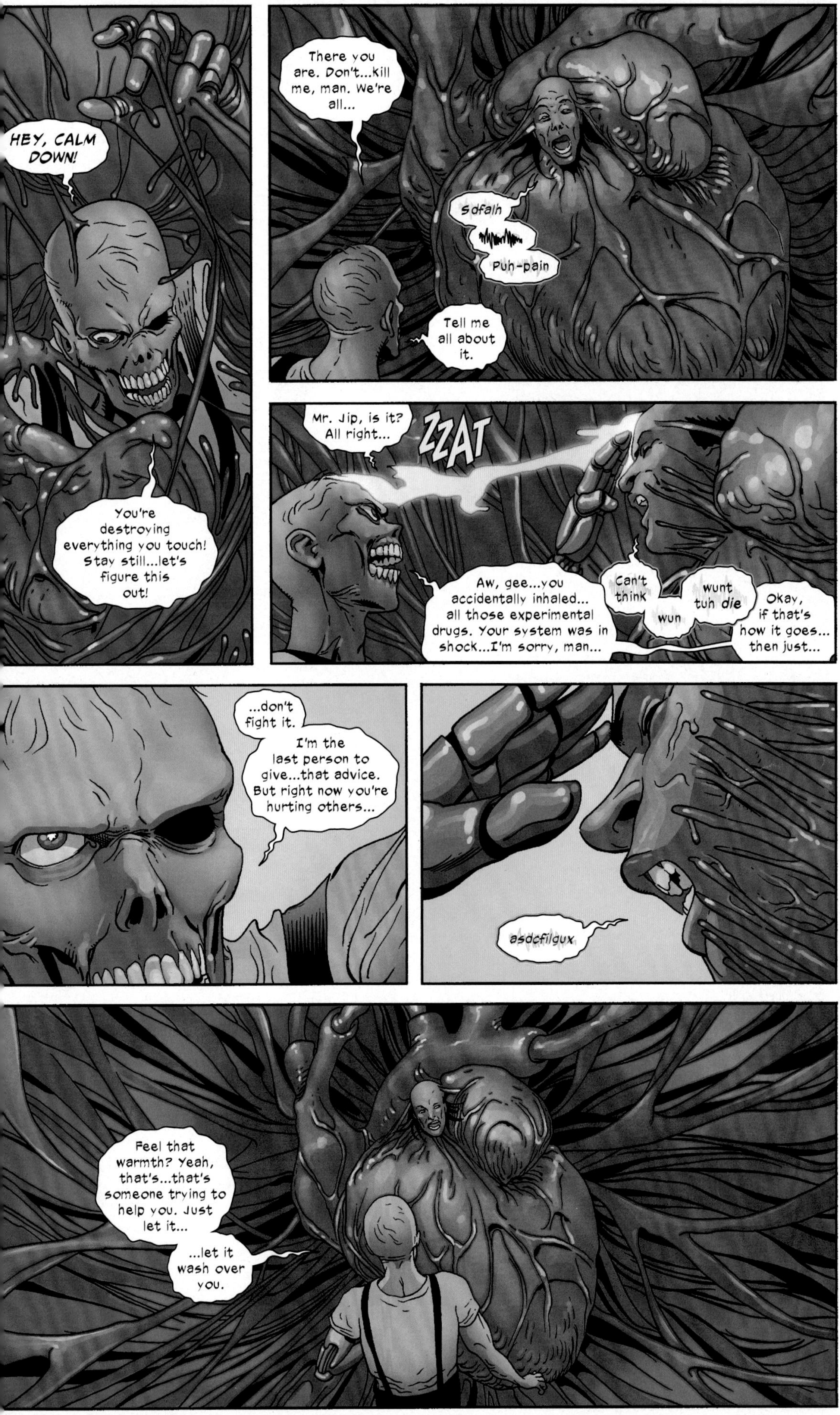

HEY, CALM DOWN!
You're destroying everything you touch! Stay still...let's figure this out!
There you are. Don't...kill me, man. We're all...
Sdfalh
Puh-pain
Tell me all about it.
Mr. Jip, is it? All right...
ZZAT
Aw, gee...you accidentally inhaled... all those experimental drugs. Your system was in shock...I'm sorry, man...
Can't think
wun
wunt tuh die
Okay, if that's how it goes... then just...
...don't fight it.
I'm the last person to give...that advice. But right now you're hurting others...
asdcfilgux
Feel that warmth? Yeah, that's...that's someone trying to help you. Just let it...
...let it wash over you.

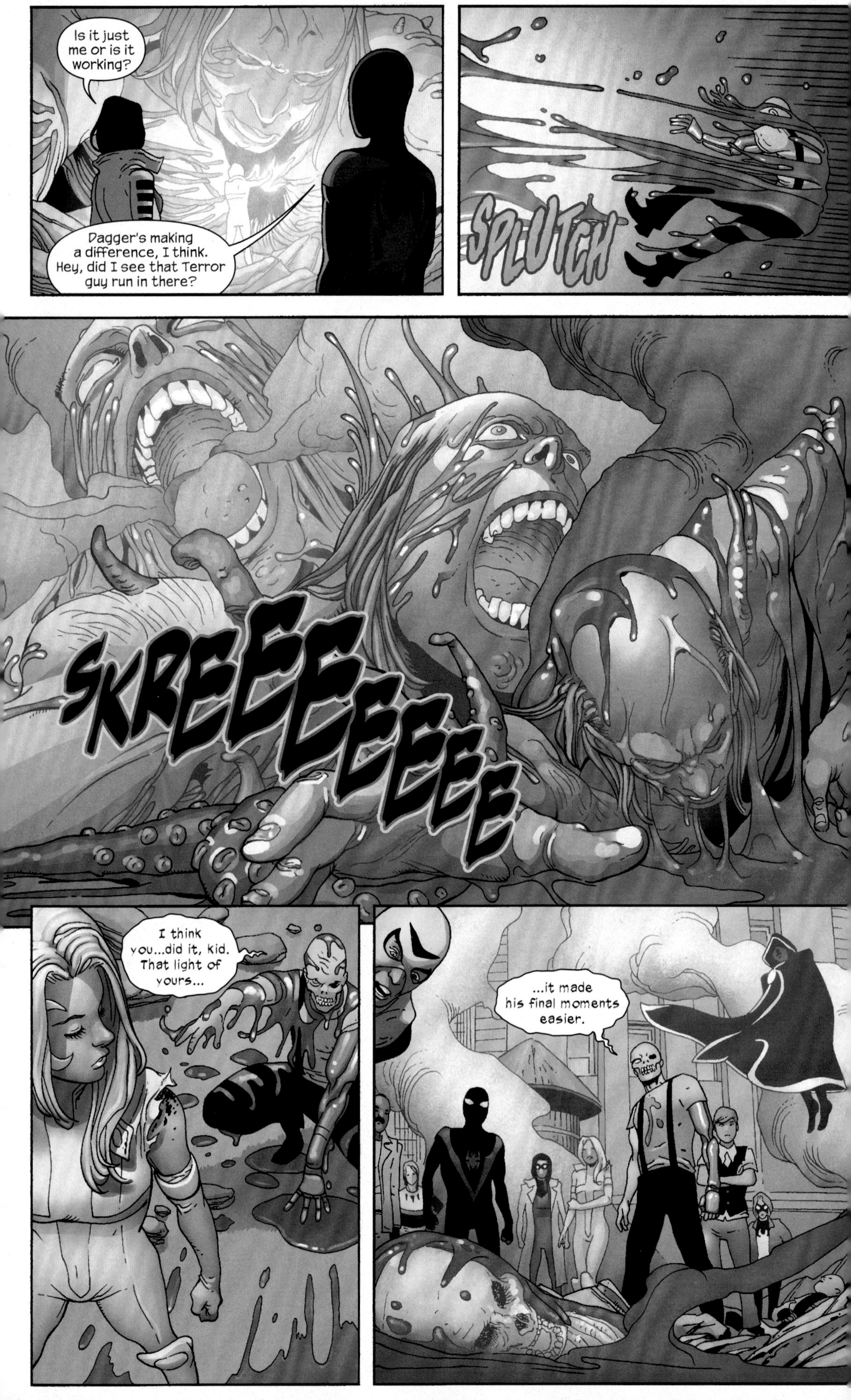
Is it just me or is it working?
Dagger's making a difference, I think. Hey, did I see that Terror guy run in there?
SPLUTCH
SKREEEEEEEE
I think you...did it, kid. That light of yours...
...it made his final moments easier.

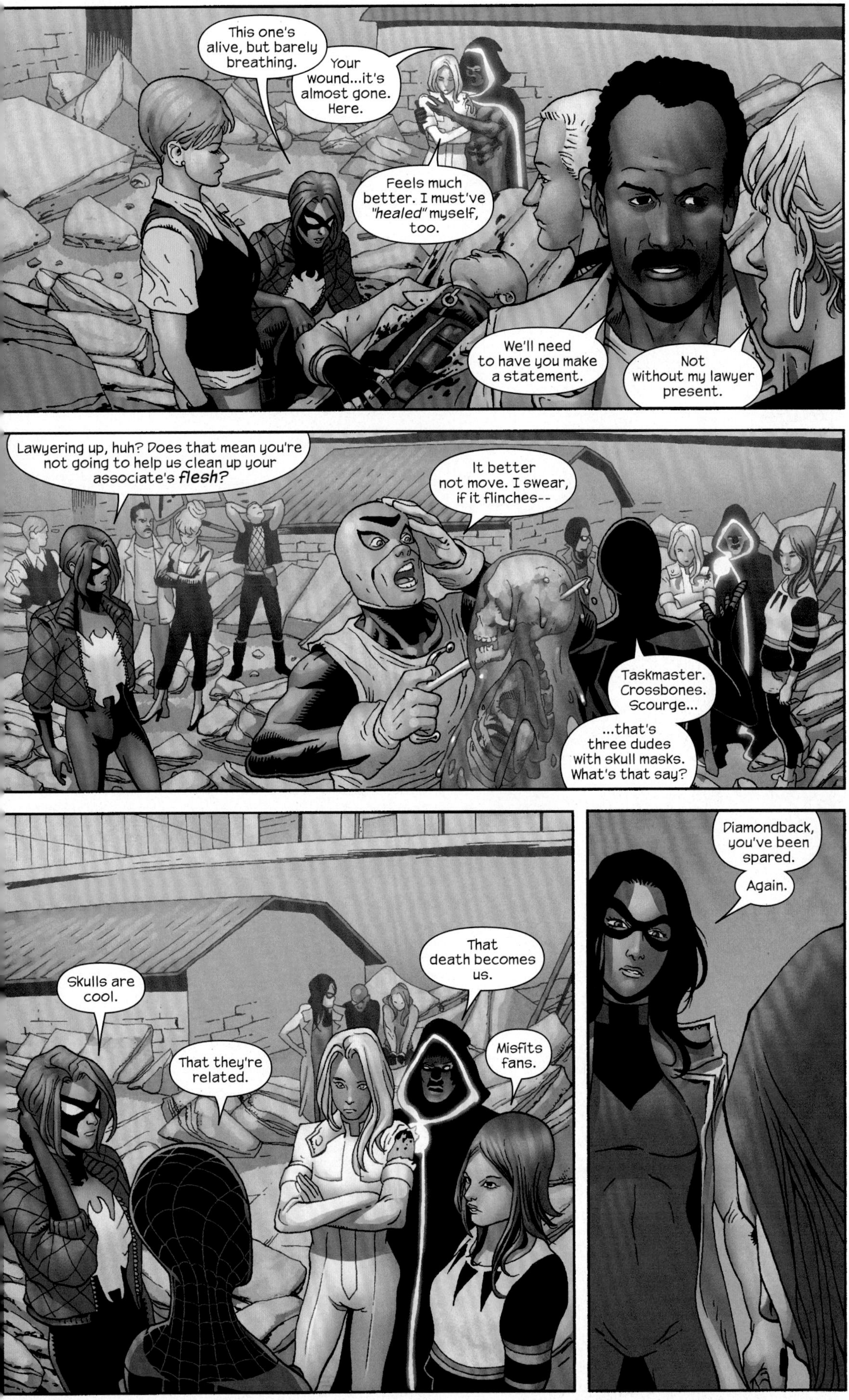
This one's alive, but barely breathing.
Your wound...it's almost gone. Here.
Feels much better. I must've "healed" myself, too.
We'll need to have you make a statement.
Not without my lawyer present.
Lawyering up, huh? Does that mean you're not going to help us clean up your associate's *flesh?*
It better not move. I swear, if it flinches--
Taskmaster. Crossbones. Scourge...
...that's three dudes with skull masks. What's that say?
Skulls are cool.
That they're related.
That death becomes us.
Misfits fans.
Diamondback, you've been spared.
Again.

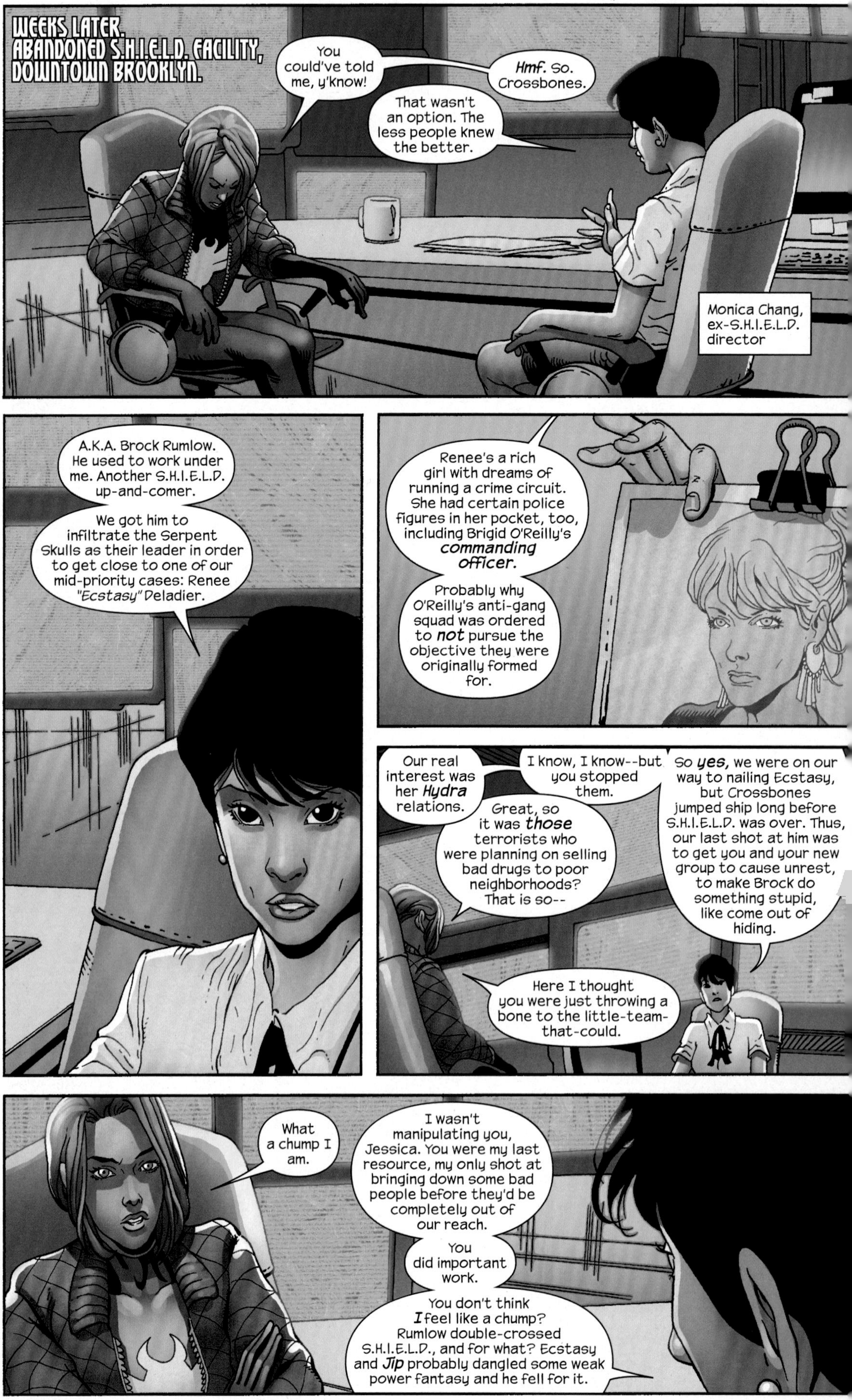
WEEKS LATER. ABANDONED S.H.I.E.L.D. FACILITY, DOWNTOWN BROOKLYN.
You could've told me, y'know!
Hmf. So. Crossbones.
That wasn't an option. The less people knew the better.
Monica Chang, ex-S.H.I.E.L.D. director
A.K.A. Brock Rumlow. He used to work under me. Another S.H.I.E.L.D. up-and-comer.
We got him to infiltrate the Serpent Skulls as their leader in order to get close to one of our mid-priority cases: Renee "Ecstasy" Deladier.
Renee's a rich girl with dreams of running a crime circuit. She had certain police figures in her pocket, too, including Brigid O'Reilly's commanding officer.
Probably why O'Reilly's anti-gang squad was ordered to not pursue the objective they were originally formed for.
Our real interest was her Hydra relations.
Great, so it was those terrorists who were planning on selling bad drugs to poor neighborhoods? That is so--
I know, I know--but you stopped them.
So yes, we were on our way to nailing Ecstasy, but Crossbones jumped ship long before S.H.I.E.L.D. was over. Thus, our last shot at him was to get you and your new group to cause unrest, to make Brock do something stupid, like come out of hiding.
Here I thought you were just throwing a bone to the little-team-that-could.
What a chump I am.
I wasn't manipulating you, Jessica. You were my last resource, my only shot at bringing down some bad people before they'd be completely out of our reach.
You did important work.
You don't think I feel like a chump? Rumlow double-crossed S.H.I.E.L.D., and for what? Ecstasy and Jip probably dangled some weak power fantasy and he fell for it.

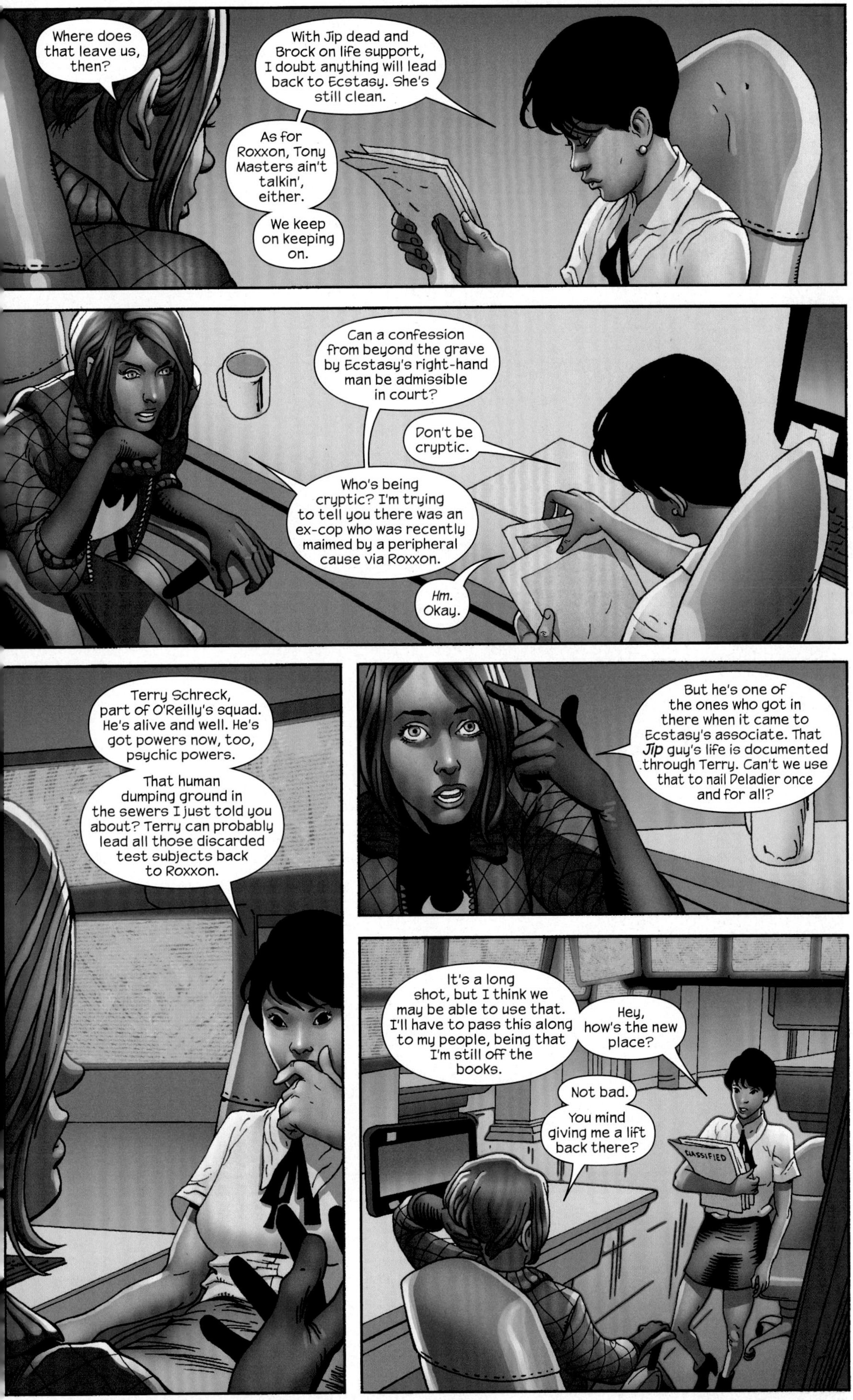

Where does that leave us, then?
With Jip dead and Brock on life support, I doubt anything will lead back to Ecstasy. She's still clean.
As for Roxxon, Tony Masters ain't talkin', either.
We keep on keeping on.
Can a confession from beyond the grave by Ecstasy's right-hand man be admissible in court?
Don't be cryptic.
Who's being cryptic? I'm trying to tell you there was an ex-cop who was recently maimed by a peripheral cause via Roxxon.
Hm. Okay.
Terry Schreck, part of O'Reilly's squad. He's alive and well. He's got powers now, too, psychic powers.
That human dumping ground in the sewers I just told you about? Terry can probably lead all those discarded test subjects back to Roxxon.
But he's one of the ones who got in there when it came to Ecstasy's associate. That *Jip* guy's life is documented through Terry. Can't we use that to nail Deladier once and for all?
It's a long shot, but I think we may be able to use that. I'll have to pass this along to my people, being that I'm still off the books.
Hey, how's the new place?
Not bad.
You mind giving me a lift back there?
CLASSIFIED

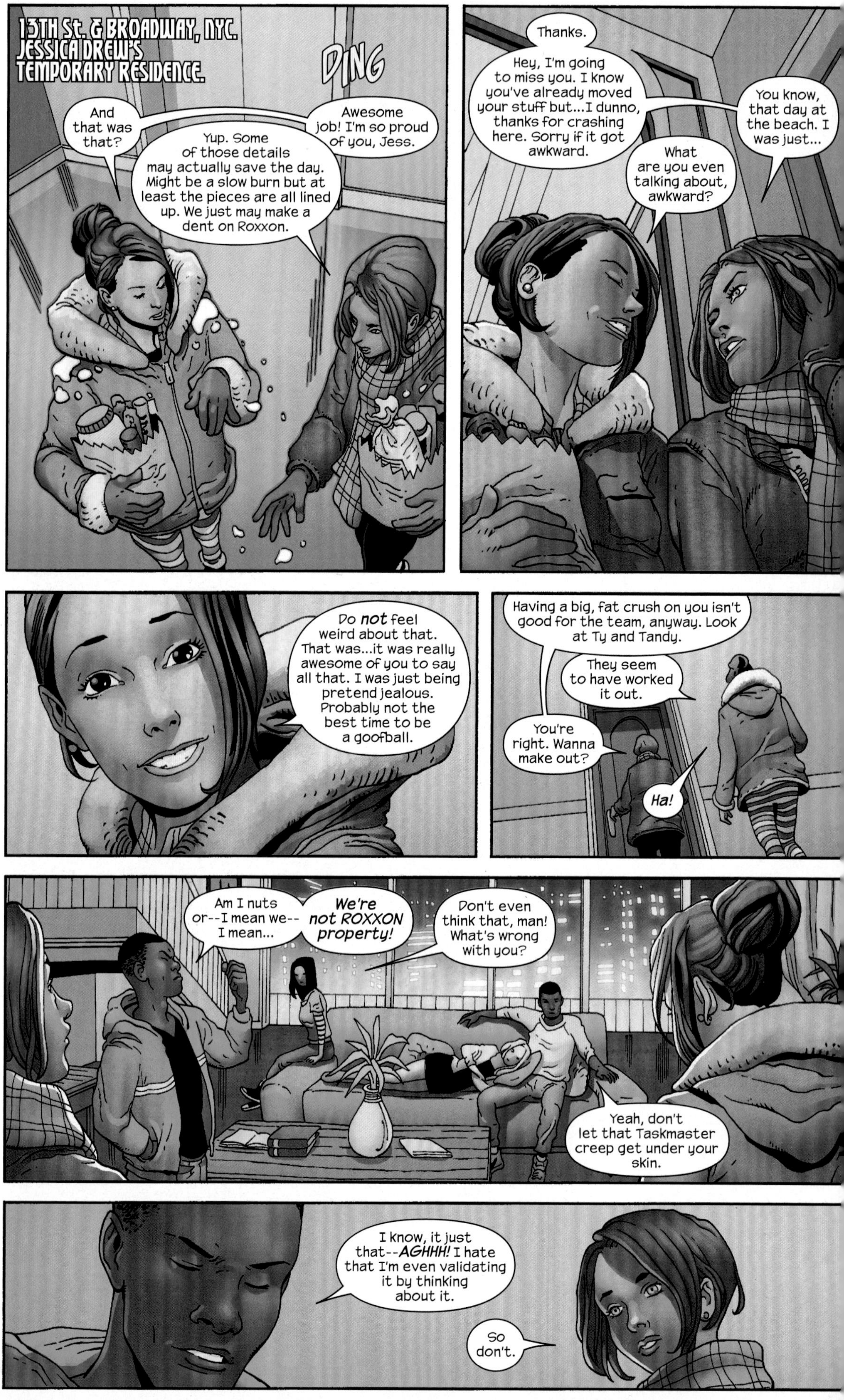
13TH St. & BROADWAY, NYC. JESSICA DREW'S TEMPORARY RESIDENCE.
DING
And that was that?
Awesome job! I'm so proud of you, Jess.
Yup. Some of those details may actually save the day. Might be a slow burn but at least the pieces are all lined up. We just may make a dent on Roxxon.
Thanks.
Hey, I'm going to miss you. I know you've already moved your stuff but...I dunno, thanks for crashing here. Sorry if it got awkward.
What are you even talking about, awkward?
You know, that day at the beach. I was just...
Do not feel weird about that. That was...it was really awesome of you to say all that. I was just being pretend jealous. Probably not the best time to be a goofball.
Having a big, fat crush on you isn't good for the team, anyway. Look at Ty and Tandy.
They seem to have worked it out.
You're right. Wanna make out?
Ha!
Am I nuts or--I mean we--I mean...
We're not ROXXON property!
Don't even think that, man! What's wrong with you?
Yeah, don't let that Taskmaster creep get under your skin.
I know, it just that--AGHHH! I hate that I'm even validating it by thinking about it.
So don't.

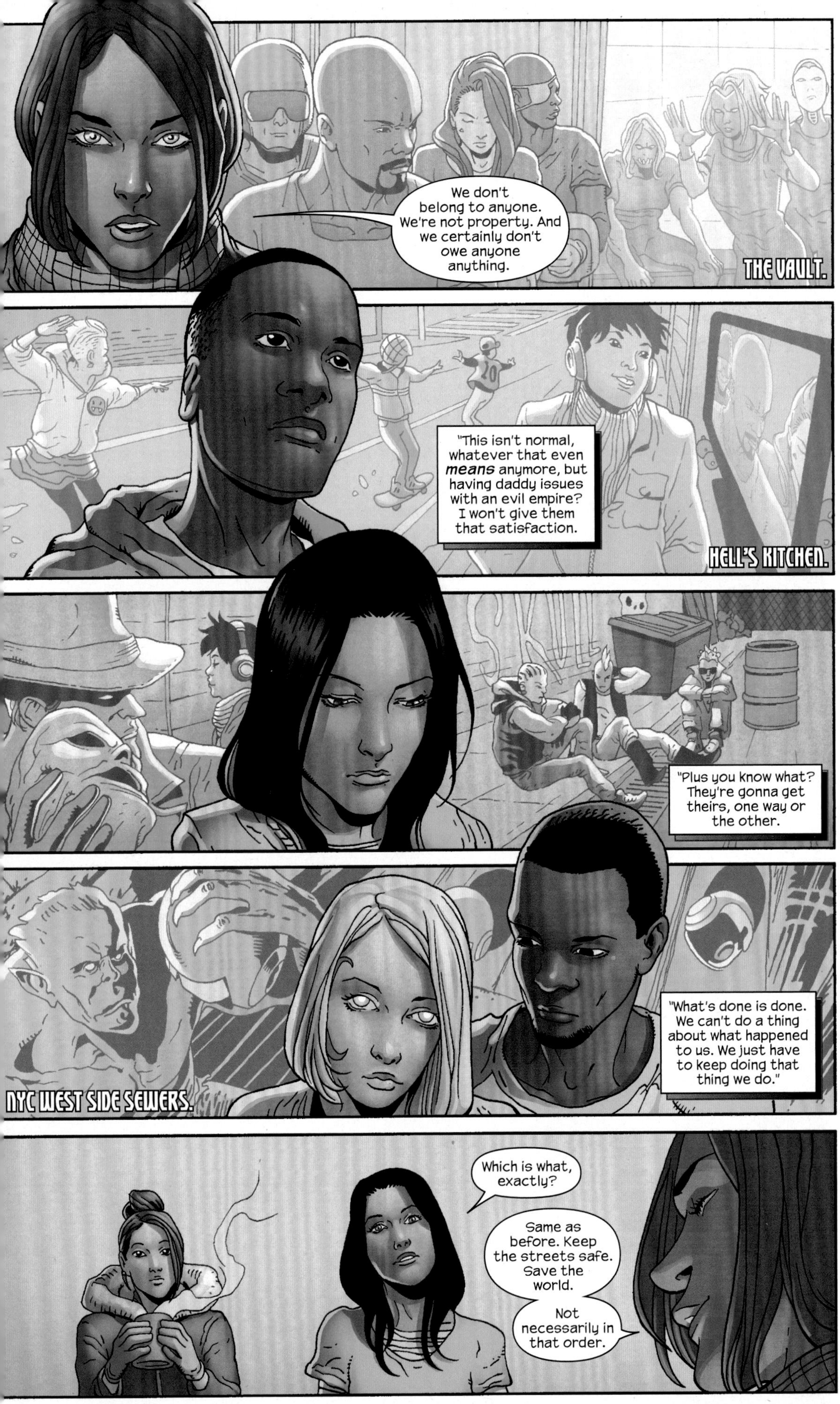
We don't belong to anyone. We're not property. And we certainly don't owe anyone anything.
THE VAULT.
"This isn't normal, whatever that even *means* anymore, but having daddy issues with an evil empire? I won't give them that satisfaction.
HELL'S KITCHEN.
"Plus you know what? They're gonna get theirs, one way or the other.
NYC WEST SIDE SEWERS.
"What's done is done. We can't do a thing about what happened to us. We just have to keep doing that thing we do."
Which is what, exactly?
Same as before. Keep the streets safe. Save the world.
Not necessarily in that order.

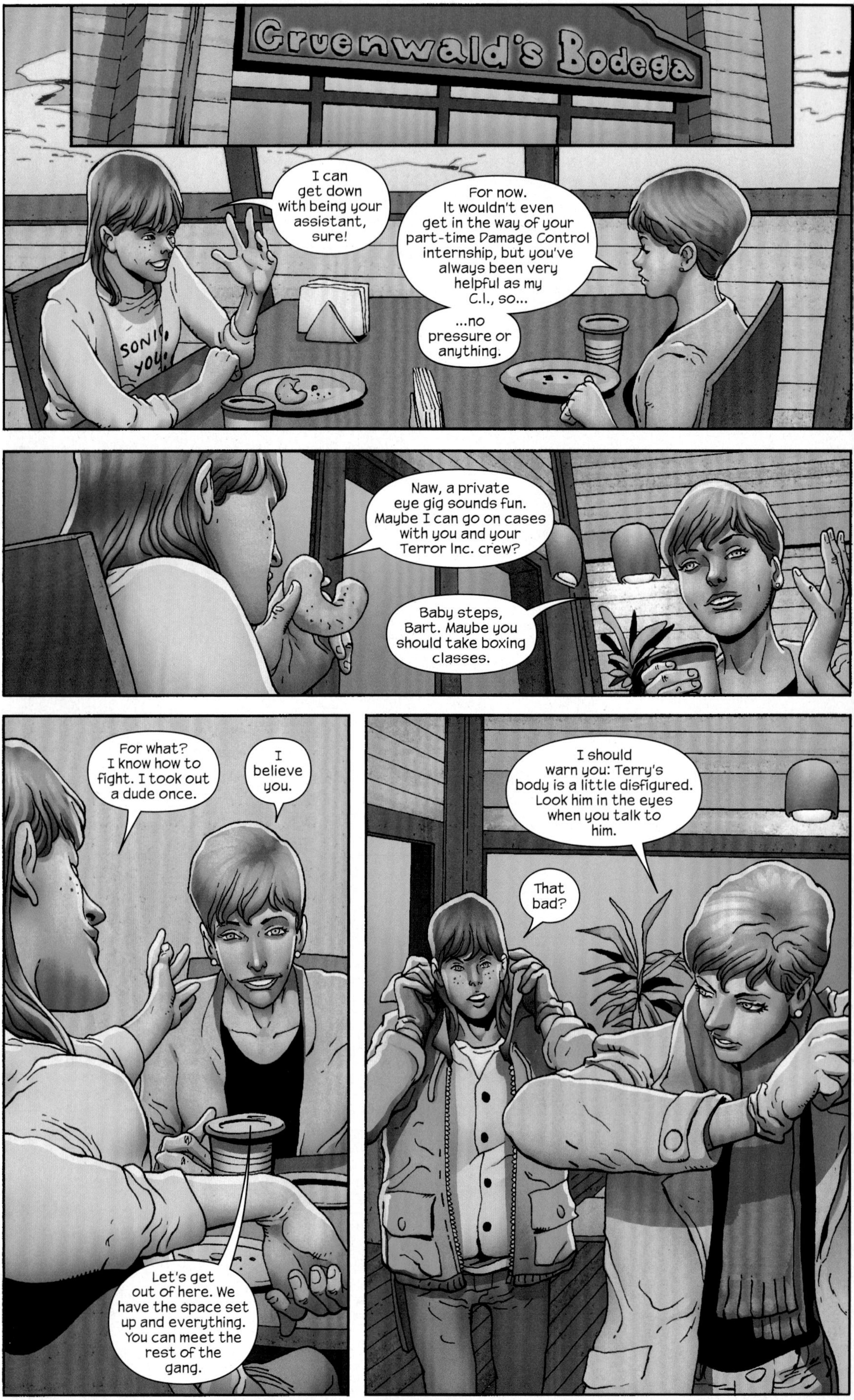
Gruenwald's Bodega
I can get down with being your assistant, sure!
For now. It wouldn't even get in the way of your part-time Damage Control internship, but you've always been very helpful as my C.I., so...
...no pressure or anything.
Naw, a private eye gig sounds fun. Maybe I can go on cases with you and your Terror Inc. crew?
Baby steps, Bart. Maybe you should take boxing classes.
For what? I know how to fight. I took out a dude once.
I believe you.
Let's get out of here. We have the space set up and everything. You can meet the rest of the gang.
I should warn you: Terry's body is a little disfigured. Look him in the eyes when you talk to him.
That bad?

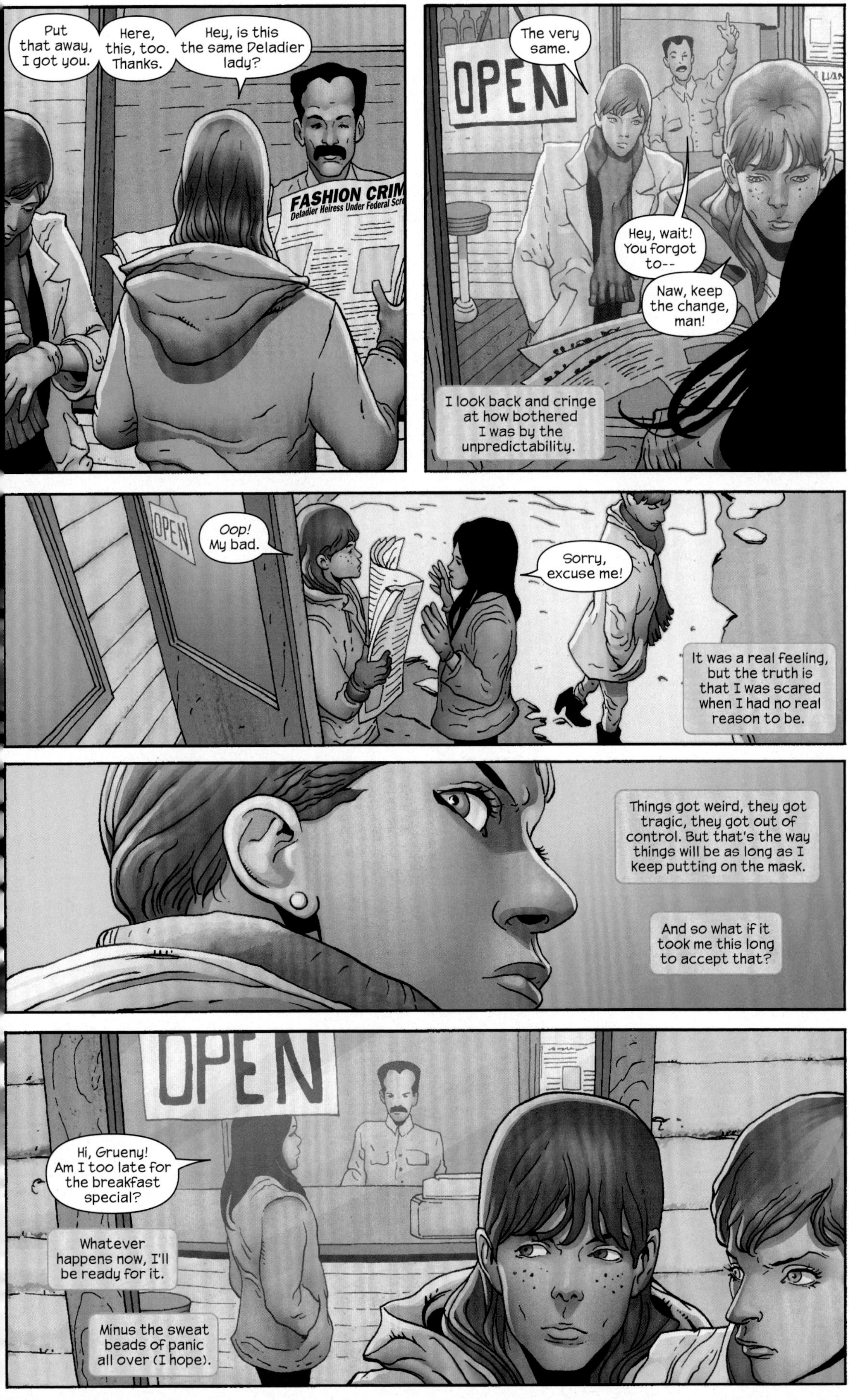
Put that away, I got you.
Here, this, too. Thanks.
Hey, is this the same Deladier lady?
FASHION CRIM
Deladier Heiress Under Federal Scr
The very same.
OPEN
Hey, wait! You forgot to--
Naw, keep the change, man!
I look back and cringe at how bothered I was by the unpredictability.
OPEN
Oop! My bad.
Sorry, excuse me!
It was a real feeling, but the truth is that I was scared when I had no real reason to be.
Things got weird, they got tragic, they got out of control. But that's the way things will be as long as I keep putting on the mask.
And so what if it took me this long to accept that?
OPEN
Hi, Grueny! Am I too late for the breakfast special?
Whatever happens now, I'll be ready for it.
Minus the sweat beads of panic all over (I hope).

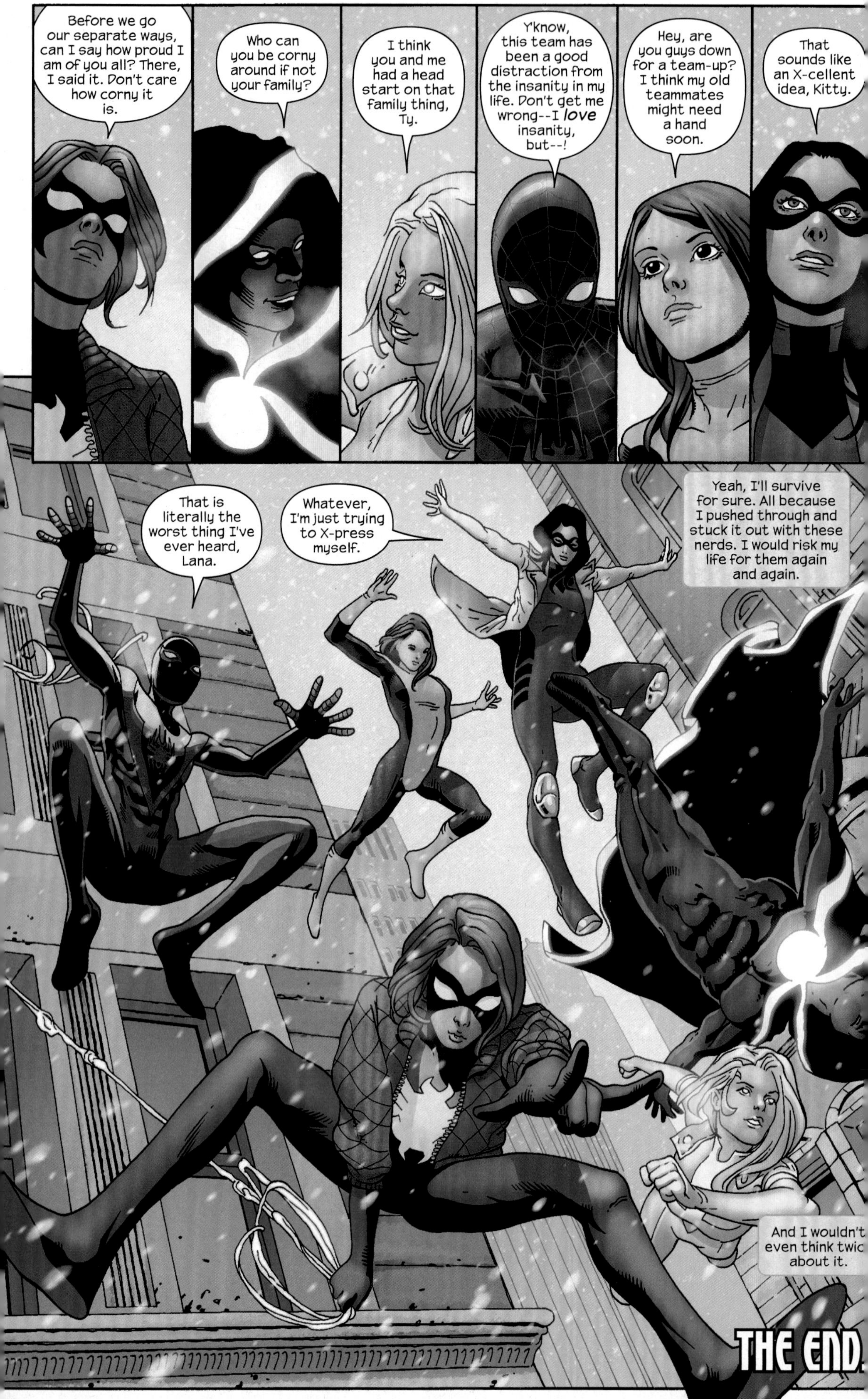
Before we go our separate ways, can I say how proud I am of you all? There, I said it. Don't care how corny it is.
Who can you be corny around if not your family?
I think you and me had a head start on that family thing, Ty.
Y'know, this team has been a good distraction from the insanity in my life. Don't get me wrong--I *love* insanity, but--!
Hey, are you guys down for a team-up? I think my old teammates might need a hand soon.
That sounds like an X-cellent idea, Kitty.
That is literally the worst thing I've ever heard, Lana.
Whatever, I'm just trying to X-press myself.
Yeah, I'll survive for sure. All because I pushed through and stuck it out with these nerds. I would risk my life for them again and again.
And I wouldn't even think twic about it.
THE END.

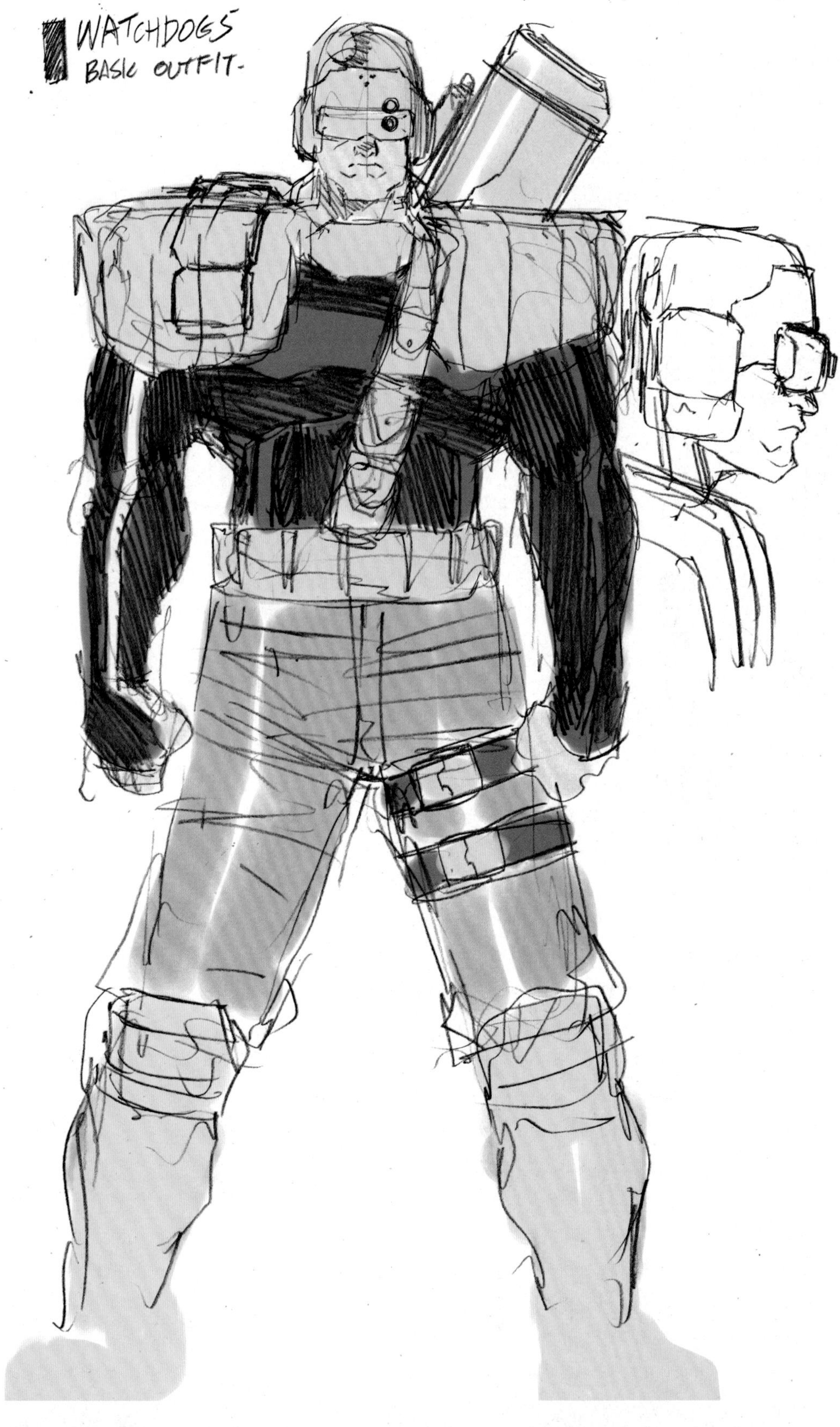
WATCHDOGS
BASIC OUTFIT-

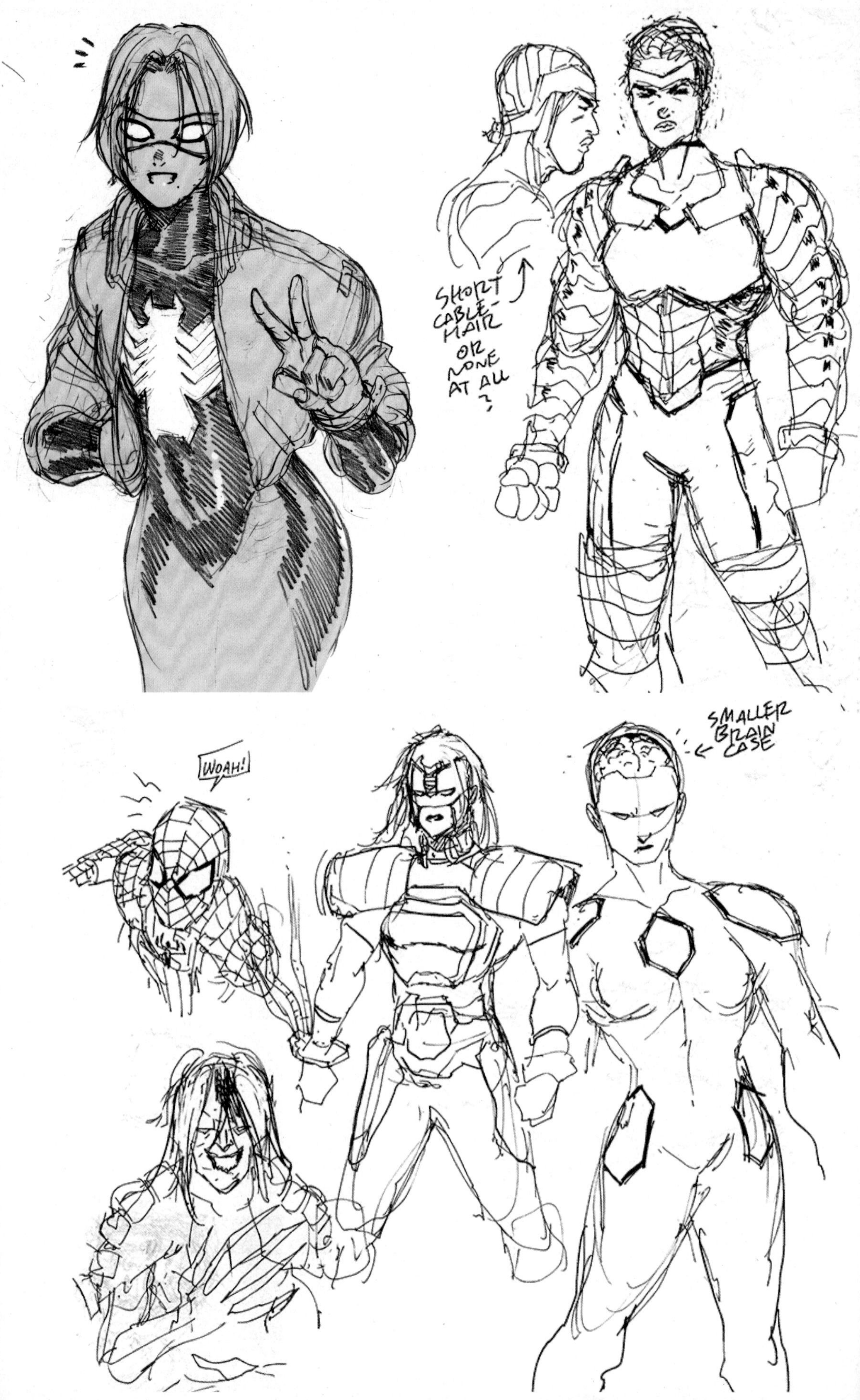
SHORT CABLE-HAIR OR NONE AT ALL ?
WOAH!
SMALLER BRAIN CASE

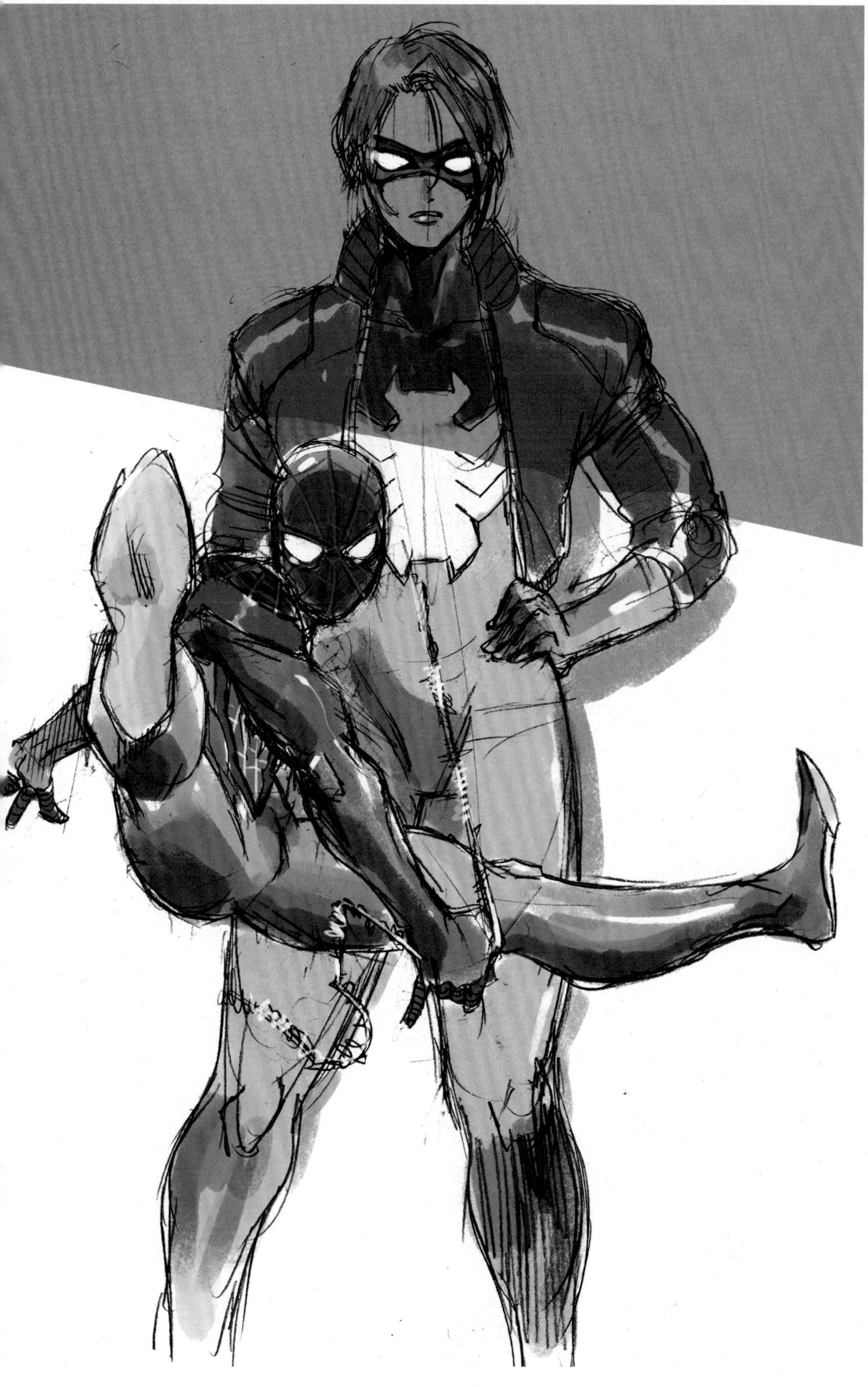

GIANNIS MILONOGIANNIS & JORDIE BELLAIRE

ART PROCESS: #7, PAGES 1-2

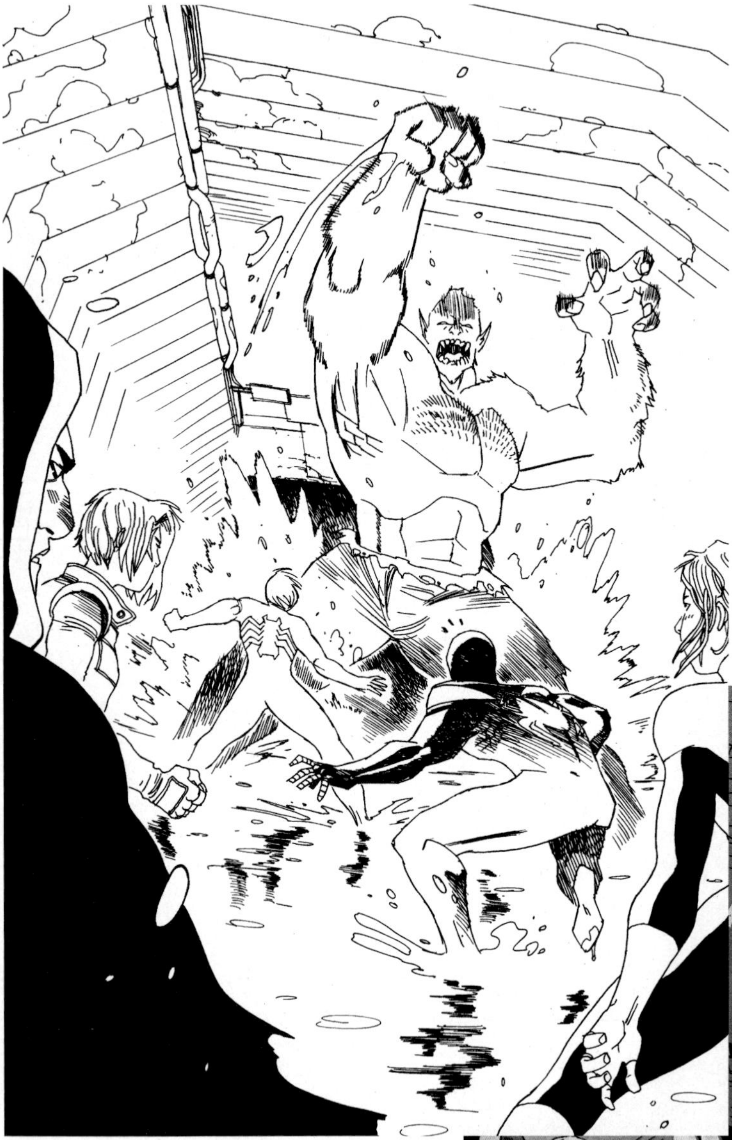

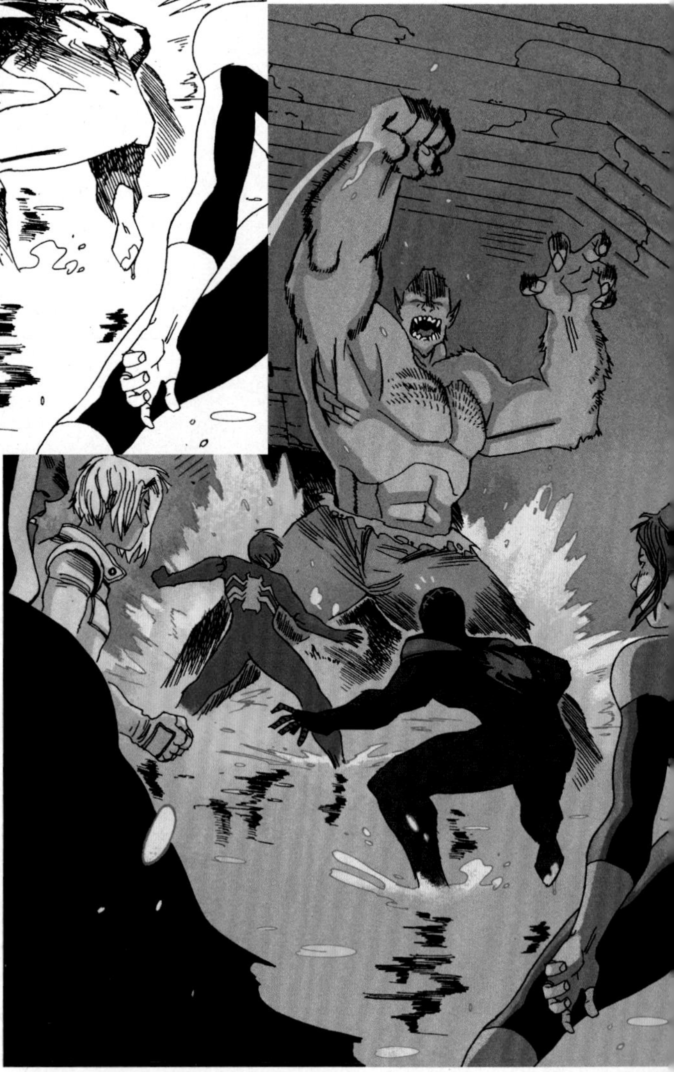

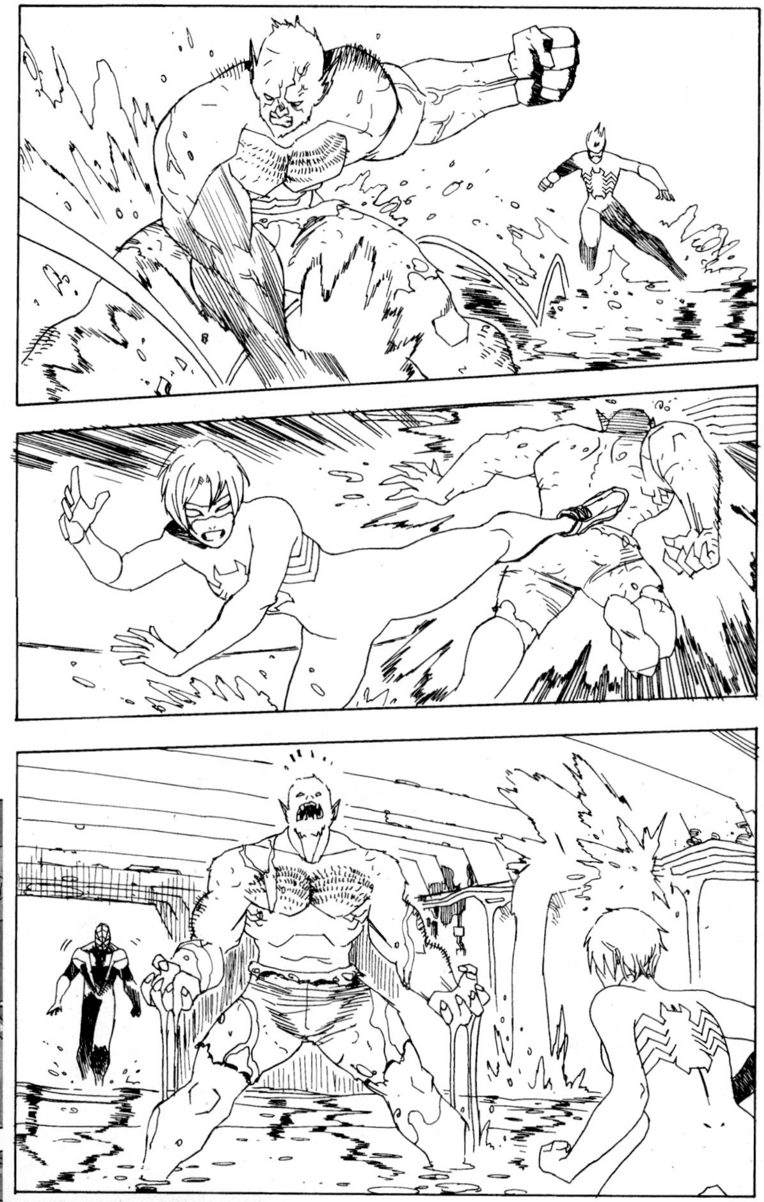

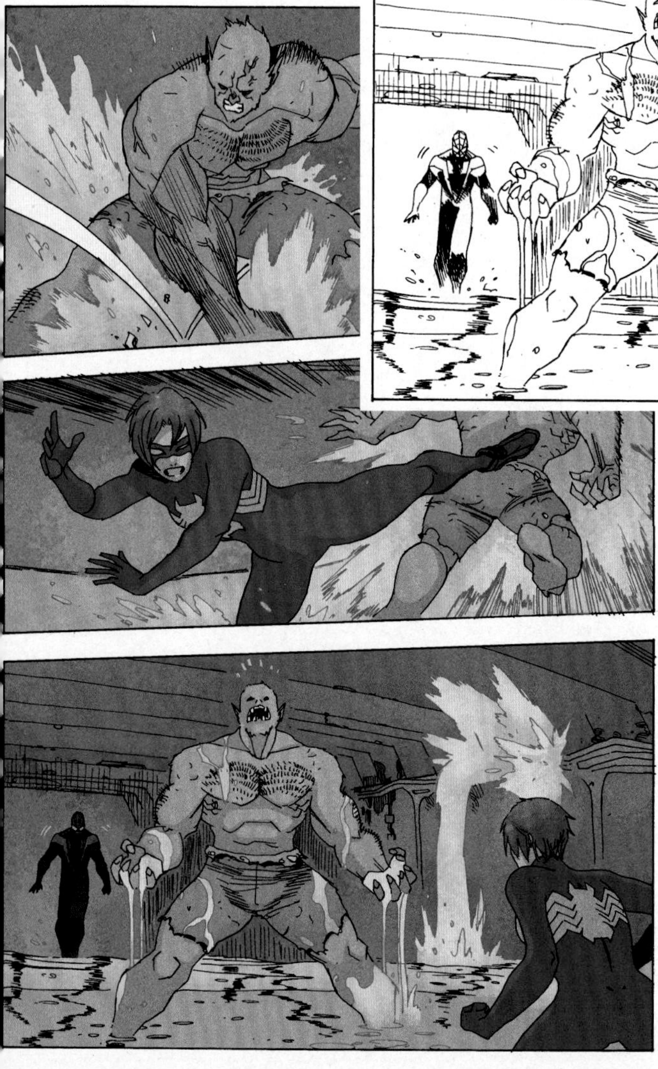

It was a risk to even dream about making this book: a new direction, a new atmosphere, and a new world that looked like nothing else before it. In mapping out twelve issues worth of story, I tried to have it all go down within these pages, eager to shine the spotlight on as many characters as I could. Sure, you can always put it in context with what came before and what comes after, but I loved the idea of this title working as its own self-contained unit. Big thanks to Emily Shaw and Mark Paniccia for allowing us to make that happen.

Give it up for to Amilcar Pinna, whose style visually defined the identity of All-New Ultimates – he took whatever impossible thing I jotted down and brought it to life with confident naturalism. And let's hear it for Giannis Milonogiannis, who tore it up for three fun and kinetic issues. That was a genuine treat, no doubt.

The rest of the crew deserves love, too: the great Nolan Woodard, colorist extraordinaire, and letterer Clayton Cowles, who indulged all of my suggestions (I'm positive that all letterers looove when writers request things like "a Dave Sim balloon"). Oh, and David Nakayama, who gave us some of the best covers on the stands this past year. Then there's Brain Michael Bendis, the Frank Lloyd Wright of the Ultimate Universe. Thanks for nudging my involvement in the sandbox you helped create, good sir. I'm honored to have taken part in it.

Hey, this is your world as well, so thanks for welcoming me and for sticking around. Every fan, blogger, collector, completist, and reader alike, you all helped make this risk pay off. Seriously, thank you for that. Let's do it again some time.

Michel Fiffe
Brooklyn, 2014

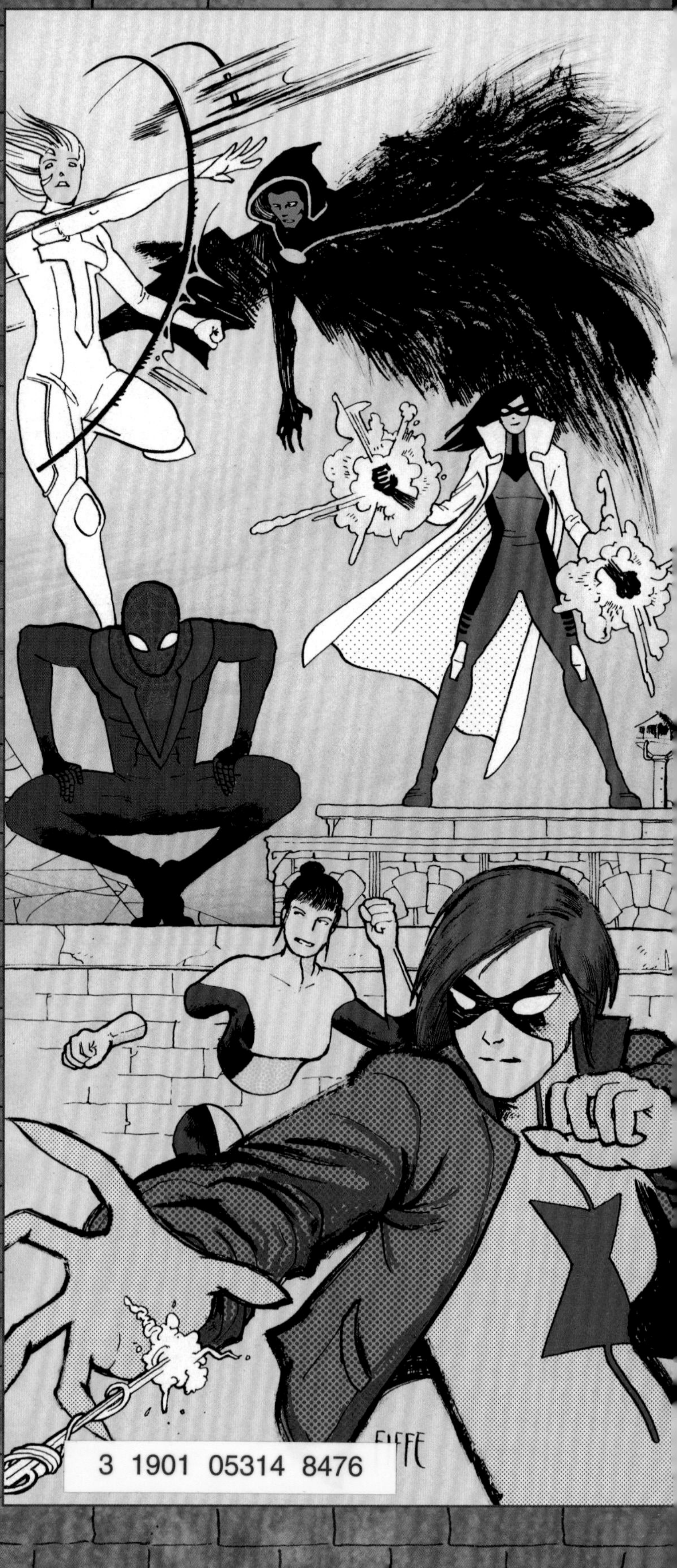
FIFFE